Autumn of Love

How the Swinging 60s and the Counterculture came to Portsmouth

Dave Allen

*To 'oscar'
with very best wishes*

Dave Allen

2017.

Moyhill Publishing

First Published in 2017 by Moyhill Publishing.

A CIP catalogue record for this book
is available from the British Library.

ISBN 9781905597758

Printed in the UK.

The papers used in this book were produced in an
environmentally friendly way from sustainable forests.

Moyhill Publishing,
1965 Davenport House, 261 Bolton Rd, Bury, Gtr. Manchester BL8 2NZ. UK

"The Ghosts of the past which follow us into the present, also belong to the present moment.

To observe them deeply, to recognise their nature, and transform them, is to transform the past."

Thich Nhat Hanh 365 Zen

Contents

SPEAKERS' CORNER, SOUTHSEA

A group of Southsea's hippies join the Salvation Army on a sunny afternoon in the Summer of Love. Nigel Grundy is seated centre foreground looking up to the left.

Photo: Roger Courtney

TRACK ONE, SIDE ONE

"Our beginnings never know our ends"

T S Eliot

In much of Britain today, the past is very much our present and probably our future, with the heritage industry a key element of the economic strategy. Heritage loves nothing more than an anniversary, so in 2017, we find ourselves exactly 50 years on from the fabled 'summer of love', one of the key periods in the decade that is often still described as the swinging sixties. How will we mark – and market – it? Will we merely exploit it? More importantly perhaps, are there still any tales to tell of that time, and any further lessons to be learned?

Those days, including how we got there, and where some of us went afterwards, is one focus of this book, which will seek to offer one or two answers to that last question. The other main focus will extend the store of histories of that time about my home city of Portsmouth; a tale that has not been comprehensively told in this way, previously. For those of us who lived through those times, it invites a certain nostalgia, an emotion that can be perfectly healthy in the right circumstances and right proportions – although not the kind of nostalgia that informs the rhetoric of current political movements, seeking to recover a mythical past, to the advantage of the powerful, at the expense of others. In the end this book is as much concerned with today and tomorrow, as with the past.

Where it does look backwards, it is not a book about the 1960s as a whole, but about a very specific aspect of it, in which (mostly) young people in (mainly) America, Britain and Europe, challenged the dominant values and behaviour of their elders in the search for a different kind of world. It is largely celebratory of a period that had a huge impact on my life, and in that sense, it is partly a personal memoir – but one which seeks to situate the particular in a broader context. In that respect, it acknowledges Sarah Hill's recent identification of the "long sixties"; considering how what happened back then was sustained and continued to develop, albeit in a less public way, and mostly far from the headlines of fifty years ago. She offers, among others, the example of Hugh Romney, better known as 'Wavy Gravy' who featured in the film of *Woodstock* as a member of the Hog Farm and since then, Hill suggests, has been

> A living reminder that the long 60s are viable … the charitable work that he has done, *quietly, individually,* and in his larger collective, is a continuation of the ideals of the short 60s (2016, 311, my emphasis)

This book is not, of course, the first on the broad topic of the swinging sixties or the summer of love, and for sure the latter's 50th anniversary will produce all kinds of other cultural reminiscences, including books, magazines, articles, television shows and of course the internet – which was not around back then, but now allows us to us to multiply, share and contest the stories of those crazy, sometimes hazy, days of summers long ago.

A great deal of what follows is about the music in those days, but it is also about more than just the music – and indeed more than just the sex, drugs and rock & roll – because it documents a period when young people in particular examined a whole range of alternatives to mainstream life in post-war Britain. Some of those alternatives were nothing more than short-lived fun, some were simply crazy, a few were dangerous, and some have led to dramatic and sustained changes.

Partly by focusing on Portsmouth, and also by examining the legacy of those days, *Autumn of Love* will challenge three widely held and frequently-published views about those days:

- That to participate in all that was happening in the late 1960s, it was necessary to be in one of the great cultural centres such as London, San Francisco, New York, or Los Angeles.
- That in Britain in particular, the swinging sixties were limited to a tiny, wealthy elite in the heart of London.
- That the whole countercultural project collapsed around the misdeeds of Manson, the anarchy of Altamont or the killings at Kent State, after which the participants mostly simply returned to 'normality'.

This tale of Portsmouth, is my latest contribution to an on-going project by a group of 'survivors' from those days of half-a-century ago, documenting popular music and popular culture in the city since the post-war return to the mainstream entertainment of the mid-1940s. While Portsmouth has generally been little more than a footnote in the major histories of popular music or the swinging sixties, it has interesting tales to tell, and this is one more piece of an emerging, and increasingly detailed jigsaw. To some degree, I use the focus on Portsmouth to raise questions more broadly about provincial experiences in Britain in those days, and I hope readers from elsewhere might recognize similar, or subtly different experiences and stories. Was it like this for you in Brighton perhaps, maybe Northampton, Cardiff or Redcar – which incidentally did have a very fine club scene back then?

I was 17 at the start of 1967, attending clubs and other venues in Portsmouth on a regular basis, listening to and learning about music whenever I could. By the end of that memorable year, I had been to my first festival, lost my virginity, spent part of the summer sleeping on beaches in the west country, smoked a joint or two and joined my first 'proper' band. All those experiences and memories – and more – have been central to the tale that follows. This apparent advantage can, however, be a double-edged sword. In the opening chapters, I will consider a variety of views from researchers, writers and media historians, some of whom are tired of hearing yet more tales of the 1960s, while others go further and contest our accounts of the period, or offer versions (usually negative) which do not coincide with what I recall of the times. But it does not follow that because I was there I am necessarily right, or that my ageing memory is infallible; I have long been comfortable with Harold Pinter's view (*No Man's Land*) that "Experience is a paltry thing; each man has it and will tell his tale of it". Where parts of this book are principally my tale of my experiences, I make no great claims beyond that. I am telling my tale of it, but if you think my version is wrong, let us hear (or read) yours.

Where my account differs from most of those critics and sceptics then, is not so much in any claim to the authenticity of experience, but in the essentially celebratory account that follows. I am grateful to have lived through those days, and indeed through much of what followed, as the legacy of those days became the "long", perhaps, never-ending sixties. It may never have been the case that all we need is love, but it never hurts to share some around – so, with love, here's to Portsmouth, and days that changed some things and some people forever.

"THEN YOU SHOULD SAY WHAT YOU MEAN"

It feels right to take my title for this chapter from the March Hare, encountered by Alice over tea on her 'trip' to Wonderland. The Wonderland that will unfold in the following pages certainly lived up to its name on occasions, and in 1967 of course, provided us with a very fine "White Rabbit", but like Alice's adventures, it also offered a fair range of bewildering, surreal and sometimes alarming experiences. It certainly alarmed the authorities on those occasions when they were not able to command as they wished – and they might well have desired to shout "off with their heads" at some of us.

I shall begin by hoping to satisfy the March Hare and anyone else who wishes to know what I might mean – although this is not always a simple task. While I begin with familiar terms like the beats and beatniks, pop and rock, or mods and rockers, the core of this book is concerned with what at the time was generally known as the underground or counterculture, the summer of love or flower power, involving what were often known as hippies or perhaps, with too strong a bias towards North America, the 'Woodstock' generation. 'Flower power' seems to me to have been a term that never survived much beyond the first *Autumn of Love* in 1967, as the petals fell, and as for hippies, I do not use that term very often, because these days in Britain at least it probably carries too many connotations of someone as hopeless as Neil in television's *The Young Ones*. There have always been suggestions that it is a term developed from 'hip'; indeed, it might well be in a general sense, although the strong link between that term and the beats, be-boppers and (original) hipsters makes any precise link feel somewhat tenuous. As Carr *et al* suggested in their book *The Hip: Hipsters, Jazz and the Beat Generation*:

> Hip is an understated state of grace that does not necessarily wish the world well … Hip has never been about hippies, nor majorities and fashions, freaks and first-withs, the flounderers after a star to steer by. It is sometimes present in the pool shark and almost always absent in the pop star … (1986, 11)

Does that help to make things clearer? Perhaps not, after all, even the spelling can confuse, with some preferring hippie and others hippy, although the plural is certainly hippies. It is worth noting perhaps, that while labels like Teddy boy, mod and rocker were previously applied fairly precisely to their respective youth groups, the late 1960s were often less clear, so that for example in the USA in September 1967, Joan Didion wrote about San Francisco's "Hippie Generation", while just a few months later Henry Gross (1968) published an interview-based book about *The Flower People*. Some of Gross's respondents were in California and others New York, but on the whole their views and life styles are very similar to those described by Didion. One, Ian, told Gross

> Like hippies don't exist man. It's just the media extension of the name. It was devised as … it's a handy label to put onto a group of people who look similar, but whom you can't classify in any one sense … I suppose the main common denominator would be the drugs … the psychedelic drugs (94).

This resistance to being labelled is a common cry. In a "Director's Foreword" to a lavish exhibition catalogue, *Beat Catalogue and the New America 1950-1965,* David A Ross (1995, 12) proposed that "words like 'beat' are generally the inventions of journalists and marketeers", can be "hyperbolic or just banal" and therefore tend to miss "the richness and complexity of cultural history". One of those beats, Allen Ginsberg, a few pages on in the same publication, nonetheless suggested it was largely the key participants, beginning with Jack Kerouac in 1948, who coined, used and developed the label. These matters are rarely straightforward and to write any kind of cultural history without employing some generic terms, however tentatively, can lead to lengthy and possibly tedious description.

Around 1967, the term underground was used fairly frequently in the media by and about those who were exploring a plethora of new ideas in the arts, popular culture, politics, and social living. By then, it was perhaps used more in Britain than in the USA, although across the Atlantic the term had been used in relation to the beats in the previous decade, and it was still attached to specific practices such as the underground films, mostly from the USA, which were screened in London at venues like the Arts Lab or Film Makers' Co-operative (see e.g. Le Grice 1977). Joe Boyd, an American promoter and producer who spent much of the 1960s in London, has written a very fine account of the period, *White Bicycles* (2005), describing what was known as the London underground in 1966 as being "worthy of its name" because "few outsiders were even aware of its existence". By the following spring, Boyd says it "flourished" as a

> Sub-culture of drugs, radical politics and music built around the
> *International Times,* Indica Bookshop, *Oz* magazine, UFO, the
> London Free School, Release, Granny Takes a Trip, the 14-Hour
> Technicolour Dream and the Arts Lab (133).

As the underground became more visible, it might, initially at least, have been seen as one of those youthful sub-cultures following their predecessors the Teddy boys, beatniks, mods and rockers, that attracted the attention of the mass media and was subsequently written about influentially by Stanley Cohen (1972), Dick Hebdige (1979) and others. I do not propose to examine the broad concept of subculture in any detail in *Autumn of Love,* but for those who wish to pursue the topic, in more recent years, Muggleton (2000) and a collection edited by Bennett & Kahn-Harris (2004) among others, have developed the thinking of those earlier seminal studies. Whether we think this new movement was initially another sub-culture or not, in a very short time, it became rather more completely a distinct cultural phenomenon than some of those other sub-cultures, which tended to restrict themselves to fashion, music, stimulants and modes of transport

Those subcultural studies were retrospective, but in a contemporary account from London, in October 1967, Peter Fryer offered "A Map of the Underground", suggesting by then, in comparison with San Francisco and Haight Ashbury, "the British Underground has its own roots, its own history and pre-history" (6). He too, recognised that on the whole, the participants "rejected" labelling as "boring" and "beside the point" – since you either 'knew' on the inside, or you did not, and remained on the outside. Intriguingly, given the anti-materialistic thrust of much of the counterculture, Fryer suggested at the time, "the whole phenomenon can be seen as a complex of business enterprises" and was "acutely publicity-conscious".

While Joe Boyd's description of the underground "sub-culture" is clear enough and fairly inclusive, it is also, not surprisingly, very London-centred and that is why in this book, like the term hippie, I have used underground where it *feels* appropriate or where that was the term applied at the time, while my preference for a general term when required, is counterculture – which I believe reflects rather better the broadening and spreading of key ideas that emerged initially in Haight Ashbury, San Francisco and the London underground. Fryer's observation about business enterprises is also useful in a temporal sense, in that there is a common tendency around the 1960s' subcultures, trends and fashions for those involved at the start to dismiss the latecomers as pretenders or perhaps part-timers. Yet it might be that to a very large degree, and particularly in terms of the late 1960s underground, that the key difference between the innovators and followers is to some degree that between entrepreneurs and cultural consumers – where the former cannot survive long without the latter, and the latter often adopt an increasingly active role in what is produced or presented.

As for the term counterculture, at certain places and times in western society over the past two hundred years, other countercultures have emerged in the sense that they either distinguished themselves from what they perceived as the mainstream, or that they were actively hostile to it. The term does not imply *necessarily* a complete break with the mainstream or dominant culture, since counter is by implication tied to those things it opposes. It is not obliged to be 'separate from', and the distinction is never unproblematic – not least because the 'mainstream' was not necessarily as monolithic as some of its opponents would prefer to claim. I hope that clear, contextualised accounts of the precise differences, whether creative, economic, political or social, will emerge through the following pages.

Some of the earliest writing about the 1960s' counterculture emanated from the USA, initially for example, through the work of Roszak (1970). Many years after the publication of his seminal book *The Making of the Counter Culture,* and in an online review of another book, *The Imagine Nation: the American Counterculture of the 1960s and 1970s,* Roszak wrote

> When I coined the term "counterculture" in 1968, I had a precise but far-too-narrow definition in mind. I meant the rebellion against certain essential elements of industrial society: the priesthood of technical expertise, the world view of mainstream science and the social dominance of the corporate community – the military-industrial complex …

By contrast with that definition, offering an emphasis on social and political "rebellion", much of this book is concerned with the mid/late 1960s developments in popular music around rock, psychedelia, the folk revival and contemporary jazz. The main focus here is on alternatives to mainstream pop music and the differences are principally in terms of musical style, instrumentation, venues, commercial intentions and media representations. Occasionally, this alternative music was overtly political, although rather more often and more simply, it provided a soundtrack to the counterculture; some of it was experimental or at least novel, although in certain cases it led up blind alleys or towards aesthetic excess.

Autumn of Love is not all music however; alongside that focus I have drawn attention to broader issues, rather more in line with Roszak's initial interests. Throughout the book, there will be references to social activities, and the various alternatives that were part of the counterculture in areas like politics, ecology, diet, education and perhaps most notably spirituality. The penultimate chapter, in particular, focuses on that topic, largely to the exclusion of music, and if the music is your sole or principal interest, you might choose to skip it, although I hope not, because I believe that the music was only one (key) element of a much broader social movement. Perhaps for some of us, music was the glue that held everything together, or the soundtrack to the bigger picture, but it was not the only thing.

And why *Autumn of Love?* Partly, obviously, because that distant summer of '67 is long gone, and those of us who were there then, are perhaps not yet quite ready for winter. As an October (Libran) child, I confess to enjoying the autumn anyway, as it can be a period of rich colours, tolerable temperatures and moments of reflection, while we prepare the short, cold, dark days. Are they coming? Maybe for us personally, as we move beyond our own sixties and into the seventies that were never so much fun, but without the autumn (and indeed the winter) there is no regeneration, and those of us who have survived can offer grateful thanks that we are here to witness it.

In part, *Autumn of Love* is intended to suggest how San Francisco, London and other cultural centres enjoyed their summer of love in 1967, while Portsmouth's was rather more stretched out, perhaps taking a year or two more to come to fruition, and somewhat in the shadow of those better-known places. I do not believe this is a problem, since it is in the nature of the provinces, that styles and fashions filter through and are often adapted for the context. As academic and punk historian, Russ Bestley suggested about the late 1970s, in a crucial sense "punk came alive … when the provincials started getting involved in it". (*Provincial Punk in Pompey* film, 2016). Here then, is a tale from the provinces about a time of extraordinary and rapid social change.

The spread of the music, ideas and lifestyles beyond those cultural centres, was of course highly dependent on the post-war growth of the media, including in the UK not only underground publications like *Oz* and *IT* (which I generally call by its full title *International Times*) but also in particular, pirate radio, the creation of BBC's Radio One, the extra television channel BBC2, and the new Sunday magazine supplements. Through them, much of the underground and counterculture became visible in the provinces and there is a feeling that some of the early participants were not too resistant to, and perhaps even welcomed the publicity. As Charles Perry, reflecting ten years on from the first Trips Festivals, said of the early days in Haight Ashbury, San Francisco

> It was a really funny time … The thing was going on by itself, but then some people wanted to publicise it. They didn't know how to publicise it exactly, so it often sounds sappy. 'Summer of Love', I think is a little sappy (1976, 3).

That was ten years after. Now we are half-a-century on, and those of us who lived through those days, like most ageing people, probably spend much of our time now looking back. The key question surely is how do we do that, and what do we do with what we find? Being nostalgic can be perfectly healthy, but is that all we are doing, or are we still learning lessons and still developing? One of the key ideas informing this book is that the most interesting members of the generation described here were almost constantly in a state of 'becoming'; undergoing regular periods of reinvention and at each point, discovering and understanding more about themselves and their world. While we are still around, there is no reason why that process should ever end.

To a large extent this book is a celebration of a time and place that meant a great deal to many people and continued and continues to resonate. That is certainly the case for me, and in that personal sense at least, *Autumn of Love* is celebratory. But as I suggested in the opening of this chapter, Wonderlands can carry their own problems, and not everyone who was there at the time is convinced that we shared the best of times – or that everything necessarily improved. I invited various friends to contribute memories and thoughts to this book and one of them, Chris Abbott, who was very much there on the Portsmouth scene in those days (and subsequently as a promoter) offered these observations:

> I think when considering that transition from Mod to 'Hippiedom', during 1966/67, you have to realise it happened over a very short time frame and for some people it was just a case of fashion and musical tastes, while for others it meant a whole change of life values. Personally, I liked some of the lifestyle and value changes, but wasn't so keen on some of the music and fashion changes! Although it didn't apply to my old mod friends, by 1967 one found oneself mixing with people whose grooming and personal hygiene left a lot to be desired.
>
> Also, the more gullible, who were obviously looking for some answers and a bit of spirituality were getting dragged into Scientology and various forms of Buddhism, possibly due to their deference to the Beatles and other pop stars who suddenly thought they had deeply meaningful messages for us instead of

getting on with entertaining! Personally, I was already pretty much a convinced Atheist. My main argument against the Hippy ethos is that a number of its luminaries used it as a control mechanism over other people – Charles Manson being a prime example. It has also produced the Hippy entrepreneurs who on the surface ran their businesses in a more cool and hip way, but were still greedy, power-hungry egotists, such as Richard Branson.

It might have changed social attitudes on many levels but it has done nothing to combat the basic inequalities in our society which are now far worse than they were pre-1967.

Chris has clearly said what he means, and since he too was there at the time, we might keep his words in mind, as we read what follows.

SOUTH PARADE PIER 1959

The pier advertises its Summer Season
with Arthur Haynes and the Beverley Sisters.

JUST MY IMAGINATION

"Imagination is more important than knowledge.
Knowledge is limited; imagination encircles the world."

Albert Einstein

*A*utumn of Love is mostly a tale about Portsmouth in the mid/late 1960s. Given its focus on the swinging sixties and the counterculture, it is not a tale that has been told previously about the city in any great detail, despite the apparently endless chronicling of that period elsewhere in the western world. One of its key themes is imagination, which was in plentiful supply at that time, and is more generally surely, a desirable element in living a meaningful life.

It might also contribute to understanding of particular places, including Portsmouth. In a fascinating exchange in Alasdair Gray's novel *Lanark* (1981) two characters discuss what they see as the apparent anonymity of Glasgow:

> "Glasgow is a magnificent city," said McAlpin. "Why do we hardly
> ever notice that?"
> "Because no one ever *imagines* living here" said Thaw.

Is that true? I am not sure about Glasgow, but Thaw goes on to explain why he holds that view, suggesting that in the case of other cities like, "Florence, Paris, London, New York, nobody visiting them for the first time is a stranger because he's already visited them in paintings, novels, history books and films", adding, "if a city hasn't been used by an artist, not even the inhabitants live there imaginatively" (243).

When I first read that extract, I wondered whether it might help to explain why, after a lifetime in Portsmouth, working mainly in the arts and popular culture, it often seems to me that what we do here might be considered unimaginative or invisible, especially in the wider world. But I'm not sure it necessarily follows that those of us who do live here are incapable of doing so "imaginatively". Perhaps it is rather that what we do has a limited audience, even within the city itself, and since Portsmouth is Britain's only island city, it might be that bounded by the waters of the Solent, what we do stays on our island; that we tend towards a certain insularity. If so, perhaps this tale supports an alternative to Gray's idea, so that in the right circumstances anywhere can be inhabited imaginatively, even if within limited boundaries.

In fact, Portsmouth does appear in popular and creative representations every now and then – for example, in the British war film *The Cockleshell Heroes,* showing the Royal Marines training on Eastney Beach, or in some versions of *Mutiny on the Bounty* which set off from, or perhaps return to Portsmouth – "Well what are you looking at? It ain't Tahiti, it's only Portsmouth" (USA, 1935). In 1953, Hollywood star Glenn Ford had to share top-billing with Portsmouth & Southsea station, threatened by a bomb in *Terror on a Train*; while David Essex and Ringo, looking back to the late 1950s, worked fiddles at Southsea's funfair in *That'll Be the Day* – although we are not told the location in the narrative. Similarly, Ken Russell never reveals in the film, that the extraordinary, overblown *Tommy* was shot almost entirely in Portsmouth – although it is not a representation *of* the city. More specifically, Turner did paint and identify a fine seascape or two around the harbour (the 'mouth' of the 'port'), and when Mrs Thatcher's forces engaged the Argentinians in the Falklands, they departed and returned on our television screens and newspapers, via that same harbour.

Portsmouth has appeared in fiction too – for example, in *Mansfield Park,* where Jane Austen described my ancestors as "under-bred" and inhabiting a "sad place" with "vile sea breezes". We don't think much of her either. Much more recently, in the television fantasy *Dr Strange and Mr Norrell,* the latter declared "I dislike Portsmouth intensely", while in the popular ITV television thriller *Broadchurch* we hear a character ask "what else do you do in Portsmouth but be in the navy or look at the ships?" One author who has offered an answer of sorts is Graham Hurley, not a native, but one who lived here for a while. He sees the city as an ideal setting for his crime dramas, and in an interview told the local newspaper, "Portsmouth is God's gift to a working novelist and particularly a crime writer. If you subscribe to the theory that society is falling apart, that it's imploding, then there's no better place to see that than Portsmouth" (20.1.2012). That view might suit his story-telling, but it is not my experience of the city that I have loved for 67 years.

Given that list, we cannot claim that Portsmouth is never 'represented', but it is a bit scattered, not very uplifting, and unsurprisingly often links to times of war – or criminal activities. A number of famous authors have links to the city, but Charles Dickens was barely out of his nappies when he departed, while Rudyard Kipling and HG Wells both had unhappy memories of Portsmouth. For the most part, Portsmouth is best known for the sea, the Dockyard and the Royal Navy, and despite recent cuts to its historic purpose, the Dockyard, the Royal Navy and ancient and modern warships still play a major role in attracting visitors to the city. That was exemplified in the early weeks of 2017 as the travel companies began seducing us with invitations for next year's holidays. *The Guardian* carried a series of their own offers around the world, including "Four Days in Bruges by Eurostar" (from £269), "New England in the Fall" (£1,179), the Canadian Rockies (£1,399) or "Mary Rose and Portsmouth's Maritime History" (three days, £369). The Mary Rose was of course a warship and alongside her, visitors will find two others from the past, HMS Victory and HMS Warrior. As a consequence, Portsmouth rarely offers itself as a natural site for much 'peace and love', but this book will suggest that there have been and still are, other possibilities.

Beyond the Dockyard, the Royal Navy and the historic ships, located principally in the south-west corner of the island of Portsea, what is the particular nature of the city of Portsmouth – or 'Pompey', as it is often called? Britain's only island city has a population of around 200,000 depending on whether you include those who are just off the island, around the M27 and over Portsdown Hill. The island itself is extremely flat, with its highest points probably two railway bridges, and after London and Hull, the British city most prone to sea flooding – with the one slight advantage that at least coastal flooding recedes rapidly with the tide.

To the east lies Hayling, another seaside island, and to the west Gosport, which shares with Portsmouth the large natural harbour that travels up past the Continental Ferry Port, to the Roman castle at Portchester. The Romans probably settled there because they could more easily defend the top end of the harbour, but also because at that time Portsea Island itself was largely marshland which over the centuries since has been reclaimed from the salt water. Five miles south of Portsmouth, across the Solent, is the Isle of Wight, which in the period we are covering, played host to three increasingly large music festivals. Because Portsmouth is an island on the southern edge of the country, it is not normally a place that people pass through, unless the Isle of Wight is their destination. Otherwise you visit for a specific purpose or you do not come – even the cross-channel ferry port is on the north-west corner of the city, accessed directly from the M27/M275.

There are popular stories about Portsmouth that are handed down through the years; how for example, when the Royal Navy was at its height there were more pubs per square mile than anywhere else in the UK, how its citizens have a commitment to the local football team out of all proportion to its achievements of the past 60+ years, and perhaps most importantly how it resembles a working-class northern town that somehow ended up in the 'privileged' south-east of England. In 2011, the Office for National Statistics published figures revealing that Portsmouth is the most crowded city in the UK with 5,100 people to every square kilometre; 20 times higher than the national average of 255 people. While being crowded, urban and largely working class, politically it is conservative even when, very occasionally, it chooses politicians of other persuasions. There have been a few Labour/Lib Dem MPs (not currently) and even a fairly recent Lib Dem council, but when UKIP made significant gains in the council elections of May 2014, they were not for the most part in the major English cities and towns, apart from Portsmouth, where they gained six seats out of 42.

In 2007, the BBC's News Channel (3.4.2007) reported that Conservative politician Boris Johnson had written in his motoring column in GQ magazine that the city of Portsmouth was " one of the most depressed towns in Southern England, a place that is arguably too full of drugs, obesity, underachievement and Labour MPs." The Labour MPs have gone, but when others from that party criticized Johnson at the time, a Conservative spokeswoman replied online that: "According to the government's own figures, Portsmouth suffers the third highest level of deprivation and the fifth highest crime rate in the whole of the South East of England."

The city is certainly not affluent. In 2013, the Office for National Statistics reported that wages in the city were among the worst hit after the recession, and the local newspaper published evidence from other sources of economic hardship (11.01.2013). Some months later the Government announced the closure of the centuries old shipbuilding in the city that has provided much of its identity – Richard the Lionheart raised a fleet in Portsmouth, but on 7 November 2013, *the Sun* carried as its front-page story "Smack in the Mouth: catastrophe for Portsmouth workers".

Inevitably this economic reality has an impact on other aspects of life in the city. In July 2010, *The News* (Portsmouth) reported the findings of the Association of Public Health Observatories that "men die younger in Portsmouth than anywhere else in the area" and that worse, in its most deprived areas, the expectancy is eight years less than in the more affluent "such as Drayton and Farlington"; both just off the island of Portsea. In 2015, Public Health England revealed that only Manchester and Liverpool have worse figures for alcohol-related deaths (*The News* 3.6.2015)

Aspiration and ambition is a major problem for young people in the city – the tale that follows of local musicians will reveal a considerable number of individuals and bands of promise, but very few who managed to compete in the national and international context. In 2014, the Department of Education revealed that fewer pupils from the city's state schools are likely to go on to University than anywhere else in the country. With the overall national figure now around 40%, fewer than 30% are from Portsmouth while only one per cent get to a more prestigious Russell Group university and none to 'Oxbridge'. Alarmingly, a few young men did travel east recently, as the Guardian reported "How the 'Pompey Lads' fell into the hands of Isis". Sadly, few of them returned to their homes in the city.

That is all relatively recent history, but this book is focused on the 1960s, and from a significant newspaper article, we know something about how Portsmouth was understood at that time. In November 1968, The Times published a lengthy article under the title "Why Pompey is under a cloud", which revealed that among the 20 biggest cities in the country, Portsmouth had

- The highest suicide rate
- The third highest illegitimacy rate
- The highest county borough rate of children in care
- "High incidences of drug addiction and venereal disease"
- 2.9% unemployment, against 1.7% in the region, and 2.4% nationally

The 1960s were a period of high employment, but even then, Portsmouth lagged behind many other places, while the article reported that 40% of male employees in the city worked in HM Dockyard, where the "wages are low and there is little competition for labour". The newer industries, like IBM were generally locating to the north of (and just off) the island which encouraged employees to move out of the city centre to the private and council estates.

Stedman (1995) has described how the heart of the city suffered considerably from bombing during the war, with damage to 80,000 properties of which around 6,500 were destroyed (1995, 1). He notes that the first task was repair where possible, so that "rebuilding in the blitzed areas proceeded more slowly" (17) and when it occurred "there was resentment at the breaking up of communities" (20). He does however suggest that one positive outcome of the delay "may paradoxically have saved the city from mistakes" experienced by other towns and cities. Even so, the eventual solution was often a relatively cheap, 1960s modernist high-rise style, of which the most (in)famous example was the Brutalist Tricorn shopping centre, car park and nightclub to the north of the city centre, which was hated by many residents, celebrated by a few, and demolished in 2004. The beauty in the city lies in the seafront parks and beaches that stretch for some miles, from the harbour mouth, past the South Parade Pier and former Royal Marine Barracks along to Langstone Harbour, looking across to Hayling Island. From the promenade or beach, the Solent is constantly full of traffic, which in the 1960s still included the bigger liners to-and-from Southampton. In those days too, the seafront still had many of the buildings and attractions of a declining holiday trade, including the beautiful South Parade Pier and opposite, the Savoy Buildings and ballroom.

IN 1968, *The Times* described how "the influence of the Royal Navy pervades" the city and in those days, British and visiting sailors in uniform were highly visible around Portsmouth. In a response to the concerns about the report, the city convened a group of politicians and Church people to consider appropriate responses. One of them, the Roman Catholic Bishop of Portsmouth, Monseigneur Derek Warlock said

> Young people need hope if they are to liberate themselves from frustration, and avoid drifting into the purposelessness of a permissive society

No doubt the Monseigneur was well-intentioned, but this story is about how some of those young people found a good deal of purpose and meaning in what he chose to call the "permissive society". The story, will also consider how, for some of us, aspects of that experience remain meaningful to this day. In that respect, this is not merely intended to be a memoir but an account of how those extraordinary times left a legacy which, to some extent at least, can be celebrated.

The Monseigneur might have been concerned about the well-being of young people in Portsmouth in the late 1960s, but one recurring theme throughout *Autumn of Love* will be the contested issue of how many, or perhaps *how few* people were ever really participating in the "permissive society" or swinging sixties, and where that was happening. It seems to be an ever-diminishing number in the versions from mostly young historians, and they seem equally determined to insist that the UK's swinging sixties took place only in a few square miles, somewhere around Kensington, Chelsea and bits of the West End, and not at all in somewhere as provincial as Portsmouth.

By contrast, this book is suggesting that at that time in the western world, many young people's lives were transformed, regardless of class or location. This transformation manifested itself through music, fashion, stimulants, technology, the mass media, disposable income, sex and social life in general, and huge numbers of young people participated in these changed circumstances to some degree, even if, for a great many, that was only occasionally or superficially. For that majority, contentedly or not, they soon moved on to an apparently 'normal' adult life.

But this is not a story about that majority. For the most part, it is about the others – the smaller yet still significant number who threw themselves into some, most, or all of what was happening, with an enthusiasm that carried its rewards and sometimes dangers. In the story that follows, I identify myself as one of those people, and most of those to whom I refer were much the same. If you do not recognise, or acknowledge that this change occurred and had a significant impact, even on provincial kids like me, then this book is probably not for you. But if you do, or think you might, or if you would like to discover more before deciding, then perhaps it is.

In 2016, the Victoria & Albert Museum mounted an exhibition, "You Say You Want a Revolution?", which displayed and examined many aspects of those times, ranging from the hedonism of the swinging sixties to the revolutionary spirit of the counterculture. In September 2016, the *Guardian* published a review of the exhibition by their regular popular music writer, Alexis Petridis, who was then a few days short of this 45th birthday, having been born just too late to have experienced anything of those times himself. Nonetheless, he suggested that was no impediment to a degree of understanding because:

> The people involved in the late 60s' counterculture have barely shut up about it since the decade ended. Few generations are as self-mythologising as the baby boomers. It's hard to imagine there's a human being out there who hasn't heard the story umpteen times (7.9.2016 p 11).

Petedris is mostly right of course; there have been hundreds of books, magazines, newspaper articles, reviews, academic papers, television programmes, films, sound recordings and exhibitions about that decade, and it might be that all the main stories have now been told. One of the more recent developments in all this documentation and reminiscence has been a backlash, generally fiercer than Petedris, against this "self-mythologising". In Britain, much of that has been led by the broadly conservative historian Dominic Sandbrook, who produced two extensive histories on the 'long sixties' (*Never Had It So Good* and *White Heat*) in which he set out, among other things, to argue that for the majority of people, the decade was unremarkable. He sums up that view on his website, suggesting "for most people in Britain, the Sixties didn't swing at all. As well as reflecting all the gaudy excitement of the period, I also wanted to reflect the lives of millions of people who felt left out or alienated by the cultural changes of the day."

By "most people" he might have been counting simply almost all of those under about 15 or over 30, but even with regard to young people, in *White Heat*, he quoted John Benson's view that most of them "spent more time in their bedrooms or at church youth clubs than they did at rock festivals or on the football terraces" (191). It's an odd argument; in some ways, a statement of the bleeding obvious. I watched my home team 'Pompey' pretty regularly in the 1960s but even if I had watched every home game in a season, that would have amounted to about 50 hours in the year – less than the equivalent of one hour per week in my bedroom. As for festivals, in the British 1960s they were pretty rare events – Beaulieu for jazz in the early years, then Richmond and Windsor every August Bank Holiday, and from 1968-1970 the Isle of Wight. Attending one of these for the whole weekend would amount to about the same number of hours as watching the football for a year, so again an evening each week at the youth club would amount to about three times that figure. Nonetheless, Benson's point apparently satisfied Sandbrook.

Like Petedris, Sandbrook (born October 1974) was commenting on a past he had not experienced, but while this is both common and entirely legitimate for historians, it can be a missed opportunity when approaching the history of a period that still has millions of survivors, who are not consulted. De Groot (2008), an American who arrived in the UK in the 1980s, has written an extensive international account of the 1960s in which he addresses this question. He refutes quite reasonably the accusation that if you were not there "you can't possibly understand", by citing the logical problem of applying that accusation to the study of medieval history. But the issue is not that simple. Without supernatural powers, it is pretty difficult to correspond with people who were around in medieval times, so other methods and resources must suffice. On the other hand, it is not too difficult to discover the thoughts and memories of participants in the 1960's counterculture by going to archives full of moving images, recordings and published artefacts. To a large extent, serious younger historians and journalists tend to do that, but the consequence is that they draw mainly on reminiscences of the 'big hitters', while there are fewer accounts like this one of young people who were participating fully in that world in their own ways, while remaining mostly hidden from history.

The account that follows, offers on the whole a fond memory of an extraordinary time, notwithstanding the foolishness, mistakes and misjudgements, which were perhaps not surprising giving the relative inexperience and immaturity of those at its heart. It is certainly not supportive of De Groot's generalisation on that same page, that examining the sixties "we see mindless mayhem, shallow commercialism and unbridled cruelty". Was that all there was? That is a very negative view, although one can find some sympathy with his suggestion that "for too long the sixties has been a sacred zone" (2008, 2).

By 2012, Sandbrook was enjoying himself to the extent that in a BBC television series about the 1970s, he proposed that "the swinging sixties only happened to about 14 people in a few privileged enclaves". Unless I am misunderstanding his use of the term "swinging", this book demonstrates that he is wrong, not only in his deliberately exaggerated number, but in terms of the kinds, breadth and location of those people whose 1960s were unlike anything that had come before. (*The Seventies* – BBC TV, 2012).

Early in the same year, the BBC broadcast a drama series called *White Heat*. The fictional narrative opened in January 1965, with the death of Winston Churchill, and featured a mixed bunch of students sharing a flat in London, the narrative moving gradually from that point to the present day. Typically, they managed to work "My Generation" into the early action and, as with the movie *Quadrophenia,* they got the timing wrong, since the record was not released until the autumn of 1965 (reaching the charts in November) – after the events depicted in both fictional pieces. But that is dramatic licence. On the weekend following the first episode (of six) in a review of the programme, the *Independent on Sunday* columnist DJ Taylor (born 1960) echoed Sandbrook by informing us that outside a small part of London, the swinging sixties was a "mythical construct", while elsewhere, "English provincial life went on practically unchanged". This provincial tale begs to differ.

In his wake, other historians and writers have joined in. In July 2013, Paul Morley suggested on the BBC2's *Late Show* that "the incredible life of the sixties has become ghostly", while on the same programme, classical historian Bethany Hughes (born 1968) was just furious:

> I'm so sick of hearing about the swinging sixties because I think that for most people who lived in that decade the party was definitely happening somewhere else … I hate all those old farts that want to talk about the sixties … it's gone … done … there's a few snaps of it left, but now is the most interesting moment we're ever going to have, isn't it?

It might be Bethany; one of the consequences for some of us who lived actively through that decade was an engagement with certain philosophies which focused very intently on living in 'the Now'. But I am not sure that is quite what Bethany means – and if it is, she might be talking herself out of a job.

Again in 2012 (what was it about that year?) *Guardian* columnist Ian Jack visited the Royal Court Theatre to see Mike Bartlett's (then) new play *Love, Love, Love.* The setting opened in 1967, and Jack described it as a "satirical attack on the good fortune" of his generation, through a tale of "personal folly and self-indulgence" (12.5.2012). He then related how his own 1960s really did not swing, even though as early as 1962 he was attending CND rallies and listening to the Everly Brothers. It is almost as though the majority of media professionals feel duty-bound to deny that many of us were having a rather fine time back then. In the play – written by a man born in 1980 – a young woman of today suggests that all we stood for then, was "being able to do whatever the fuck you wanted" and Jack felt himself "excluded" by that view of his history. Less predictably perhaps, so do I, and I will endorse Jack's view that beyond such narratives, even "more rigorous" non-fiction history "has a habit of excluding many of the people who lived through it".

It seems that this might never end. As we were poised to go to print, novelist Anthony Quinn wrote a piece in the Guardian (11.03.2017) marking the 50th anniversary of the release of Antonioni's *Blow-Up*. He opened by asserting that the 1960s of the "public imagination" was "quite different" from the reality, adding, if you were there in the 1960s, "you didn't hang out in Carnaby Street", you didn't "trip on acid while driving a Lotus Elan" and "you didn't swing". Well it was always wiser not to mix driving and tripping, and for sure I knew no one who drove a Lotus, but once again someone who was not there (Quinn was born in 1971) was telling those of us who were, just how it was.

One commentator who *was* there and claims to have had a swinging time, was the painter Bernard Cohen (born 1933) who took a rather different approach which nonetheless seems to deny the experiences of those who came along a little later. In an entry in a 1991 Arts Council catalogue, for the 1960s' art exhibition, *Ready Steady Go,* Cohen suggested that the "swinging 1960s" were experienced by

> The creative people who had lived through World War Two and the period of austerity that followed it … Suddenly one realized that all kinds of people thought and perceived with the same spirit. Only politicians and economists appeared to remain unchanged (23).

That seems fairly positive, but then Cohen claims that it "swung from about 1958 but became as predictable as musak by 1963 …" If he was right, even the Beatles, Twiggy, Radio London, David Bailey and the real *Ready Steady Go!* arrived 'after' the swinging sixties ended, which is hardly consistent with the way the term is generally used. It is not however, untypical of the way that certain people tend to claim a widespread cultural phenomenon for themselves and their elite group – often defined merely by age. We shall meet that attitude more than once, in the story that unfolds here – while this tale will seek to be far more inclusive and open.

It might be true that almost all the tales of the 1960s to date have been produced by those who, like Cohen perhaps, were part of the "few privileged enclaves". There were such groups for sure – and some of them at least deserve their place at the heart of the tale of what occurred, but in part, *Autumn of Love* is an attempt to tell a different tale of a provincial city and to some extent, one provincial boy who grew up there in these very interesting times. That boy, and others like him, had a feeling that something really was happening back then and if he did not always know quite what that was, unlike Mr. Jones, he endeavoured to find out. Often that search was successful, which has had remarkable consequences for the life that followed, and so the second purpose of this publication is to consider the legacy of that decade – and in particular the positive legacy.

As we are noting, there are others who will tell the opposite tale, and of course some of the criticisms of those times are legitimate and warrant repeating, for there is no value in nostalgia drifting into sentimentality. One fairly vehement public critique can be found (online still) in a BBC television programme from 2004, *Why I Hate the Sixties*. The programme begins with a voice-over informing us "The sixties are the iconic decade" when "the myth was created before the decade was out", following which the writer and journalist Peter Oborne proposed that "everything was supposed to have got better, but actually almost everything got worse." Well Oborne lived through the 1960s but, born in 1957, only reached his teenage years as the decade expired, so maybe there was a certain resentment in his generalisation, a sense of missed opportunities for a boy on his way to public school and Cambridge University? In the same programme, writer and journalist David Aaronovitch echoed Sandbrook's views, stating that "the swinging sixties probably only ever existed somewhere in a triangle between Carnaby Street, King's Road, Chelsea and Abbey Road", while a similarly dismissive view was taken by the writer and critic Mike Phillips who suggested, "once you got outside that small magic circle in the centre of London, nothing swung. It was the same as it was in the 1950s, only with a few more jobs. The sixties? Rubbish".

In Phillips' case, a rather more revealing, and poignant moment occurred later in the programme with its focus on Enoch Powell's infamous "Rivers of Blood" speech in 1968. Phillips is a black man who arrived in Britain from Guyana in his teens in the 1950s, and discussing Powell, revealed that for him the 1960s were "pretty terrifying times", an understandable and entirely legitimate reason for his views. But however inexcusable racism and related violence was in the 1960s, it does not follow from that one young man's experience, that the 1960s were simply "rubbish", any more than Oborne's claim that "almost everything got worse" stands much scrutiny.

It would help in many of these cases if such generalisations were accompanied by some degree of definition and even the occasional example. It might be for example, that Oborne, who generally works for publications on the right of centre, considers that "almost everything" that got worse, included all the 'liberal' legislation of the decade. Perhaps instead, he wishes that homosexuality and abortion were still illegal and punishable by imprisonment, or that divorce laws always favoured the husband; while talking of punishment, perhaps we should forget the prisons and start hanging people again, like that nice Timothy Evans? Does he wish that the Lord Chamberlain still controlled theatres, or that censorship could protect his wife and servants from pornographic literature like *Lady Chatterley's Lover*? Perhaps he resents the setting up of the homeless charity Shelter in the light of the BBC television Loach/Garnett drama *Cathy Come Home*, or personally not being selected for National Service when his time came? While he benefitted from a fine education, maybe he regrets the creation of a number of new universities, the expansion of higher education and the planning of the Open University? Ultimately, I wonder whether he was even happy to appear in a television programme broadcast in colour, since presumably he prefers black & white television, and while I know he has a sporting interest in cricket, perhaps he did not care about England's footballers winning an international tournament for the only time. He does not tell us.

In terms of sport, David Araonovitch more recently reviewed the V&A 'Revolution' exhibition for *The Times* (9.9.2016) and noted how, apart from the 1968 Olympics' Black Power salute, sport was absent from the otherwise fairly comprehensive show, because Aaronovitch suggested, the exhibition "recognised … what changed, but not what (for most people) stayed the same". This is a common but wholly erroneous view – sport changed alongside many other things. For example, I have written a book, called somewhat cheekily *Forever Changes* (2016), about what happened to English cricket in the 1960s and beyond. In that decade, the authorities introduced the first one-day limited overs competition and the first Sunday League (both sponsored), abolished the old distinction between amateurs and professionals, were forced to address the issue of apartheid in South Africa, and enabled counties for the first time to instantly register star overseas cricketers such as Garry Sobers, Clive Lloyd and Barry Richards. Meanwhile English 'soccer' abolished the maximum wage, lost a key right of transfer case to footballer George Eastham and introduced substitutes for the first time. BBC Television's broadcasting of Test Matches had become a regular event in the late 1950s, while the BBC introduced *Match of the Day* in August 1964.

Revolution was 'in the air' and had an impact in many spheres – even among the most traditional.

Back in the television programme, *Why I Hate the Sixties,* Peter Hitchens suggested, that "in the 1960s, we chose the wrong future and we're still living with that", while the Conservative journalist, Sir Peregrine Worsthorne, pointed out that Harold Wilson's dream of a New Britain forged in the white heat of modern technology had failed; although he acknowledged that there was a new Britain, "culturally, socially" and in "religious and moral terms" – whether he approved of that change was less clear. There was a general condemnation of the architecture and urban planning of the 1960s, and this was a stronger section since it was accompanied by clear examples and documentary footage – although no doubt others might wish to offer an alternative view. There is a legitimacy too, in the argument that not only were the 1960s better in Britain if you were white but also if you were male, with entirely valid points about the relatively poor treatment of women, although oddly (typically?) these were presented mostly by three men, Aaronovitch, Phillips, and academic Terry Eagleton.

Elsewhere in the programme, the change from selection to comprehensive schools was considered a disaster, although no one questioned whether grammar schools really were always so exemplary, or addressed the impossibility of a truly *comprehensive* system in a country that continues to enable the better-off to purchase private schooling. There was also a general rubbishing of any interest in those forms and practices of spirituality which were then new to most in the west. In those "tie-dyed days of illusion" the "mix of drugs and meditation", was for Eagleton "amorphous and incoherent" and for Oborne, an often articulate and interesting commentator, just "bollocks". Chapter 14, in particular, will offer an alternative reading of those views.

Aaronovitch suggested "in the 1960s we dodged the big questions" but the programme ended with the little ones; an idea that purely for financial reasons everything was 'fixed' to enable England's footballers to win the 1966 World Cup, and the suggestion that the pop singles chart successes of Rolf Harris with "Two Little Boys" and Englebert Humperdinck's "Release Me" somehow demonstrated that even the claims for the quality of popular music in the 1960s were misguided. That last argument did offer two examples but this was hardly rigorous 'case study' research to authenticate a particular view. In fact, it was "bollocks"; ignoring for example, that through this period, sales of 45rpm singles were in decline, as sales of LPs overtook them and went on rising, while also forgetting one essential and sometimes overlooked point about popular music in the 1960s, which was that for many young people, the thriving, today almost unimaginably active *live* scene was as important – perhaps even more important – than the records. *Autumn of Love* will offer considerable evidence for that being the case, at least for a substantial minority of young people.

Taken together of course, this collection of media professionals constituted precisely the kind of elite commentators that they were themselves prone to criticise for creating the myth of the sixties. Do I mean therefore that they were entirely wrong, that their arguments were without merit or foundation? Not at all. There are many claims for that period as with any other, that do not stand up much to scrutiny, and it might well be in some respects at least that our present is indeed the "wrong future"; it often seems like the wrong something in 2017.

Not everything that occurred in those times was wise, fair or sustainable, but the 1960s opened up a world of possibilities for me and others like me, even in the provinces. Some of those possibilities we have pursued with enthusiasm ever since, some we have abandoned when our appetite was sated or because they proved poor choices, and some, even now, we are working to understand. Since I lived through the 1960s from the ages of ten to twenty in, for the most part, relatively comfortable circumstances, it might not be surprising that I view them with some fondness. Ultimately, through the rest of this book, I wish to take issue with Sandbrook's assertion that during that decade, "change came rather slowly to provincial towns" (2006 p xvii) by describing the changes that we experienced in provincial Portsmouth. I will suggest that I was not alone in finding it rather more rapid, more exciting and more interesting than he and others, imagine.

VIEUX CARRE JAZZ BAND at the RENDEZVOUS CLUB, 1961

This is probably the original venue in Ashburton Road Southsea.

'60s CITIZENS

Very often the media and cultural commentators use the phrase swinging sixties without any clear definition – it is assumed we know what they mean, yet we have seen in one instance that Cohen defines it as ending in 1963, before most people assume it began; it was for example, 1966, before the American *Time* magazine's often mentioned 'tribute'. In fact, Sandbrook, in his second volume, devoted a chapter to the topic, but in keeping with his broad views of the difference between a London elite and the rest of us, he called it "The Swinging City" – and unsurprisingly, that city is not Portsmouth (238-261).

His chapter describes the fashionable areas of the capital, certain elite clubs (Sibylla's, the Ad Lib, Scotch of St James) and well-known individuals from that time, including members of the Beatles and Rolling Stones, Mary Quant, David Bailey, Jean Shrimpton, and Michael Caine. Broadening his vision to the "Swinging Sixties", Sandbrook declared that its "bible" was nothing less than the "Sunday colour supplement", which appeared first in the *Sunday Times* in 1962, and within two years, in the *Observer* and the *Sunday Telegraph*. Through such publications, we had access to some of the latest news, even in the provinces; my father, for example, took the *Observer*. Sandbrook refers also, to the view of historian Jerry White (243) that the swinging sixties' "temples" were "the boutique and the discotheque" – we had them in Portsmouth too, as well as some clubs and shops in London that we could afford, and which we could reach easily in a couple of hours.

The question of affordability is of course significant and Sandbrook suggests that "it was impossible to be a fashionable Londoner without money" (241). There is a truth to that in terms of the specific fashions to which he is referring, and which were the preference of the cultural elite, but it ignores the possibility of a certain hipness that is less dependent on 'having' and rather more on 'being' – a kind of being that was rooted in knowing of a certain sort, which was neither new nor even that difficult to find. It had resided for decades in the mythology of the 'starving artist; the literature and poetry of the beats and those who came after; in the behaviour of the more 'authentic' of their followers, the beatniks; and by the 1960s, in the fine art courses of some (independent) colleges, and in the new, mostly amplified music of young people, who began with little more than a determination to find the 'right' sounds and modes of expression. This mode of being did not cost the earth, and it was not something you could buy. An early example, can be seen in the film *Momma Don't Allow* with 'ordinary' young jazz fans, leaving work to see Chris Barber's band in the early 1950s in a north London club. When a car full of youthful 'toffs' arrives, they are tolerated despite their demonstrable lack of awareness of how to dance or fit socially with this sharp scene. It was ever thus. If you have to ask, then probably you do not know.

A few years after that film, anticipating what was to come, Colin MacInnes published his celebrated novel *Absolute Beginners* (1959) in which the anonymous leading figure, a young stylish photographer, is in looks and attitude essentially a prototype mod. He describes his unlucky half-brother Vernon who is "one of the last of the generations that grew up before teenagers existed" (37) and is dismissive of the "full-fledged Teddy boy condition – slit eyes and cosh, and words of one syllable, and dirty finger nails and all" (43). On the other hand, he is impressed by "a young coloured kid called Mr Cool … (who) wears a beardlet and listens to the MJQ and speaks very low" (50). At a time of racial tensions in London and elsewhere, our narrator gravitates towards black London culture, not least because

> When the teenage thing began to seem to me to fall into the hands of the exhibitionists and money-lenders, I cut out gradually from the kiddo water-holes and made it for the bars, and clubs and concerts where the older members of the jazz world collected (61).

By the mid-1960s, many of those same clubs had become home to the mods and their soul and rhythm & blues. Also in 1959, Basil Dearden directed the feature-film *Sapphire* about the murder of a black woman in London who had attempted to pass herself as white. The film appeared immediately following the Notting Hill race 'riots' and explored the nature of contemporary British society with the two leading figures, white police officers, attempting to discover who was responsible for the murder.

Sapphire was genre fiction, if based on very real contemporary social issues, while again in 1959, Karel Reisz, who had also made *Momma Don't Allow* with Tony Richardson, directed the documentary *We Are the Lambeth Boys,* about teenagers (boys *and* girls) attending a south London Youth Club (and shot in the summer of 1958). The participants are all white and living mostly in the local council blocks; the majority have left school and are in employment and while, as in *Absolute Beginners,* there is a somewhat forbidding gang of Teddy boys ("Smithy's Mob"), the majority of these teenagers dress in more up-to-date, and generally smart fashions. At one point, there is a very interesting session in the club where a group of the boys discuss clothes and one expresses the importance of spending perhaps 15 guineas (£15.75) to ensure you have the best and latest suits – probably about one month's take-home pay then. They do not all agree, and even those that do, would not have thought of themselves as mods, but they anticipate the same concerns for clean living and looking their best – even for a normal night at the Youth Club. They are very definitely 'ordinary', mostly working class teenagers, and by no means wealthy, albeit with disposable incomes.

There were similar examples in the early 1960s. It is not apparent that the young artists shown in Ken Russell's 1962 BBC Monitor film *Pop Goes the Easel,* including Derek Boshier from Portsmouth, are particularly wealthy, although some would become so, but they clearly exhibit a certain hip attitude which through the tragically brief life of Pauline Boty, manifested itself beyond the artist's studio, in cinema, fashion and advertising. Another young art student, Barry Miles came to London from Cheltenham, and by 1966 was involved in publishing *International Times,* helping to run the Indica Gallery and Bookshop and eventually became one of the major chroniclers of the times in a broad range of publications covering the UK and USA, and many of the key figures and events of the 1950s and 1960s. In a recent catalogue, Andrew Sclanders (2017) listed a book inscribed by Miles to his friend and collaborator in the early London underground, John 'Hoppy' Hopkins, in which Miles wrote "To Hoppy, I remember when we were all beatniks together at Westbourne Terrace, love Miles".

One of the key points about these representations and memories, is the extent to which so many of the participants shifted through various phases and tribes in the world of contemporary teenagers and young people. *Absolute Beginners* and *We Are the Lambeth Boys* both depicted Teddy boys as if they were stuck in outdated subcultures, and there have always been those who even decades later, continue to pursue identities as mods, rockers or punks, all of which tend to become more fixed as time passes. But many other young people who immersed themselves in those groups at the time, were excited by processes of transformation. Sometimes this is interpreted as a tendency to fashion-conscious fickleness, but it can be seen also as an openness to new ideas and opportunities – as Portsmouth mod Ian Hebditch told Paolo Hewitt (2000)

> The only people who had anything of validity to say were those who shared your beliefs. There was this sense that you were right

but you were constantly moving on and breaking new ground. You didn't want to stay where you are (my emphasis, 78).

Prior to the highpoint of the mod years in Portsmouth between 1964-1966, another group that might be seen as archetypally transitional, came from the city, and were featured in another BBC television documentary film, one of a series of six made in 1963 by John Boorman, under the title *Citizen 63*. Each film selected an individual from a range of contexts, and subjects, and Episode Three, shot through the spring and summer and broadcast in September 1963, was about a young woman student from Portsmouth, Marion Knight. She was 18, and, post-school, studying Nursery Nursing at John Pounds Secondary Modern School, in the dockyard area of Portsea. Marion lived in one of the city's densely populated streets, just around the corner from me, had been adopted and was raised by parents who were committed members of the Salvation Army. Boorman (2003) suggested retrospectively that she was "rebellious" but with qualities of "leadership and grace", adding, she and her friends "thought of themselves as beatniks, a faint echo of the Beat Generation", while Boorman found them "more interesting than the mods and rockers then emerging in all their decorative banality" (100). In fact, a number of this group would participate fully in the Portsmouth mod scene within a year or two, and by the late 1960s might have been more easily described as hippies.

When Boorman was making his film in 1963, beatniks had already made an impact on mainstream media and news reporting for some time. As early as November 1959, an episode of BBC Television's *Hancock's Half Hour* entitled "The Big Night" poked fun at these young people by featuring Tony substituting beatnik garb for normal Saturday style. Then in 1960, the BBC's news magazine, *Tonight,* ran a feature on 'real' beatniks in Newquay being chased away because of their long hair and generally scruffy appearance. In the introduction to the piece, Alan Whicker described how at the height of the summer there might have been as many as 50 beatniks in the town, and Newquay council urged local businesses to ban them from access and employment, and sought to turn them out of the town. 'Wizz' Jones, one of the interviewed beatniks, subsequently became a successful folk singer, appeared regularly in and around Portsmouth and across the country and is still playing and recording – including a scheduled appearance at our local Wickham Festival in 2017. In 1965, a cinema short, *Primitive London,* described the 'peacock' tendency and group identity of the mods, contrasting that with the beatniks who prided themselves "in their non-conformity". A pub clip showed folk singer Emmett Hennessy and harmonica player Ray Sone (ex-Downliners Sect) performing the American folk song "John Henry", while alongside them, 20-year-old long-haired, unemployed Michael described himself as writing as yet unpublished poetry.

Presumably all the bigger towns and cities had their own beatniks, as they had Teddy boys and later mods & rockers, and all these groups tended to exercise the civic minds, as reflected in the local press. In 1960, Portsmouth's *Evening News* reviewed *The Beatniks* an American movie showing in Fratton Road's Troxy Cinema and depicting, "young rebels, living like there was no tomorrow", while around the same time, a British offering, *Beat Girl* starred pop singer Adam Faith. A few years later, the newspaper looked back on the days in Portsmouth, when the Saturday night Rendezvous Jazz Club opened in a disused church in Ashburton Road Southsea and described its "steaming walls and beatniks by the dozen". Of course, most of them returned to school, college or work on the following Monday morning, although one interesting arrival, probably in the summer of 1962, was a London beatnik that Marion Knight and her friends met on a CND march and again at a jazz festival. He played a little music and had ambitions in that direction, but he spent that summer in and around Portsmouth, sometimes sleeping in a tent on Portsdown Hill, or making friends around Southsea, who provided alternative places to 'doss'. His name was Rod Stewart, and interestingly when he came to write his recent autobiography, he had clear memories of a similar spell in far 'cooler' Brighton, but somehow had forgotten all about his summer in Southsea.

In mid-July 1961, the *Evening News* ran a series called "When Youth Drifts" which examined issues like under-age drinking and sex, drugs, the impact of working mothers and "the Beatniks and their Followers". In a city pub, reporter James Bayes found an "authentic" beatnik who was only too ready to dismiss look-a-likes as "part-timers". That would be a common theme among all the fashionable groups of the 1960s and beyond. Then on Friday 5 October 1962, the newspaper published a 'Kay Stanhope' women's feature about a group of local beatniks including poet 'Holy' Peter, 18-year-old with "multi-patched jeans" and Johnny, in a duffle coat. They disputed the label beatnik insisting they were "individualists" and criticised the fashion-conscious "pretence of art students". They claimed to live "on the road", sometimes sleeping under South Parade Pier, saved money on haircuts and shaving but could not understand why Portsmouth people did not accept them, or their opposition to materialism, class divisions and race hatred. However principled and truthful those claims might have been, in the final weeks of 1964 there was a report of two men sought for an armed hold-up on the A3. They were being linked to a young Waterlooville woman, who was described as a "runaway beatnik". Her mother said that she had seven

'O' levels (GCSEs) and a decent job, but bored by "very dull" Waterlooville, had gone to live with other "beatniks" in Southsea.

A review of an episode of "Citizen 63" shown the week before the Portsmouth episode, appeared in the *Observer*. It was about a police inspector, but reviewer John Gross (8/9/1963) who had hoped for "a stormy evening", found the inspector's opinions "conventional but mild". He suggested the programme was "technically up-to-date" but in terms of the documentary fashion of the time proposed, "the trouble with cinema-verité is that it all depends how interesting your verité is". For Gross, the following week's episode showed an "improvement" with a "portrait of an intelligent, idealistic girl from Portsmouth, who … has taken up the CND, more or less as a way of life". Gross praised in particular, the photography of a beach party and concluded enigmatically that the fairground scene showed "nature catching up with art, or at least with Tony Richardson" (Theatre/Film Director – notable for the Oscar winning movie *Tom Jones* in 1963). In November, *The Times* summed up the series positively, with the view that human material is best approached on television as "people in close-up", an achievement of *Citizen 63*. "The result did not add up to an anatomy of Britain but … it introduced an exciting equivalent of cinema verité".

Boorman later recalled "the country was in turmoil as the sixties began to swing … I was observing … a significant shift in society, a revolutionary itch" (99). He added that in the series, "we were probing the lives of ordinary people (but) I tried to do it with style and imagination, with juxtapositions, so that it transcended the 'people to people' idea."

In the Portsmouth episode, Marion Knight and her friends were shown as firm advocates of various strands of left-wing politics; they supported CND; preferred jazz, folk music and Ray Charles to the transience of current pop hits; sang folk songs together, danced the jazz fans' stomp; wrote poetry and wore contemporary fashions which clearly hinted at the gradual transition from beatnik black to more tailored mod. Marion, training to care for young children, made a number of thoughtful observations about sex and its conse-quences among young people and outside marriage, some of which were either misrepresented in the editing, or misconstrued by those watching. It caused a considerable local incident in Portsmouth at its provincial best (worst?).

In his autobiography, Boorman recalled, "it is hard to convey how shocking all this was to the nation. There was an outcry. Yet Marion was honest and she argued her position so cogently there was sympathy for her too" (101). The *Evening News* printed a number of reactions and subsequent responses. One main letter was headed, "This teenager was not typical of Portsmouth

Youth" (17.9.1963) as two 16-year-old girls "and friends" complained of "this appalling portrayal of our grand city and its young people" which showed "a collection of barely disciplined youths, exposing thoughts and pursuits, which we deplore". They added it was "a completely appalling and false portrayal of an average citizen" – although it never claimed to be "average" anything. A reply (20.9.1963) argued however that the film was "enlightening" because Marion and her friends were "typical of a new and large group of citizens which exist throughout the country … holding bold if misguided views (and) a very different outlook … from most people".

The mother of one of the nursery children was dismayed by the implication that the young children shown on screen were "backward … difficult … from broken homes … illegitimate" (*Evening News*, 14.9.1963). She was sure that most were "happy (and) normal". This emerged as an issue of editing and construction, as the BBC stressed that the general comments were not applicable to the children at that nursery. Portsmouth's Councillor Bateson investigated, but had "no intention of attempting to apply censorship". He reported that Marion would elsewhere make it clear that "her views are different from the majority of her schoolmates", adding her views were "unconventional" but "sincere"

In the same edition, Marion's Headmistress, Mary Bray, described the programme as "first class", confirming Marion's comments about the children were from "her previous experience in a residential nursery". The mother acknowledged that Marion's general comments (alongside shots of the nursery children) were not specifically about those Portsmouth children depicted, but told the *Evening News*, "it is still my considered opinion that this fact was not made at all clear by the BBC" (19.9.1963).

Beyond this particular controversy, the documentary can be seen as representing a group of provincial young people in touch with new ideas, fashions and attitudes in a way that some commentators would have us believe were never seen outside the capital, even five or more years later. It was a different kind of cutting edge from the more hedonistic and better-funded version characteristic of the celebrity circus of swinging London, but what it was not, in any respect, was life as it had been, even just a few years earlier. This was perhaps because of the extension of further and higher education, perhaps because almost all young people had (some) more money to spend; perhaps because entrepreneurs and the media were exploiting young people's tastes for new fashions in everything in the cultural sphere, and because of the very recent end of National Service. That might have had a bigger effect on young men than young women, but for two decades the majority of men around the age of 19 or 20, had gone off to serve in a uniformed, ordered world which must have had a significant impact on everyone's life when they departed and then returned to 'civvy' street. Now that was over and, however subtly, young men found themselves in a different world, which was not suddenly disrupted by the call to arms; even if that meant sometimes, no more than spending 18 months in Aldershot, Catterick – or Portsmouth Naval Base.

None of the foregoing is to argue that Portsmouth was at the heart of the swinging anything in the 1960s, it is simply to contest the idea that provincial life in the UK back then was unchanged from previous decades. By the end of 1964 on the south coast, we had the Sunday colour supplements, *Ready Steady Go!* on our television screens, Radio Luxembourg and 'Big L' on our new transistor radios, coffee bars, juke boxes, youth clubs, and rhythm & blues clubs, which booked many of the leading London acts, while the Beatles and Rolling Stones had both visited the city more than once. In addition, while this particular world was populated mainly by young people, since many of them (like me) still lived at home, it hardly left our parents, other relatives, neighbours or teachers, untouched or unaware. I had a maiden aunt in her fifties at this time, who was Head of History at a local grammar school. She had absolutely no interest in popular culture, but would occasionally tell her pupils that she knew all about the Beatles and Rolling Stones from her nephew! For better or worse, the world was changing more rapidly than ever before, and a lot of people knew about it, including some who were not terribly keen on the idea.

THE HONEYS

Around 1960, on tour with Scottish pop singer Jackie Dennis ("Lah Dee Dah"), the Portsmouth trio sign autographs for their fans.

Photo courtesy of the Honeys.

THE YOUNG ONES

I was ten years old when the 1960s began, living with my parents and younger sister in a semi-detached house in Festing Road, Southsea – just a few minutes walking distance from the Canoe Lake, Southsea seafront and South Parade Pier, which in those days were the favoured destinations for visiting holidaymakers. Next door to us was a guest house that catered mainly for the working families who came from other bits of England to smell the sea air, eat candy floss, watch the 'Bathing Beauty Contests, and laugh and singalong to the end-of-the-pier shows with Tommy Trinder, Ted Ray the Beverley Sisters and other giants of British 'light entertainment'.

For four years, I went to the junior school around the corner in Albert Road, just past the beautiful and long-gone Southsea Odeon. Then in September 1958 I was sent across the city to the junior department of Portsmouth Grammar School – boys only, and preparing us for a seamless transition to the bigger boys' 11+ version across the road. By January 1960, I studied Latin, sang hymns and recited prayers every morning, loved cricket and was only slightly less fond of football. My dad was a local government clerical officer, working in Portsmouth's Fire Stations, my mum, once a librarian, was now a mum, while in their spare time, my parents visited our ageing relatives most Saturdays, watched the two television channels (but mostly BBC) in the evenings, and ran the local Sunday School. My mum came from a northern coal-mining family, my dad's family had been small shopkeepers in Southsea. We were therefore a bit lower middle-class, mixed with a strong dash of northern Methodist/socialist working-class.

The generation before mine, older brothers or sisters and mostly born during war time, had encountered (or ignored) Bill Haley, Elvis, James Dean, Marilyn Monroe, Jack Kerouac, Jackson Pollock, Marlon Brando and various other innovators – all of them Americans. Meanwhile, what were we British up to? One of them, the accomplished British jazz drummer Tony Crombie, who had played quite regularly at Southsea's Savoy Ballroom, briefly forsook the dance bands and his modernist mates like Ronnie Scott, and attempted to produce an equally lucrative English version of Bill Haley & his Comets, called Tony Crombie & his Rockets. They made records and movies and toured the country, although it did not work out for them and Crombie went back to the jazz and dance bands. Nonetheless, in September 1956, with considerable attention from the music weeklies, they made their debut as Britain's first-ever professional, recording rock & roll outfit – and that debut was a week's residency at Portsmouth's Theatre Royal. It was rare rock & roll triumph for my native city although, approaching my seventh birthday, I knew nothing about it at the time. Crombie's fate was soon sealed, largely because of the emergence of younger stars who attracted the teenage audience, including Tommy Steele, Cliff Richard, Marty Wilde, Billy Fury and the others, but despite that, Portsmouth can forever claim to be the birthplace of live British rock & roll – another triumph for the provinces, precisely because we were the provinces. After a week in Portsmouth, 'warming up', the Rockets were promoted to the London Palladium, the (very minor) silver screen in *Teach You to Rock* (1956) and a tour of the country.

1956 was one of those extraordinary years of change in the arts and popular culture in Britain. Alongside rock & roll, the British created their own home-grown version of American music, skiffle. From our traditional jazz scene, Ken Colyer, Chas McDevitt and Lonnie Donegan performed and recorded versions of American blues, country and folk songs, which caused great excitement as it enabled a generation of often modestly talented young people to begin performing as well as consuming popular music. In addition to skiffle's new popularity, Elvis Presley first hit the British 'hit parade', while the film *Rock Around the Clock* was released to a (literally) riotous reception. A few months earlier, James Dean had starred in *Rebel without a Cause*, while in theatre, 1956 was the year of *Look Back in Anger* at the Royal Court Theatre and in visual arts and design, the seminal ICA art, design and architecture exhibition *This Is Tomorrow*. Beyond mainstream cinema, the British "Free Cinema" documentary group held its first screening at the National Film Theatre and among the first three films screened was *Momma Don't Allow*, that film previously mentioned, about a night at a London jazz club with Chris Barber's Band – including Lonnie Donegan.

In popular music, vinyl 45 rpm 'singles' and long-playing albums were supplanting breakable 78 rpm discs, while the guitar moved from an accompanying instrument to an increasingly dominant role in contemporary acts, thanks to greatly improved amplification. In Portsmouth, a grammar school boy called Paul Pond had his guitar and so too did some of his peers, and while Pond would always love the blues, his pals were enthralled by the new sounds of skiffle and rock & roll. One of them, Colin Olford described their music as "the cement" that held them together socially, for "nobody else had anything like this", and it became a key element in a broader Southsea scene, that would lead some directly into the folk revival that followed in the early 1960s. While the sound was mainly acoustic, they found a way of experimenting with simple amplification, and they met on weekend evenings in the cellar of a friend's home. Colin, later a GP in Portsmouth, recalled it as an innocent time, with "no booze" and certainly "no drugs", although there were "fags of course and an evening of bopping/jiving" to the latest rock & roll records.

There were a few gigs too, mostly at youth clubs, around Southsea and up into North End. The boys were generally successful academically and content to keep their weekend and evening activities separate from school life – with one notable exception, for the young Paul Pond went up to Oxford University, to read English, departed rather rapidly to immerse himself in the growing British rhythm & blues scene in London, and having changed his stage name to Paul Jones, became the singer in Manfred Mann, with whom he enjoyed a string of hit records through the 1960s. He is still performing with a version of that band (the Manfreds), another called the Blues Band, and for some decades has been presenting BBC Radio's regular Blues programmes.

There was another local skiffle group called the Krewnecks, who partici- pated in a skiffle contest on Southsea Common, which was reported under the heading "Summer Fair at Southsea" in the *Evening News* on Monday 19 August 1957. This was principally a fund-raising event for two local youth clubs in Kingston and Brookfield Road and many of the Krewnecks' friends came to support them. Colin remembered "hot competition between the two leading bands", but the Krewnecks "came a very close second", while the winners, the Mick Glover Group went on to greater local success after converting to amplified rock & roll. They appeared on local television, and after Mick had departed for National Service, renamed themselves the Live Five, landing a cameo role in the film *Expresso Bongo* starring Cliff Richard. Meanwhile the Krewnecks played in another skiffle competition at the Savoy Ballroom, on a night when one of Britain's top live dance acts, the Ted Heath Band, topped the bill.

In Southsea in the late 1950s, music was one key element of the broader teenage social groups. Apart from each other's houses, there were the youth clubs where the skiffle groups sometimes played, and more frequently a growing number of Southsea coffee bars, including the Manhattan Coffee Lounge & Grill towards the top end of Palmerston Road, Figaro's in Osborne Road and, in particular, the Coffee House on the corner of Marmion Road. As one group moved beyond their teenage years and often towards a certain kind of 'respectability' or social convention, the next batch of teenagers were always poised to take over, with their current musical interests and fashions. Around 1960, the Coffee House was where guitar players Jon Isherwood and

Pat Nelson would meet on the embryonic Portsmouth folk scene, which included elements of a localized beatnik/CND culture. One person who remembers this next phase, Donna, later sang in the folk clubs herself. She recalled that in 1960 she was 13, and at that time in Portsmouth,

> The atmosphere was very much the jazz era with people evolving from the constrictions of conformity. People from all backgrounds were aspiring to become artists, musicians, singers and poets – the feel was very 'Left Bank bohemian'. There was a feeling of rebellion and people looking for something different from their parents who had fairly recently been through a war.
>
> My parents paid for me to go to a little private school in Woodpath, Southsea called Walker's College. It was a strange mixture, special-ising in shorthand & typing in the top part of the school (actually a large house) while on the lower two floors we did history, English, art etc.
>
> Outside the college gates each day was an array of what were known as beatniks with such names as Holy Tony, Creeping Jesus and Gypsy Dave – bearded long-haired young men who were probably what was known as 'on the road'. I believe some of them had occupied the houseboats at Eastney. I was most definitely not on the road and returned home to my comforts every day.
>
> In Palmerston Road, Southsea, very much the 'in place' was the Coffee House on the corner of Marmion Road. We would drop in while supposedly following the teacher to tennis on the seafront – few of us ever made it! The coffee house was full of the 'in crowd' who were a few years older than me – probably 17/18 and that's where I first remember seeing Jon Isherwood. He always had his guitar with him and I would listen to him while eating minestrone soup, which along with frothy coffee and lemon meringue pie was the piece de resistance of the coffee house.
>
> Pretty soon I was going to the Rendezvous jazz club on Saturday nights in an old church hall in Ashburton Road, Southsea. Different jazz bands were popular at the time – Chris Barber with Ottilie Patterson, Ken Colyer, the Back O' Town Syncopators and more commercial bands like Acker Bilk and Kenny Ball and most played at the Savoy or South Parade Pier (Sunday nights). Then I started going to jazz on Friday nights at the Railway Hotel near

Fratton Bridge – the pub was nothing at all but it turned into a really popular music venue, and on Mondays there was a thriving folk club.

The folk scene became very vibrant with many venues opening, featuring new and innovative artists. The venues included The Cobden Arms (Arundel Street), The Talbot (Goldsmith Avenue), the Black Dog at Havant, while the students held a club in the pub at the end of Locksway Road, the Thatched House. But for me, the Railway was the best. All the up-and-coming artists appeared there including Jon and Pat who were at the forefront of the scene in Portsmouth; both were charismatic in their own way. Jon could hold an audience, was an excellent showman and always liked a drink to give him an edge. Pat was well spoken and as a performer he was very controlled and slick – he was a very pleasant man who unfortunately did not live a long life. He had his own BBC radio folk show for some time.

My personal 'Eureka!' moment came one Monday when two visiting American folk singers appeared at the Railway. They were Rambling Jack Elliott and Carolyn Hester. I still remember his long blonde hair and leather fringed jacket and her in an Indian buckskin outfit with high boots – that was it for me. I had always danced and sung but now I wanted to sing folk. I didn't have to wait too long as a few weeks later three young men knocked on my door saying a mutual friend had said I could sing and would I join their band the Country Strings.

I practised with them for a while and we started doing floor spots. The Railway Folk Club witnessed a lot of great artists including Alex Campbell, Long John Baldry and Diz Disley, a brilliant jazz and blues guitarist and a fantastic character who later played with Stephan Grappelli. One of my favourites at the time was a local jug band called the Levee Breakers who sang slightly risqué songs like "My Man's a Deep-Sea Diver". There were also more traditional artists like Martin Carthy, Bert Jansch, Louis Killen and Davy Graham.

Donna has mentioned the Folk Club at the Railway Hotel, where Paul Jones and the early Manfred Mann appeared in Portsmouth as well as residencies at Kimbells ballroom. This signalled the start of the local rhythm & blues boom, reflecting in particular what was happening in the London clubs around 1962.

The band offered an interesting musical combination, representing the various strands of this new boom; Manfred Mann and Mike Hugg (drums & vibes) had begun playing modern jazz together, Mike Vickers was a multi-instrumentalist, and Tom McGuiness had played in the Roosters with Eric Clapton. Paul Jones, having started out playing skiffle, then had a spell as a cabaret singer with a dance band in Oxford, played in a duo with Brian Jones, and in London, sat in occasionally with Alexis Korner's Blues Incorporated. That famous breeding ground for key figures in the first British blues boom was itself a combination of musicians from skiffle, folk, and traditional and modern jazz, plus a bunch of aspiring young singers.

Donna described the Coffee House on the western corner of Marmion Road as an 'in place' at the start of the 1960s, and Graham Laker remembered it as one of the first "frothy coffee bars with those huge Italian machines and sold coffee in glass cups and saucers". Through the 1960s, there were a number of such venues, especially in Southsea, mostly with exotic names like the 'Milano', 'Esperanto', Manhattan or 'Delmonico', and the fashionable location tended to move around. There was one, currently called The 'Wave Maiden', midway along the south side of Osborne Road and Graham recalled:

> I'm pretty sure its first incarnation as a coffee bar was around 1962 as 'The Beachcombers', decorated with lobster pots and fishing nets and frequented by 'arty-farty' types and the local beats. It then became the 'Keyhole' and was the main mod hang-out for Southsea. We started going there in 1963, when it was run by a posh bloke called Charles. He had a white English bull terrier which used to escort him to the bank each morning. The cheapest drink was a glass of orange juice for eight pence (about 4p) which we'd try and make last the whole night. Charles got wise to this and used to come around the tables feeling the glasses, and if yours was 'warm', you had to buy another one or get out. There was also a bouncer there, a greaser type called Barry, and at the sign of any trouble, the offender would be hurled out the door (quite literally) and be left sprawled across the pavement. It had also had an amazing jukebox as, apart from the usual stuff it also had records by the Miracles, Louisiana Red, Booker T & the MGs, Bo Diddley, Jimmy Smith and many other greats.

Around 1960, many of the more apparently hip people were fans of jazz, and tended to be somewhat dismissive of rock & roll and commercial pop music. While the label jazz implies a single genre however, it disguised real tensions in those days between those who looked back (traditionalists) and those who looked forward from the inventions of the 1940s (modernists) – and all of that is without entering into further ideological splits between traditional and 'revivalist' fans! The tensions became physical just along the coast from Portsmouth, at Lord Montague's annual jazz festival in 1960, and BBC television was there to broadcast the rioting 'trad' fans who were demanding an end to modern group, the Jazz Five, and the delay in waiting for the television cameras to prepare to broadcast a performance by Acker Bilk's Paramount Jazz Band. After the weekend, our *Evening News* carried the headline, "Beaulieu Back to Normal After Jazz Riot" and a photograph of "bearded beatniks" among the fairground debris, following the 'riot' on the previous Saturday night. On the Sunday, Bank Holiday visitors to Beaulieu were apparently "content to be amused by the antics of 'beatniks', 'weirdies' and 'ooblies'". On the following Thursday, the newspaper carried a letter from Ernie Sears, promoter of Portsmouth's Rendezvous 'Trad' Jazz Club and Secretary of the Portsmouth Area Jazz Federation, who explained, but did not condone the riot, suggesting the need in future to segregate the "various jazz idioms".

Among those at Beaulieu was Portsmouth musician Colin Wood and his friends Al Straughan and Paul Plowman. They travelled on motorbikes in the usual protective clothing but Colin recalls "we did, of course, wear 'beat' attire when we got close – and also had cider flagons that were *de rigeur*". While Colin was a traditional jazz fan, he was also playing bass guitar in local group the Renegades who, as was the fashion, started out covering instrumental hits by the popular acts like the Ventures, and Shadows before adding vocalist 'Danny Raven' (David Boltwood) to perform rock & roll classics and recent hits by Ricky Nelson, Cliff Richard and others. Also from the early 1960s, Graham Parker, was the drummer with local group the Conchords and their typical pre-vocalist, instrumental repertoire included Duane Eddy's "Peter Gunn" and "Because They're Young", the Shadows' "Apache", "Dance On" and "FBI", the Ventures' "Walk Don't Run", Sandy Nelson's "Let there be Drums" and the Surfari's "Wipeout", which he recalls practicing "for hours in my bedroom". On the whole, vocalists came along a little later and one challenge for them recalled by Dave Pittard, then drummer in Barry & the Zodiacs, was that in some pubs, such as the city centre's Golden Fleece and Goldsmith Avenue's Talbot Hotel, there seemed to be a licensing law allowing amplifiers but denying vocalists the use of microphones!

Other popular local rock & roll acts in Portsmouth in the late 1950s, included the Cadillacs, the Hi Fis, the Denver Four, the Tremors and then the Hot Rods, the For-Tunes, the Residents (later the Furys), Brothers Scarlett, the Southern Sounds and the Rivals. There was also Portsmouth's very own 'girl' trio the Honeys who appeared around the country and abroad on bills and tours with

Cliff Richard, the Beatles, Helen Shapiro, Bobby Vee, Adam Faith and many others. Sadly, they never recorded. One local act that did go into the studio was Frank Kelly & the Hunters with a number of single releases, and again they appeared on a number of early 1960s package tours.

With the exception of occasional national chart hits like "Take Five" by Dave Brubeck, modern jazz was always something of a cult interest in Portsmouth, although once the city's bombed Guildhall had been re-built and re-opened in the summer of 1959 it hosted a number of significant jazz concerts including Brubeck himself, Miles Davis, Sarah Vaughan, Gerry Mulligan and for the traditionalist, Louis Armstrong, Ella Fitzgerald and the British acts like Acker Bilk, Chris Barber and Kenny Ball. The latter acts enjoyed a couple of years of commercial chart success and those bands and other traditional ensembles also appeared frequently on South Parade Pier, particularly on Sunday evenings.

The advent of the electric guitar, and the new songs and youthful singers of the late 1950s however, meant that rock & roll, and in the 1960s, its offspring British beat, pulled the next generation of potential fans away from jazz, whether 'trad' or modern. The *Evening News* of 1 August 1960 carried a juvenile court story about a 14-year-old girl who said she went to a rock 'n' roll club in the city every night, while her Probation Officer told the court that her mother "was going around with coloured sailors in a fairground". The court found that the girl was "in need of care and protection … and was placed under supervision for three years", including a nightly curfew of 10.15pm. These rock & roll clubs were probably mostly coffee bars with juke boxes.

While 'trad' briefly enjoyed commercial success, a possibly more authentic version continued to attract a following in the local pubs and clubs, notably the Rendezvous, which moved from Ashburton Road for brief spells at the Dockyard Club and South Parade Pier, before settling in the Oddfellows Hall in Kingston Road. But the story of the girl and the "rock 'n' roll clubs" was indicative of the rapidly changing fashions in popular music and the broader culture. In the mid-1950s, to a large extent, the live popular music option in a city like Portsmouth consisted of dance bands, some jazz (mostly traditional) and variety shows which would mix musicians with dancers, comedians and novelty acts. In 1956, with the resolution of a twenty-year Musicians' Union dispute, American Bands toured again – Stan Kenton was the first to visit Portsmouth coming to the Savoy – while skiffle stepped out from interval entertainment with the traditional jazz bands, to a brief fashion in its own right. Some skiffle records even sat alongside rock & roll chart hits that year by Elvis, Bill Haley, Fats Domino, Little Richard, Carl Perkins and others. There was also a brief fashion for calypso, led by Harry Belafonte and then, by the late 1950s, for younger, smoother pop singers (Ricky and Bobby and Billy – and Cliff of course). Neither was it the case that one fashion simply replaced another. After the advent of rock & roll, many dance bands struggled economically, but they have never disappeared completely and even today, 50 or 60 years later, it is possible to find exponents of most of those styles and genres out there, performing with audiences that often dress appropriately and indulge in a certain nostalgia – sometimes for periods and fashions they never experienced first time around.

By 1962, electric guitars and the fashions that accompanied them were displacing if not replacing bowler hats, clarinets and trumpets, and the jazz audiences divided. Those that truly cared for it, continued to find jazz locally performed in pubs like the Cobden Arms in Arundel Street or the smaller clubs like the Cellar Club in Hampshire Terrace or the Oasis in North End, while the bigger names, like Ball, Barber, and Bilk carried an audience with them for decades. In the world of pop, 1962 came to an unsurprising end with Cliff, Elvis and the Shadows in the UK Hit Parade's top three, and for the first seven weeks of 1963 it was instrumentals all the way with the Shadows, followed by their 'old boys' Jet Harris & Tony Meehan, topping the charts.

Then, suddenly, while many familiar names continued to enjoy success, a new sound swept the world of British pop music. In late February 1963, the NME announced that the Beatles had knocked Jet & Tony from the top of the charts with their second release "Please, Please Me". During the rest of that year, they would return with three more chart-topping singles, and other Merseyside/Manchester acts to appear in the Top Thirty for the first time were Gerry & the Pacemakers, the Searchers, Billy J Kramer & the Dakotas, the Hollies, the Swinging Blue Jeans, the Big Three, the Fourmost, and Freddie & the Dreamers. Add in groups from elsewhere like Brian Poole & the Tremeloes, Bern Elliot & the Fenmen, the Dave Clark Five and Johnny Kidd & the Pirates and it was clearly one of those key transitional moments

Portsmouth joined in, as the Beatles visited in March and April1963, and then in September 1963, the Rolling Stones appeared in the city for the first time at the Savoy. The message was filtering through from London that to survive, the jazz clubs and some jazz musicians had to cater for the new generation's preference for British rhythm & blues. After three good years, the Rendezvous Club was struggling and it closed temporarily in 1963, but Ernie Sears got that message, and in early 1964, the posters went up around town for the Rendezvous "Rhythm & Blues" club on a Saturday night with two groups – usually a local support act, plus artists like Alexis Korner, Long John Baldry (who not only brought Rod Stewart with him, but sacked him there), Graham Bond, the Animals, Jimmy Powell and Downliners Sect. The new audience included the first wave of Portsmouth's mods.

I do not know whether Sandbrook, Aaronovitch and others would wish to concede that what has been described so far constitutes one example of the embryonic swinging sixties, but it is surely beyond argument that this was unlike anything that had gone before – especially in its accessibility to any young people who choose to participate. Something was going on.

The new rhythm & blues acts at the Rendezvous were, like the beat groups, largely guitar-based bands or at least in the case of Graham Bond, bass guitar and drums, but it was still something of a 'cult' scene that differentiated it from the more mainstream pop acts appearing at the Savoy, and on the Guildhall's package circuit. New fashions in western popular culture often begin as cults, limited to a minority; the knowledgeable 'in crowd', while those that come later are often dismissed for sacrificing the integrity of the earlier versions. It is an over simplification of a more complex cultural process. George McKay (2003) for example has written about the tendency of a number of popular music academics to be dismissive of traditional jazz as nostalgic, and catering largely for an ageing white middle-class audience. But McKay points out that this ignores the innovative nature of the early British performers, beginning with George Webb's Dixielanders in London from 1943, and its subsequent central role – particularly through the marching bands – in the CND movement and other left-wing causes of the late 1950s. Even in *Citizen 63*, Marion Knight and her hip pals are seen dancing the stomp to musicians performing in the traditional jazz style, although it would not last much longer, as they too transferred their interests to the rhythm & blues scene.

In early 1964, the Beatles led the 'British invasion' of the USA, while in Portsmouth's mainstream pop venues at the time, you could have seen the Searchers, Dusty Springfield, the Rolling Stones, Shirley Bassey, the Dave Clark Five, Billy J Kramer, Joe Brown, Dionne Warwick, the Crystals, Adam Faith, Manfred Mann, the Kinks, the Isley Brothers, Carl Perkins, Cliff Richard, Dave Dee and others. It was the time too when the British folk revival was growing in the provincial clubs, including around Portsmouth, mainly in pubs like the Railway Hotel, Star Inn, and Talbot Hotel, while the Guildhall presented concert appearances by Muddy Waters, Ray Charles, Rev Gary Davis, Sister Rosetta Tharpe and other black American artists. Add to them the regular rhythm & blues club acts and life was becoming pretty varied, and pretty exciting too.

JON ISHERWOOD, TED WENHAM, FRANK HURLOCK & OTHERS

This is the original 'Ballads & Blues' Folk Club
at the Railway Hotel Fratton, 1962.

Photo courtesy of Dorothy Wenham.

THE FIRST TIME I MET THE BLUES

In the early 1960s, I became increasingly interested in popular music, girls, and alternatives to school uniform. In the summer of 1963 – my first full year as a teenager – I encountered the Rolling Stones for the first time, and in two key respects it affected my life significantly. The first time had nothing to do with hearing their music, but was simply a photograph in a long-forgotten magazine – was it *Pop Weekly*? I cannot be sure, but it was certainly one of those smaller glossy magazines, not *Melody Maker* or *NME*. Wherever it appeared, I remember quite distinctly where and when I saw it. We were on holiday, staying with my aunt in Chesterfield. I had bought the magazine and, waiting at a bus stop, I was flicking through the pages when I came across the photograph of the group playing live at a festival in Battersea earlier that year; an afternoon that showed them quite clearly looking 'bohemian' in dark clothes, roll necks, suede jackets, hair brushed forwards, over ears, touching collars – and not a smile to be seen. By contrast, in the background, a group of very straight looking guys in suits and ties stood around watching the band. You can find the photo online.

At this point, my favourite band was the Beatles who made fine music, and introduced me to a range of American rhythm & blues acts with whom I was not previously familiar. I saw them twice at our Guildhall in 1963. Despite their appealing irreverence, Chelsea boots, and fringed 'Beatle cuts', Brian Epstein had replaced their rocker leathers with suits, while by Christmas 1963 he had fixed them up with a two-week London Christmas show, featuring other 'Merseybeat' acts, Rolf Harris and the 'loveable mop-tops' in short, under-rehearsed sketches. By contrast with that shift towards 'showbiz', I found the Rolling Stones of 1963, surprising and exciting. There was something about that bohemian look that struck a chord, and while I could not have articulated it at the time, their appearance seemed to imply something significant about a specific world view – authentic or not.

This feeling contrasted with my experience over the previous five years at a school that cared so desperately to ensure that the *uniform* we wore everyday was absolutely that. Masters and prefects (17/18 year olds) could pick on you for wearing coloured socks, patterned shoes, unconventional tie knots and especially not wearing your cap off the premises – and they could beat you for the last of those offences, as well as many other misdemeanours. I became used to this pretty quickly, including the injustice of it on occasions. For example, our huge playing fields at Hilsea were divided from the former barracks that served as changing rooms by a long row of rose bushes. These were punctuated by gaps, but which gaps you were allowed to walk through was governed by strict hierarchical rules. One day, when I was about twelve-years-old, I walked off the field after playing cricket, enjoying a conversation with the master in charge of our game, and as he went through one of the 'special' gaps, I went with him, continuing to talk – until an older master inter-rupted us, pointed out what I had done and told me to report to him at break *the next day,* for a beating. He quite deliberately left me to worry about that all night, and at twelve, I did worry, but it was the kind of experience that left me with a very clear view of authority, justice and indeed the ethos of that school in those days – although it is a very different place today. Incidentally, the master who inflicted that double punishment was teaching us a few months later, around the time of my 13th birthday and during the Cuban Missile Crisis, and he quite clearly told us that we might not be back the following week for the next lesson. So, there I was, embarking on my teenage years, learning that my elders and betters, could be sadistic, frightening but not necessarily right.

We also had a virtually compulsory cadet section (I was a sailor) with its own uniform inspections, and transgressions there could also be punished by a beating – Martin Richman and I were once so punished for "mutiny" after refusing to keep marching on a 'Drill Parade'. By the end of my school career I had been beaten sufficiently often not to care much, although it was always pretty odd being beaten by a boy maybe just one or two years older than me, and merely confirmed my life-long suspicion of people who seek power and/or enjoy punishing others. I suppose what I saw in the Rolling Stones, suggested in a barely understood way, an alternative. Eventually that view came to be concerned with more important issues than a school cap.

School uniform also complicated travelling around the city by bus or 'bike'. A fellow grammar school boy, Paul 'Oscar' Wild, recalled

> Having to ride my bike through what is now Somerstown, with my straw boater on my head certainly attracted plenty of expletives! After a while, I was accepted, probably because a lot of my mates lived around the Somers Road area, and it became acceptable to just put up with the 'stop me and buy one' taunts.

Almost as soon as the Sunday magazine sections appeared 'Oscar' paid attention to them and recalls one occasion when:

I took a picture from a *Sunday Times* colour supplement to my local barber in Elm Grove, to be told that my hair wasn't right for the style! It's an excuse I've used many times since. I then went to Debonair in North End/Hilsea where I got something like it, but coming out of the barber's I was spotted by a school prefect who reported me for not wearing a cap in the street and I got four with the slipper!

Portsmouth Grammar School was a day school that aspired to be a public school, and embraced solidly middle-class values, although we pupils were a far more disparate lot than is the case today with fees now of around £13,000 per annum (ours were less than £2 per week). There were plenty of boys there who had some interest in popular music and maybe even current fashions, but another fellow pupil Nigel Grundy wonders why it was

That from such a large school, so few PGS pupils found the Southsea nightlife exciting? There were a few boys and girls from the other grammar schools out in the evenings, so maybe the lack of PGS people may have been due to a complete lack of interest, or it may have been due to parental control, I know I had to be secretive about my movements. As the 1960s progressed things got easier and a couple of years later there were more PGS and ex-PGS people around. As far as fashion went, at school it was easier to be a Mod. With a compulsory Combined Cadet Force requiring us to wear Army, Navy or Air Force uniform to school one day a week and frequent uniform inspections, there could be no digression from the standard, but those of us in the know would remove a single diagonal thread from our ties, exposing a thin black line and some of us wore CND badges on the reverse side of our school blazer lapels.

Having seen the photograph of the Rolling Stones, I wanted to hear them, and I liked their first single, "Come On". I was too young to have noticed Chuck Berry first time around, and his songs, initially via the Beatles and Rolling Stones were a revelation – alongside Eddie Cochran he is one of the finest at portraying teenage life; one of the first great singer-songwriters. The Rolling Stones' version of his song might almost be seen as an early prototype for what became garage/punk; it is not 'great' in any objective sense, but it had some energy. The really interesting track for me however was the 'B' side "I Want to Be Loved" written by Willie Dixon and recorded initially by Muddy Waters. It was pretty good in itself, but crucially it took me off on a lifelong adventure with the post-war Chicago blues. It was not long before I was buying the real thing, and even starting to play a bit of music.

At the start of 1964 I was 14, and popular music and popular culture were becoming increasingly central to my life. I read *Melody Maker* every week and enjoyed its mixture of pop, rhythm & blues, jazz and folk. I had also taken my first faltering steps as a 'musician', singing and drumming with a very talented guitar-playing classmate Pete Gurd. When I bought the "Countryline Special" EP by the wonderful Cyril Davies something about the sound of the 'blues harp' struck a deep chord with me, and I bought my first Echo Super Vamper for 10/6d from Courtney & Walker at the top of Commercial Road. Apart from my voice, it became my instrument for life. These days I play Lee Oskars at about £40 each.

In Portsmouth, a new rhythm & blues club started at Kimbells, Southsea, initially organised by the Concorde Club over Southampton way. There was a Sunday night residency initially featuring Georgie Fame & the Blue Flames, plus mid-week nights through to July. Apart from Georgie Fame, it featured acts like the Graham Bond Organisation, Rod Stewart with the Soul Agents, Alexis Korner's Blues Incorporated, Jimmy Powell & the Five Dimensions, Chris Farlowe & the Thunderbirds, John Lee Hooker touring with John Mayall's Bluesbreakers and on one occasion, Eric Clapton in his last days as a member of the Yardbirds.

Among local bands, there had been significant changes with the members of the Renegades. While Colin Wood took his bass guitar to work with the excellent, jazz-influenced rhythm & blues style of the J Crow Combo with saxophonist John Crow, the other Renegades reformed as a four-piece rhythm & blues band the Dynamos. In January 1964, 'Spinner' in his weekly *Evening News* pop column described them as "just about the most popular group in the whole of the Portsmouth area" but while he was positive about the various guitar-based acts, there was less cheer in the suggestion of a "lean time ahead for Portsmouth's jazz lovers", with the local jazz club having "faded into obscurity in the last 18 months" and the city becoming "noted for its apathy towards modern music". It would not be so with the next generation.

By March, the newspaper was publishing criticism from the older jazz fans of the new British rhythm & blues as nothing more than a variation of rock & roll, having "little connection" with the real thing, while promoter Ernie Sears admitted that the Rendezvous was not trying "to satisfy the purists" because "we cater for a larger number". Such a debate begs the questions of what exactly we mean by any 'pure' form of a genre and, if we can answer that, whether exposure to a diluted version (if it is that) nonetheless encourages new fans to seek out the 'real thing'. I would suggest that the latter view is entirely consistent with my experiences when I first heard the Rolling Stones, and then started going to live gigs at the Rendezvous and elsewhere. From that, has come a life-long love of the blues in all its forms.

The first British rhythm & blues act I saw live was the Pretty Things, with their mix of fairly raucous covers of Jimmy Reed, Bo Diddley and others, matching their wild appearance, which I remember with delight causing something of a stir among Southsea's holidaymakers on the promenade when they arrived to play at South Parade Pier in mid-summer 1964. They were not particularly subtle, but at 14 I loved them. A couple of months later, my first visit to the Rendezvous coincided with a visit from the Moody Blues who had just released their cover of Bessie Banks' "Go Now". In blue suits and neat hair, they looked like a tidy alternative to the Pretty Things but they were exciting live, and one of the songs I particularly enjoyed was an up-tempo version of Sonny Boy Williamson's "Bye Bye Bird" with Denny Laine on harmonica and vocals. A few months later, I bought a single version of the American original, coupled with "Help Me". Sonny Boy Williamson's recording is more restrained – as were most of the blues originals covered in those days – and these days those originals are almost always my preference. Around my 15th birthday however, I had a taste (albeit short-lived) for the wilder, raucous British rhythm & blues.

That manifested itself most obviously on the number of occasions I saw Downliners Sect. They had a repertoire very similar to the Pretty Things and indeed toured with Jimmy Reed at one point, although I do not think they were with him when Jimmy Reed played at Kimbells – a gig that Graham Laker recalls with great affection. With regard to Downliners Sect, I particularly liked their original harmonica player Ray Sone, although he soon departed. While the early Rolling Stones' albums featuring their live repertoire, stand scrutiny today, it is not quite the same with Downliners Sect, although, as with "Come On", they did somewhat anticipate the garage sound that was a precursor of punk. For a brief spell, I loved them, and bought their first album and a couple of singles as well as an EP recorded live in London which is qualitatively perhaps the worst record I've ever owned! It sounds as though it was recorded on a domestic reel-to-reel at the back of the noisy club (Studio 51) and having hardly ever played it, I was delighted decades later to sell it for almost £100 to a dealer at one of the big record fairs they held at the Pyramids. The tracks appeared eventually on a compilation CD.

The London rhythm & blues scene was pretty varied, given its frequent dependence on three chords, 12 bars and four beats to a bar. I went to the

Rendezvous for less than one year albeit not every week (sadly, I missed Little Walter) but in addition to the wilder, guitar and harmonica bands like Downliners Sect there were a variety of (modern) jazz influenced acts who depended very little on lead guitarists, including the Graham Bond Organisation (post-John McLaughlin), Georgie Fame & the Blue Flames and the rather fine first version of Alan Price's post-Animals Band. Long John Baldry was probably the most accomplished jazz/blues vocalist, and one of the most impressive acts was the Spencer Davis Group who explored a broad range from folk-blues through rhythm & blues and soul, to remarkable covers of Ray Charles, mostly sung by the superb Stevie Winwood. Between them, these bands encouraged me to explore a broad range of American music across blues and jazz.

Most of it was music from previous years and decades and many favourite songs came from the classic post-war Chicago recordings on Chess, often put out in this country on the pink Pye label, including my first blues album, around Christmas 1964, called *Rhythm & Blues All Stars*. It had tracks by Muddy Waters, Sonny Boy Williamson, Elmore James, Jimmy Rogers, Jimmy Witherspoon, Little Walter, Memphis Slim and Buddy Guy's awesome version of the Little Brother Montgomery song "First Time I Met the Blues". Jack Bruce sang a version of that with the Graham Bond Organisation, a very fine band that I always felt suffered somewhat from the quality of Bond's singing.

While most of these bands were exploring a range of blues and modern jazz sounds, the (original) Moody Blues did something else. Listening to their old recordings today, suggests they were an efficient band with a good lead singer, but very dependent on material which was sometimes a bit 'ordinary'. Where they scored for me was in their exploration of more recent American soul and rhythm & blues, with melodies that generally suited English voices better than what Muddy Waters has called the 'deep' blues. I do not have a set list for that evening at the Rendezvous, but what I remember most clearly are the references they made to James Brown as they covered tracks from his great *Live at the Apollo* album. I had never heard of James Brown and it was another example of how these British acts were important in alerting us to new musical artists and styles, at a time when it was difficult to find much on the radio – even Radio Luxembourg in the evenings. Very soon afterwards I bought the James Brown album. The original Moody Blues, incidentally sounding nothing at all like their very successful late 1960's version, performed tracks like "I'll Go Crazy" and "I Don't Mind" by James Brown, "I Don't Want To Go On Without You" – the Drifters, "Can't Nobody Love You" – Solomon Burke, "Something You Got" – Alvin Robinson and of course Bessie Banks' "Go Now", which would soon take them to the top of the British charts.

There was no DJ at the Rendezvous and I cannot remember much in the way of records – just a main act and usually a local support band, such as the Challengers, the Roadrunners, the Soul Society or the Sons of Man, who would later become Aubrey Small. The latter's album from the early 1970s was supported by Radio 1 DJ 'Whispering' Bob Harris and it has been re-released recently by *Record Collector* magazine, while they have re-formed for live gigs and more recording. Back in the mid-1960s, all these local bands were playing classic rhythm & blues or soul covers of the period, as were the Dynamos, who through the summer of 1964 reached the final of ITV's group talent show *Ready Steady Win!* Sadly, they did not, but they got through the audition, heats and semi-final, and appeared on the finalists' compilation album. It is a characteristic of the Portsmouth scene that so many bands like the Dynamos or Aubrey Small over the years have found themselves on the verge of breaking through to the next level, yet for whatever reason it has not quite happened. The first time I wrote about Portsmouth music, I called the book *Almost*. Sadly, it still seems to apply in 'almost' all cases.

The Classics were another local band that favoured rhythm & blues and built a strong reputation in the region. They were described in a feature by *Hampshire Magazine* in March 1964, playing a gig in Whitchurch. Their drummer Tony Ransley and bass guitarist Pete O'Flaherty would soon replace the same in the Roadrunners, as the latter reformed as Simon Dupree & the Big Sound, while Classics guitarist Ian Duck joined the Soul Agents and then Elton John's backing band Hookfoot – I think he might have been Mr Bloe in his 'Groovin with …' hit record days. Mike Devon & the Diplomats famously supported the Beatles at the Savoy one Sunday evening in April 1963 – lending their drum kit to Ringo when his failed to arrive – and after Mike left to sing with the Arthur Ward band, the group too shifted towards rhythm & blues, but in their earlier days their repertoire was fairly typical of the beat groups who would mix rock & roll, current pop hits and even the occasional Broadway show tune (as the Beatles did with "Till There Was You"). Mike Devon & the Diplomats' set included some 'Merseybeat' songs such as "I Saw Her Standing There", "There's a Place", "I Call Your Name", "Sugar & Spice", and "I'm Telling You Now" as well as Chuck Berry's "Roll Over Beethoven", & "Memphis Tennessee" and other songs from the USA that many people covered back then such as "Keep Your Hands Off My Baby", "Do You Love Me", "I Can Tell", "Searchin", and "Love Potion No 9". Guitarist Pete White of the Furys, another popular local band of the time recalls a similar set of covers – again 'Merseybeat' songs by the Beatles, Faron's Flamingoes, the Mojos and Gerry & the Pacemakers as well as popular records by Chuck Berry, Buddy Holly and Eddie Cochran, a couple of British stars Cliff Richard ("Move It") and Johnny Kidd ("Shakin' All Over") and otherwise mainly American records – Bobby Vee, Ben E King, the Beach Boys, the Crickets and others. Pete now looks back on that set as

> A rag-tag bunch of crap that seems like a band in transition with an unsure direction. At the start, we struggled and made the change from instrumental to vocal group and seemed to have some wild swings in what style we played. We did veer towards some oddball stuff; almost at one point into just Top 20 type stuff and Beatles, with an exploration into almost Folk music then into Beach Boys ("I Get Around"). In 1963, we had pretty much left the instrumentals behind and were transitioning into the typical black leather and white shirts – the Hollies look we all had back then. We played many of the standards and the hits of the time.

The Furys had started out a few years earlier as the Residents, so they were already fairly experienced, and from those early days, there is a delightful if rather faded photograph of them performing to the school hall at Eastney Secondary Modern, which is full of teenagers dancing – yet Pete says

> I don't think we targeted the dancers; we just played along and they danced anyway. I think there always was a percentage of guys and girls who hung out at the foot of the stage, but back then they danced to anything. It was a couple of years before the crowd became mainly watchers, and I think that was due to the shifting beats and strangeness, as the musicians became more self-indulgent.

For me, those early days and months of seeing bands live, especially in the rhythm & blues clubs, were very influential. I am talking about the music of just a handful of bands, few of whom enjoyed sustained or significant commercial success, but I came to recognise very quickly that music mattered, although I had not yet realised that it was not necessarily the case, or at least not to the same degree, with the majority of my peers who were living through this glorious period in popular music. In terms of performing music, I had no great talents beyond my first tentative steps on blues harmonica, but I could sing, I enjoyed it. For a while I did so in the school's choir, where we sang works by the likes of Schubert ("The Trout"), Purcell's "Nymphs and Shepherds" (what did *that* mean to a 20th century city boy?) or grand pieces like Handel's oratorio "Judas Maccabeus" in Portsmouth Cathedral. Previously there had been a rather different formative experience around 1956/7 which I have recounted previously, about a rainy playtime at Highland Road School, when a group of my classmates entertained us with a rendition of "Rock

Around the Clock". Most people loved it and reacted accordingly but inside I was envious – partly because I did not know the song or what it meant at that time, but mostly because I wanted it to be me – and not in the ensemble, but out front, as the lead singer.

The chance came because of that school friend Pete Gurd, who even in his early teens was a fine guitar player. We hooked up and after I had a brief but enjoyable spell as his drummer, we switched for financial reasons from any hope of forming a 'beat' group, to the cheaper option of a folk-blues duo – not least also because we liked what we were hearing of that style of blues. This began happening through 1964 and had much to do with Pete's older sister Anne, who was a student of languages at the College of Technology and dressed accordingly, in that mainly dark, unadorned style still favoured by those of a beatnik disposition. Her hair was much like Joan Baez's, and her boyfriend we have already heard about, Portsmouth's star folk singer Jon Isherwood. He encouraged Pete to turn to acoustic guitar and showed him some new blues runs, so although he did not generally play or sing in that style himself, it gave us a clearer way to develop; now we could play acoustic blues with just a guitar and harmonica.

In the early days, we were influenced for the most part by available recordings of black American musicians like Sonny Terry & Brownie McGhee, Leadbelly, and Big Bill Broonzy, while there was also a British folk-blues scene in the mid-1960s, based mainly in the folk clubs. It could not match the rhythm & blues club scene for audience size or commercial potential, and unlike the Rendezvous and similar London clubs, the blues element was only ever one (small) part of a fairly eclectic scene. I say "fairly" as that depended on the 'folk-police', those inheritors of the ideology of MacColl/ Seeger and others, who tended to define what was and was not legitimately considered 'folk' music, and who might sing what – determined generally by place of birth or domicile. In an extreme case for example, I gather that coming from Portsmouth, I should have been singing sea shanties. It is a view that persists to this day. For many years in Portsmouth there has been a very good acapella male group called the Portsmouth Shanty Men. In late 2016, they appeared on Gareth Malone's BBC2 series *The Choir: Gareth's Best in Britain*. He quite liked them, although did not select them to progress, but he said of them:

> I am looking for people that represent the region and I feel like those guys absolutely represent this region. They're from Portsmouth, they've got the right sound they are shanty men, they've been singing these shanties for 40 years".

I know some of the Shanty Men, I have seen them a few times over those 40 years they sing well, and they are good guys. On the other hand, I have lived in Portsmouth for 67 years, and I have no sense that the majority of my fellow citizens would ever identify sea shanties as 'representing' *their* Portsmouth. What it represents perhaps is the Portsmouth of Nelson or *Mutiny on the Bounty,* 200+ years ago. The Shanty Men are recreating the music of a past they do not inhabit, just as Pete and I were doing the same, playing blues – there is no difference, it's simply a matter of preference, yet according to some of the more extreme 'folkies', sea shanties should have been my cultural heritage.

Fortunately, given my particular fondness for black American music, I never witnessed that hard-line attitude in the Portsmouth clubs in the 1960s and 1970s, when the folk clubs flourished. Jon Isherwood and Pat Nelson often sang Irish 'rebel' songs, at least until the troubles reignited a few years later, there was a regular bluegrass band the Cumberland Echoes, Donna identi- fied her fondness for a local jug band, Southsea guitarist Barry Roberts was moving towards an accomplished classical style, while his pal, ex-Marine Barry Gordon played the banjo, and by the mid-1960s, someone would usually offer a Dylan or Paxton song from the USA. Occasionally there were even sea shanties, and *very* occasionally Pete and I were allowed to sing one or two folk-blues in the floor spot, a wonderfully democratic feature of folk clubs which survives to this day.

What was the British folk-blues scene like in the 1960s? For a start, it was beginning to be a boom time for blues record re-releases, and when the pirate radio stations started, Radio 390 offered us the Mike Raven Show where you could hear the best of the originals of the genre. Most significantly, some of the finest of the old blues players were being brought regularly to Europe. The Blues & Gospel Caravan of 1964 came to Portsmouth Guildhall and was also broadcast live on ITV from a disused Manchester station. Paul 'Oscar' Wild went to the Portsmouth concert and described it as "orgasmic", adding that mentioning it

> Fills me with nostalgia. What a night that was – I remember it in all its detail. It's just such a shame that we 'peaked' at such a young age. We'll never see a line-up the likes of that again.

One of the few genuine musical regrets of my life is that I did not go, although I did eventually see most of the main performers, including the Rev. Gary Davis, who returned the following year with Josh White and Buffy Sainte Marie. A couple of years after that, an Art College trip to London enabled me to see and hear live, Skip James, Bukka White and Son House along with

Little Walter and Sonny Brownie & Brownie McGhee. By that time other blues players like Sonny Boy Williamson, John Lee Hooker, Howlin' Wolf and T-Bone Walker had toured Britain and appeared on television, while various publications by Paul Oliver (e.g. 1968), plus others, including LeRoi Jones (1963) and Charles Keill (1966), as well as regular coverage in *Melody Maker*, the jazz magazines and the specialist blues 'fanzines' (*R&B Monthly, Blues Unlimited*) made it possible to discover so much about this previously obscure genre in Britain.

The relevant British players who appeared on the folk scene, divided into two groups. Some were the star names for whom the blues – particularly blues guitar-playing – was a significant part of a broader repertoire. The most obvious examples included Bert Jansch, John Renbourn and 'Wizz' Jones (who all appeared in Portsmouth) and the superb and innovative Davy Graham (who I think did not). There were also visiting Americans like the remarkable Doc Watson (who appeared at the Railway Folk Club) and Ramblin' Jack Elliot who, like Dylan, drew heavily on Woody Guthrie and also blues and folk songs and styles. In addition to these highly talented, eclectic and innovative performers, there was a smaller group of folk musicians on the circuit who played almost exclusively acoustic blues. Particularly popular in the mid-1960s was Gerry Lockran who came to the Railway frequently, his pals Cliff Aungier and Royd Rivers, plus just a couple of years later the wonderful Jo-Ann Kelly, a diminutive lady who filled the room with her powerful renditions of the blues – seemingly Memphis Minnie reincarnated. Jo-Ann's brother Dave Kelly has played for decades with Paul Jones in the Blues Band, and was also a solo acoustic blues performer who appeared in that guise at Portsmouth's Brave New World in 1968.

The folk club scene was always quite different from the Rendezvous and other rhythm & blues clubs. Folk clubs were generally fairly brightly lit, the drug of choice was alcohol, especially beer, people rarely danced as the audience sat in polite silence during performances, amplification was not unheard of but rare, and for some the highlights were opportunities to join in with choruses (e.g. "Wild Rover" or Tom Paxton's "The Last Thing on My Mind") or the raucous shouting of "Fine Girl You Are!" It seemed jolly rather than hip, at times a bit like a lively Sunday School outing, with the remnants of beatnik culture, a hint of CND and broadly left politics – and a fair smattering of college scarves, whether the wearers were students or not. There were certainly more beards than were to be found on the mod scene and they were not early versions of Hipsters – in Portsmouth, one of them belonged to Phil Tree, who could sing all ten verses of Bob Dylan's "Desolation Row". By comparison with some of the dance halls and mod clubs, it all felt rather safe.

The UK's folk revival mirrored that of the USA, although to a large extent the music's origins were different, despite the shared impact of Bob Dylan's early albums. In terms of the main musical focus of this publication on the psyche-delia of the late 1960s, the American folk revival had a far bigger impact, with the majority of musicians in the Byrds, the Lovin' Spoonful, Janis Joplin and the San Francisco bands having started out playing folk. The American revival is reputed to have owed a huge amount to the appearance in the 1950s of the albums collected and issued – not entirely legally – by artist and film-maker Harry Smith, the *Anthology of American Folk Music.*

Harry Smith's collection was described by Greil Marcus in the reissue booklet, as a "dubiously legal bootleg" collating the "old weird America". The simple story is that Smith began collecting old 78 rpm records in the 1940s of the great tradition of American vernacular music – folk, blues, country, gospel, religious under three broad headings; Ballads, Social Music and Songs. Marcus suggested that in creating the anthology, Smith "made his own country", while

> The whole bizarre package made the familiar strange, the never known into the forgotten, and the forgotten into a collective memory that teased any single listener's conscious mind

While Marcus was referring in this case to folk recordings, mainly from the 1920s and 1930s, that's not too far away from a definition that might fit the psychedelic music we shall consider later. Smith's anthology was not for the most part overtly 'political' music, but like the old English song "Nottamun Town", it offered 'strangeness', and a world beyond the rational, beyond the real, inhabiting the imagination. In the same vein and the same piece, John Cohen one of young revivalists from the three-piece Lost City Ramblers which formed in 1959 with guitar, fiddle and banjo, said that the Anthology "gave us contact with musicians and cultures we wouldn't have known existed", adding that those older musicians "became like mystical gods to us". It is not insignificant that this broadening of knowledge and understanding was rooted in technology – in the ability to record and preserve and circulate the past/other – almost precisely as technology in other guises was dismantling the particular and local that produced such cultural riches.

Smith's original anthology of 84 records appeared on six LPs, and the black and white artists included Clarence Ashley, the Carter Family, Furry Lewis, Mississippi John Hurt, Henry Thomas, Blind Willie Johnson, Gus Cannon's Jug Stompers, Blind Lemon Jefferson, the Memphis Jug Band and Sleepy John Estes. I have selected those named anticipating that they might be the most familiar to British readers. If not, I am doubtful whether others such as the Williamson Brothers & Curry or Frank Hutchinson will ring any bells, although their traditional songs, "John Henry" and "Stackalee", might be familiar. I would know nothing of Harry Smith's anthology for some decades yet, in fact I became aware of his art and film-making first, but looking back to the 1960s, I can see that some of us were engaged albeit less clearly, on a similar enterprise in the UK; we were collecting, preserving, sharing and even performing these 'strange' sounds and songs from other times and other worlds. In doing so, we were challenging the monolithic, manipulative and essentially commercial mainstream.

There are enthusiastic stories of that Harry Smith album – a 'box set' before there were such things – underpinning the American acoustic folk revival, and enabling young, mostly white players to develop repertoires which they could claim offered some authenticity for themselves and their audiences. It is important to acknowledge however that not everyone shared the view that it had such an impact. Just before I completed the first draft of this book, editors Ross Hair & Thomas Ruys Smith (2017) published a collection of writings about the Anthology and in their introduction offered a number of alternative or dissenting views, including those of Samuel Charters, blues scholar and later producer for the albums of Country Joe & the Fish. Charters described Harry Smith's collection as "fine and fun – but no big deal" (6), pointing out that when it appeared, a number of those tracks were already available elsewhere, while the anthology was "expensive and largely unavailable to a commercial market". Bob Dylan too suggested that most young folk singers did not live lifestyles conducive to record collecting in fixed home addresses, although as with my peers a decade later, hearing something, was not necessarily the same thing as owning something. There was a great deal of sharing and collective listening, and a great deal more variety on American radio.

These alternative views are valuable because Harry Smith's Anthology is one of those artefacts of post-war popular music that is the subject of a growing mythology and reification. I will suggest later in this book that the same point applies to the Beatles' album *Sgt Pepper's Lonely Hearts Club Band* – like Harry Smith's collection, an important and influential album but perhaps less seminal or, in the latter case, original, than history claims.

If access to such old Southern recordings – and they were all records made for commercial sale – provided a sense of authenticity that is a notoriously complicated concept. If the performers and their audiences, generally, young, often white, frequently middle-class, read the new performances as authentic then perhaps we had to revise our ideas of authenticity and meaning? How could that be? While pondering such questions, we might at least identify why young people were seeking authentic experiences in popular culture. Was it perhaps in contrast to the often culturally anodyne, materialistic and politically unstable world they saw themselves inhabiting in Eisenhower's USA? And was the British experience similar?

There was no equivalent to Harry Smith's anthology in Britain, but what we had of course was hundreds more years of tradition – since Smith's anthology was culled entirely from records, it was by definition the music of the previous 50 years. Britain had the extensive archives of the Cecil Sharp House, offering a similar sense of authenticity, which was not apparent in commercial pop music, and always more complex to claim for the British blues. In addition, the folk music scene might seem 'safe' and somewhat polite, but it was certainly more politically engaged than the emerging mod club-based scene.

As 1964 turned into 1965 I was going occasionally to folk clubs, usually with Pete, very occasionally to perform briefly, which was always a thrill. For some reason, I have a clear memory of rehearsing at his home in London Road on the Saturday morning of 30 January 1965, as the funeral of Winston Churchill was broadcast on BBC television. It seems now to be a moment symbolic of the changing times – and not merely for the two of us – although I suspect at the time Pete and I were probably simply concerned to get to terms with our versions of "Key to the Highway" or "Living with the Blues".

In Portsmouth around that time, there was a newspaper story about a "beat group" vocalist who was fined £30 for the possession of cannabis, although the mods' preference in 1965 was generally for the expansion of time, rather than consciousness through a variety of amphetamine-based pills. February 1965 should have seen the return of the (now) chart-topping Moody Blues to the Rendezvous but they did not arrive, and police with loud hailers were called to inform the queueing crowd, while the Sons of Man and Roadrunners entertained for the evening. The next night, Kimbells' Sunday rhythm & blues club continued with the promising but ill-fated Mark Leeman Five. Through February, visitors to the two rhythm & blues clubs included the Memphis Four, Ronnie Jones & the Night-timers, Georgie Fame & the Blue Flames and Cops & Robbers but the key moment – one of *the* key moments in the city's popular music history – came on Thursday 25 February 1965 at Kimbells, Osborne Road. From Brighton, Rikki Farr, son of boxing champion Tommy, and his friend Robin Beste, arrived in the city to open their new club, which they called the Birdcage, and on that first evening featured Rikki's brother Gary Farr and his band the T-Bones.

I was not there, indeed I am not even sure I knew about it as, for a month or two, I maintained my loyalty to the Rendezvous. Kimbells' Sunday night club had co-existed contentedly with the Saturday nights at the Rendezvous for the best part of a year but they were not really clubs in the sense of a venue like Soho's Marquee Club, with single owners and open up to seven nights each week. They were simply weekly events, run by promoters who hired the venue and booked the acts. Rikki and Robin were, for starters, closer in age and attitude to their mod punters than the older jazz guys who had read the runes and switched to rhythm & blues. Crucially too, they knew that in London the taste for blues-based bands playing Jimmy Reed, Chuck Berry and the Chicago Chess guys (Muddy, Wolf, Sonny Boy etc.) was changing. We had heard that through those covers by the Moody Blues and Georgie Fame & the Blue Flames, and it was apparent from some of the tracks on the second Rolling Stones album; the older sounding blues-based rhythm & blues was shifting subtly towards a more contemporary soul and jazz influence.

At the Birdcage, the move away from the older, 'deeper blues', was indicated with the following bookings of Chris Farlowe & the Thunderbirds and Ronnie Jones & the Nightimers. Jones, a black American ex-pat had sung with Alexis Korner, while Farlowe, under the pseudonym Little Joe Cook, had released a much-admired version of "Stormy Monday Blues", but both singers were part of that move towards soul, characteristic of London's Flamingo and Scene Clubs in particular. Their bands' sounds were changing too, with the inclusion of saxophones and organs – as with the Blue Flames, or in April, the first appearance in the city of Zoot Money's Big Roll Band.

Initially, there was no obvious conflict between the Birdcage which ran on Thursday nights in its first summer of 1965, and the Rendezvous on Saturday nights. I was still very much a schoolboy and I suspect the reason I went to relatively few early Birdcage gigs, as Nigel Grundy has suggested, was some kind of domestic veto on school nights – whereas Saturday nights were permitted. There was one notable Thursday however, when I indulged my continuing loyalty to Downliners Sect and bought a ticket to see them at the Clarence Pier Ballroom for an annual apprentices' dance (GEC). I guess there was a relatively sharp young man organising that bill, because in addition to the resident support band of drummer Arthur Ward (vocalist Mike Devon), second on the bill was a fine rhythm & blues band from Southampton, the Soul Agents, featuring their vocalist Rod Stewart. I have three distinct memories of him that evening: firstly, he and his band (who released a couple of fine singles on Pye) with a fine organist Don Shinn, sounded rather more sophisticated than Downliners Sect; secondly, he looked the epitome of the stylish 'peacock' mod with a rust tweed jacket and longish back-combed hair; and thirdly, after he had played his set, he was approached by Rikki Farr and Robin Beste, who had wandered across Southsea Common on a fine late May evening. After a brief conversation, he went off with them; I thought nothing more of it.

But he had gone to sit-in with the Birdcage act that evening, the Brian Auger Trinity. At around that time the Melody Maker, published an article called "The Men Jazz Lost to Pop", listing drummer Bobbie Graham (also working as a producer with the Pretty Things); organist Dave Davani who described his fondness for the "natural fusion of R&B and jazz"; two Rendezvous favourites, Graham Bond and Georgie Fame, plus Brian Auger who said

> We play a brand of R&B and commercial jazz. I think we appeal to the more sophisticated R&B fans … It was originally going to be a Jimmy Smith sort of thing, but we have evolved into our own style.

Rikki and Robin developed a plan either prior to the evening or as a result of it, that they might put together a revue-type band based around Brian Auger's Trinity, but with more than one singer – which is how the Steam Packet evolved gradually, with 'Rod the Mod' leaving the Soul Agents and teaming up again with his old boss Long John Baldry and a third singer Julie Driscoll. The management idea did not work out for the Birdcage pair, but briefly they did acquire Portsmouth's J Crow Combo and at one time also discussed pairing their fine singer Chris Ryder, with Ms Driscoll.

Rikki almost certainly led the way in the management front, not for the most part with happy consequences. The J Crow Combo, had already appeared on the London scene, notably at Tottenham's Club Noreik where they played an all-nighter with the Who. Locally, they also played with Graham Bond at the Guildhall for a College of Technology dance and on Sunday night at Kimbells with the original Yardbirds, including Eric Clapton. Then Rikki and Robin saw them in Andover, took them over and in no time, had dispensed with or lost the services of everyone except singer Chris Ryder and drummer Graham Hunt. They teamed them up with two Williams brothers from Southampton on guitar and bass guitar and cut their name to the Crow. It did not work, but signing and then reorganising bands became characteristic of Rikki's management style; it would happen again with the Action and then with Heaven.

Nonetheless, in their brief reincarnation, the Crow did participate in one of the big nights in Portsmouth in 1965, when they supported the Who, for their first city appearance, at the Savoy Ballroom on Southsea seafront. Through the spring and early summer, the Thursday night Birdcage Club had been building its mod audience, and in mid-June, they presented future favourites Jimmy James & the Vagabonds for the first time, and two nights later, the Moody Blues as the first Saturday night at Kimbells. That worked well, so the following week came the embryonic Steam Packet and then Ronnie Jones with a new band the Blue Jays. From Thursday-Saturday, 8-10 July, there were three consecutive nights at Kimbells with respectively, the Shevells, the Vagabonds and Ronnie Jones again, followed by the Who, which was moved to the larger Savoy Ballroom on the Sunday night – an evening packed with all the local mods among 1,000 attending, rewarding the courage to go for four consecutive nights. It was also, unusually, enlivened by a huge punch-up at the back of the hall which did not interrupt a very loud performance by the stars. The Birdcage regulars were a lively bunch but mostly too cool and too smart to start fighting – although there was one 'interesting' evening in the club, with a somewhat brief and bloody visit from the Southampton mods. It was pretty much a 'one off' inside the club, while the rockers stayed away.

During the rest of July, support began to disappear from the Rendezvous, despite the planning of a celebratory fifth birthday event in August, with former local heroes Manfred Mann. At the Birdcage, over the weeks following the Who, came the first appearance of the Action who would rival the Vagabonds as the club's favourite live act, and another very popular booking saw the return of Chris Farlowe & the Thunderbirds, plus the T-Bones, Ronnie Jones and the first soul act from America, Inez & Charlie Foxx ("Mockingbird") backed by Zoot Money's Big Roll Band. That was my first and very enjoyable experience live of the more contemporary sounds from the USA, followed in August, by the Chess label, "Soulful Dress" lady, Sugar Pie Desanto, then another black 'ex-pat' soul man, Herbie Goins. Next along came a couple of British bands: Alex Harvey's Soul Band and the In Crowd, whose early singles covered material by Otis Redding and James Brown, but in their next incarnation as Tomorrow, would be one of those bands like the Who, who led the club scene away from American soul and rhythm & blues covers, towards something more British and more original.

At the Birdcage, unlike the Rendezvous, there were not usually any local support acts. Instead one of the locals, Pete Boardman – known as 'Brady' for his imitation of a victim of the television character Brady, *the Invisible Man* – eventually became the resident DJ at the Birdcage, playing a broad selection of mainly danceable singles from the new soul sounds of the 1960s. He worked in a legal office in Hampshire Terrace and could be seen midweek in Weston Hart's record store in Arundel Street, picking up the new releases on labels like Motown, Stax/Atlantic, Chess, London American and (the British) Sue, which had been started by Guy Stevens and was re-releasing many top American tracks. While mostly British soul and rhythm & blues bands performed at the Birdcage, the records were almost exclusively American.

One of the characteristics of the mods was that they generally dressed in a way that others would recognise, while appearing smart and 'respectable' to their parents and other adults. They took great care over how they looked, from their hair on down; for example, Dave Pittard remembers going to Ian's barber shop above Smartwear "virtually every Saturday around 1963/4", although getting there, meant "running the gauntlet" past shop owner Gerald Garcia who tried his best "to sell you a couple of shirts and a jumper – we had to be quite rude sometimes otherwise we would have ended up skint, before we'd even had a haircut". At one point Dave ordered a new bespoke suit, and Graham Laker recalled him being "the fussiest guy I've ever seen … the suit was sharkskin, very shiny material; he'd already had four fittings for it. I'd go in with him every Saturday and he'd say 'it's puckering up there. send it back'. They'd have to re-cut it and start again". Dave still has that suit and very fine it is.

Sometimes the mods were more flamboyant of course; there were for example the longer back-combed (boys') hairstyles on such as Bob Dunford and Barry 'the Gnome' Atkins who was reputed to have demonstrated the style to Rod Stewart. Keith Dolan recalled Dave Pittard's suit and, wondering whether it came from 'Shanghai' Jackson in New Road, mentioned that Barry Davies, one-time singer with Dave in Barry & the Zodiacs, had a silk silver suit made there. Dave Pittard replied that 'Shanghai' was rather expensive but that Barry's suit "was fantastic – silver mohair and silk", while even better was his camel overcoat – "almost ankle length". Dave was with Jeff Searles, when he first saw Barry wearing it in Commercial Road, enhanced by a white silk scarf, prompting Jeff to shout "oi Steptoe!", despite which Keith and Dave still recall the outfit with admiration.

Despite the occasional 'ostentatious' outfit, on the whole, mods, unlike Teddy boys, rockers and beatniks, were visible to others 'in the know' without generally drawing attention to themselves by their appearance. By contrast, they were certainly noticed during the Bank Holiday seaside 'riots' during 1964/5, although there was not much of that in Portsmouth; it probably came closest on Bognor's seafront at Easter 1965, with a number of arrests. Apart from violence, the other growing concern reported by the media, was recreational drug use. In a talk at Portsmouth Rotary Club, Mr E Inglis warned that "increased drug taking was resulting in more crime" and he identified the mods and rockers taking "tablets for kicks", while his reference to the possibility of "growing your own" hinted at the start of a preference for cannabis.

During the summer of 1965, the Rendezvous struggled on with appearances by most of its more familiar acts like Downliners Sect, Jimmy Powell and Graham Bond. They even tried a switch to Friday nights with the main night at the Birdcage now on a Saturday. Graham Bond broke the attendance record at the Rendezvous, but it was a brief reprieve, although the performances of John Mayall's Bluesbreakers, the Alan Price Set and the Spencer Davis Group were greatly admired, while Geno Washington's Ram Jam Band made a first appearance in a rare concession to the increasing shift from rhythm & blues to contemporary soul. There was a cheeky exchange of adverts in the local *Evening News,* referring to "Rikki's taxi service", organised to persuade those arriving in Kingston Road to move on to Southsea. Ronnie Wood's Birds played Kimbells Sunday night rhythm & blues club before it focused more on local acts like the Shamrocks, Klimax and Crow before fading away. In its place, Monday nights at the Savoy offered an interesting menu including the Animals, Them, the Yardbirds and Steam Packet. The Who were scheduled for Gosport's Thorngate, but they never arrived.

Through the spring and summer of 1965 there were big names at the Guildhall but some ticket sales were poor. With two houses, the evening's capacity exceeded 4,000, which might have been too large to fill, although it is likely that young people generally preferred the freer atmosphere in the clubs, where the acts played longer sets. One unsurprisingly successful exception in mid-July featured the Walker Brothers, the Steam Packet and headliners the Rolling Stones, but other visitors included the Motown Revue which failed to attract a large audience, and it was a similar case with the Yardbirds and Kinks who came together in May, followed by Donovan and the Pretty Things, while the Byrds' concert was cancelled due to poor ticket sales, despite their number one hit with Dylan's "Mr Tambourine Man". Bob himself caused some excitement at the USA's Newport Folk Festival in late July, performing with the driving blues band of Paul Butterfield. There is a recording from Newport of them performing "Maggie's Farm" which exemplifies as well as any, the contrast between his merely amplified album version, and a few months later, truly electric 'rock' sounds.

Folk music in Portsmouth in 1965 offered less volume than Dylan at Newport, but there was plenty of it, with clubs opening up in various locations. In the *Evening News*, Spinner suggested "life is all action in the folk world which at last seems to be moving towards the long-forecast boom". In late June, with *the Evening News* more frequently carrying front-page headlines about the Vietnam War, he reported the opening of the Loft Folk Club as "the sixth since Christmas" in the city. There were concerts too, including Julie Felix and Rambling Jack Elliott at the Guildhall, Caroline Hester at the Oddfellows and an interesting mix of fellow Americans on one evening, with Rev Gary Davis, Josh White and Buffy Sainte Marie. In the clubs, there were a number of popular local performers plus visitors including Martin Carthy, Gerry Lockran, Nadia Cattouse (a sell-out), Derroll Adams, Red Wilmot, Derek Serjeant and Steve Benbow. In mid-July, there was a 'World Folk Festival' along the coast at Beaulieu, with a fine bill including Tom Paxton, Julie Felix, John Renbourn, Shirley Collins, Bert Jansch, the Watersons and the Spinners. Perhaps the great local folk event was the appearance of legendary American guitarist/singer Doc Watson at the Railway, a fine guitarist whose performance was rooted in American folk, blues and country. There was also a growing taste for singer-songwriters including Americans like Tom Paxton and Paul Simon who both appeared in the Portsmouth clubs, but in many cases, folk fans were keen to connect with older traditions and older performers. The other aspect which was utterly alien to the 'modernists' was the rural aspect of the folk culture – even if only implied in the dense streets of Portsmouth. That would be inherited by some of the more peaceful elements of the late 1960s' counter-culture

On Friday 20 August 1965, the Vagabonds' gig at the Kimbells Birdcage was cancelled because the dance hall was suddenly unavailable. The T-Bones did appear the following night, but with the hiring problems increasing in Osborne Road, the *Evening News* carried a "Very Important Announcement" on that Friday evening about the imminent opening of "a revolutionary club, the like of which has not been seen outside London". It would be the second incarnation of the Birdcage in the former Court School of Dancing, just south of Bransbury Park, Eastney, and it opened its doors on the following Thursday with a double bill of the Steam Packet and the Action – all for 5/-. Jimmy James and the Vagabonds then returned on the Friday, Ronnie Jones on the Saturday and from their home just around the corner in Eastney, the Shulman Brothers' Roadrunners on Sunday (3/-). One figure involved in helping to acquire the premises was Tony Harris who had links with Soho's Flamingo but continued to live in Southsea until his death a few years ago. Dave Pittard recalled him "living in Havelock Road" and then later, "buying the house next to the Hereford Hotel in Kent Road, where he opened the cellar as a gay club".

In August 1965, Manfred Mann played the Rendezvous' birthday party, although it was rather more like a wake, with fewer than 400 in attendance. There had been just 80 for Alan Price and 220 for Graham Bond, as soul edged out the older sounds of rhythm & blues and traditional jazz, although the steady shift to the Birdcage had as much to do with fashion, atmosphere and the attraction of a real club, as opposed to a hired large old hall with poor acoustics, in the middle of town. The Rendezvous announced a closure to "re-shape our future" but that future never came, although the name was revived deliberately with the Rendezvous independent cinema in the same venue in the 1980s, as part of the Hornpipe Arts Centre. The Birdcage was simply the 'in' place and in the *Evening News*, Myles Strong, already a Birdcage regular, suggested that while the Rendezvous had a "definite taste", "the

Birdcage is run by a person who is alive", which suited him and his friends who wanted "something new".

The "taste" of the Rendezvous was clearly derived from Ernie Sears' fondness for traditional jazz and three-and-a-half years of successful promoting of the same. The jazz and blues roots of bands like Graham Bond Organisation, Georgie Fame & the Blue Flames, Alexis Korner, Zoot Money, or Long John Baldry & the Hoochie Coochie Men suited the transition from jazz, but the increasingly popular soul sounds were closer to pop, with some of those singles – such as "Reach Out I'll be There", "Midnight Hour" and "Rescue Me" – reaching the British Top Ten. Further, as the mod fashions spread from London across the country, disseminated not least by ITV's *Ready Steady Go!* those styles changed rapidly too.

Richard Barnes, in an introduction to Terry Rawlings' *Mod: A Very British Phenomenon*, suggests, that mod is the only "teenage movement … that years later can be looked back on without any embarrassment" – and as partial evidence he notes how the fashions and preferred musical styles have persisted and revived throughout the decades. For Rawlings, those first mods reacted against much that was mainstream at the turn of the sixties in favour of modern jazz, espresso coffee bars, Ivy League, Italian and French styles and food, scooters, the new mini and "all things sexy and streamlined". Despite an early depiction of Marc Feld (Bolan) with slicked-back hair, the early mods (male) soon discarded hair cream in favour of a continental 'crew cut' or college boy style. Crucially, they were the first generation to avoid the short-back-and-sides brutality of National Service.

Mods did not seem to believe in much beyond living for today, or maybe tomorrow night. Barnes suggested, they were "strictly hedonistic (and) not particularly altruistic", adding

> Although dismissive of their parents they didn't necessarily want to rebel or change the political status quo. Theirs was a revolt into style.

He also saw it as "male-led", suggesting, while the girls looked "deliberately less feminine … the boys looked more deliberately so". This was true to a degree, although since 1979's revival, mod has become less of a 'peacock' style and more uniform, sustaining through the decades the principles ("clean living under difficult circumstances") but losing some of the variety and individual innovation that occurred in the mid-1960s. There were set styles of course back then, and like almost all the teenage boys who participated in that scene, I ordered my made-to-measure suit (blue, single-breasted, single vent, £15 from Alexandres in Commercial Road). I worked in the school holidays to raise that money – the post office every Christmas, photographic printers or *Evening News* seafront sales in the summers, but it was difficult having fun and keeping up-to-date otherwise on pocket money and holiday jobs. Are you wondering about a Saturday job? Sadly, we went to school on Saturday mornings and played sports most Saturday afternoons. Once the suit arrived – and my peers already in work would have more than one – I augmented it with button-down shirts, a paisley tie and pocket handkerchief, and black brogues. I do not often make such an effort these days, but 'versions' of all those items are still in my wardrobe – albeit the suit is now off-the-peg and rarely worn if I can avoid it.

Beyond the individually tailored suits, there was variety and innovation. Sometimes the options were relatively cheap – in a services' city we could raid the Army Surplus Stores for ex-army parkas for the scooter boys; black PVA macs and ex-navy reefer jackets, but increasingly the clothes were more stylish (if less robust) and bought either from the Portsmouth boutiques like Smartwear or Hym, or on trips to London – probably not Carnaby Street, more probably King's Road or the east end for full-length leathers. Among the more varied styles, I owned a camel reefer jacket, hipster jumbo chords and a particularly neat rust herringbone tweed pair. Not all the clothes came from the newest boutiques, some came from more traditional shops; for example, Graham Laker worked in a very upmarket outfitters and tailors in Palmerston Road (south), MacDonald, Woods & Mortimer, while my dad's closest friend from Southsea schooldays, was Percy Brookman, an independent gents' tailor in Elm Grove. From him, in particular, I bought fine shirts with detachable collars.

Although mod probably was "male-led", there were two broad styles for the girls around the Portsmouth clubs. The first was long-hair, short skirts, a style similar to that of the *Ready Steady Go!* presenter Cathy McGowan or perhaps (blonde version) Marianne Faithful. Then, following the look of someone like actress Jean Seeberg in Jean-Luc Godard's *Breathless*, there was the short-haired look, initially elfin but which, in long leathers and clumpy shoes could look less sylph-like and almost asexual as they danced together around their handbags. But soon, Twiggy, Biba (founded 1964) and the like, would encourage new and more varied styles.

1960s mod was, at its best, characterised by invention and variety – albeit *always* clean, unlike some of the 'trad' fans, beatniks or rockers. One example of the variety was what was called 'Pop Art' by those in fashion and music. This had a tangential link to the painting and sculpture which in Britain and the USA had its origins in the 1950s, and had been partly and entertainingly captured in Ken Russell's documentary *Pop Goes the Easel*. Pop art was, influenced by contemporary advertising, mostly hard-edged, using white or bright, often primary, colours; it appropriated flags, targets, stripes and arrows and complemented the brash guitar/drum sound of bands like the Who, Small Faces, Action and Creation – a cult band whose best-known song "Painter Man" was about being an art student.

In early July 1965 – a fortnight before they appeared at the Savoy – the Who's guitarist Pete Townshend attempted a description of the musical version of 'Pop Art' in the *Melody Maker* ("Well What Is Pop Art?"). He suggested it was "re-presenting something the public is familiar with, in a different form" although his example of jackets made from the Union Jack was about fashion not music. He added

> We stand for pop-art clothes, pop-art music and pop-art behaviour
> … we don't change off stage. We live pop art.

Pressed on the matter of pop-art music, Townshend described how, using standard equipment, he produced "jet plane sounds, Morse code signals (and) howling wind effects". He suggested that previous examples of pop-art records included the sound effects on records by the Shangri-Las or Twinkle and referred to the Who's next single "My Generation" as "really pop-art. I wrote it with that intention". It would be released some months later, in October 1965, and Townshend added that "not only is the number pop-art" but it also "anti middle-age, anti boss-class and anti young-marrieds!"

A couple of months later (28 August) in a follow-up article, the *Melody Maker* revealed the cost of Pop Art (minus the hyphen now) with an obvious reference to the wrecking of £150 guitars and the expenditure of £100 per week on clothes. Townshend had been an art student, influenced somewhat by Gustav Metzger's 'auto destructive' art, which manifested itself on stage in his guitar-smashing antics. The new article suggested that the Who's stage act was "the closest pop music has ever got to the happening", a reference to the growing interesting in 'live art' and events through the decade. In May 1966, the Who appeared at the NME's Poll Winners' Concert and reviewer Keith Altham said of their performance,

> I don't know that it was music; it was more like watching violence
> put to rhythm. But unquestionably it stood out as the most
> remarkable performance in the second half … even though the
> Beatles and Rolling Stones were to follow.

The Who continued to appear fairly regularly at the Birdcage over the next few years, returning to Portsmouth in 1974, as Ken Russell shot *Tommy* in various locations around the city.

HERBIE GOINS at the BIRDCAGE CLUB EASTNEY 1966

Photo courtesy of Cathy McGuigan

SWEET SOUL MUSIC

While the earlier, more subtle, mod styles now stood alongside the sharper, brighter impact of Pop Art, Biba and the mid-1960s boutiques, a major event in London signalled something new, rather different and initially less fashion-conscious. Improbable as it might seem to younger generations 50+ years later, this event was a poetry reading to a large audience at the Albert Hall on Friday 11 June 1965, and it is often cited as the event that heralded the start of London's counterculture.

The event featured many of the UK's more prominent young poets and was stimulated by the London visit of American Beat poet and countercultural 'guru', Allen Ginsberg, upon which a small group of people decided they must organize a venue for him to read in public. Not lacking ambition, they booked the Albert Hall and invited other poets to join the reading. The ticket, for 11 June 1965 read "The Poets Co-operative presents Poets of Our World; Poets of our Time". The event was somewhat hastily put together with a degree of bravado, but thousands arrived and in addition to Ginsberg, other poets included Alex Trocchi, Christopher Logue, Michael Horowitz, Gregory Corso, Adrian Mitchell, Pete Brown, and Stevie Smith. Barry Miles and his wife Sue were involved in the planning and organization and he recalled

> Incense and pot-smoke wafted into the dome, bottles of wine and chillums were passed around. A dozen or so bemused schiz-ophrenics brought along by anti-psychiatrist RD Laing danced to music heard only in their own heads and blew bubbles from pipes…(Ginsberg) opened the event with a deep-voiced Tibetan mantra (Miles 2002a, pp 58-59)

Jonathan Green (1999) has recorded how the event is often seen as the start of a new phase, as some members of the audience, "faces adorned with psychedelic colours", handed out flowers. There was a good deal of dope smoking and poet Simon Vikenoog was surely not the only person on acid" (143). On the other hand, Green tells us that, "many British beats…saw it as the culmination of that society rather than…its inception", on the basis that any "true alternative thrives on exclusivity" (39). For those older participants, from this point, "the 'alternative' began to wither, (and) began believing its own myths, recycling its own propaganda" (142). Maybe it was simply a matter of age and experience whether you saw it as the beginning or the end? It would not be the last time such views would be expressed by people a mere handful of years older than those who came after.

Two months after the poetry event, in early August 1965, the Who were one of the pop acts who appeared over the three days of the Bank Holiday National Jazz & Blues Festival at Richmond. In 1961, the first of these annual events, organised by the Marquee Club, had followed Beaulieu in offering a mix of the best of British traditional and modern jazz, including the bands of Chris Barber, Joe Harriott, Alex Welsh, Ken Colyer and Tubby Hayes. By 1964 some of the same acts returned, while the bill now included the newer rhythm & blues club groups such as the Yardbirds, Georgie Fame, Manfred Mann and the Rolling Stones, with the latter headliners on the Friday evening.

The 1965 festival offered even more acts with a rhythm & blues or soul influence, including the Graham Bond Organisation, Georgie Fame, the Vagabonds and Ronnie Jones, while some were more pop (or perhaps Pop Art) oriented. There was still jazz on Saturday and Sunday afternoons but in the evenings, alongside the Who, came the Moody Blues, the Yardbirds (with Jeff Beck), the Mark Leeman Five, the Steam Packet, and the Spencer Davis Group. The final act was particularly interesting; the Animals Big Band. The normal five-piece rhythm & blues group was augmented by a brass/reed section from the cream of British jazz, including Ian Carr and Kenny Wheeler who were the arrangers. Their set consisted principally of rhythm & blues classics such as "Let the Good Times Roll", "Roll 'Em Pete", "Outskirts of Town" and "Talking About You". It was a welcome experiment, albeit one that was too expensive to repeat. Over 40,000 people attended during the weekend, including Mr & Mrs J Lennon and Mr & Mrs G Harrison, and these annual events on London's outskirts, which moved each year more towards pop and rock, are frequently overlooked when people trace the histories of the pop/rock festivals; this one was two years before California's legendary Monterey Pop. Around the same time as the 1965 festival, the NME ran adverts suggesting "Carnaby Street Goes Floral" with exotic button-down shirts for the boys at 50/-. The accompanying image showed a neat hairstyle and a tie, so this was still in the mod realm, but it was a softening from early mod, or the hard-edge style of pop art, and perhaps a first hint of what might follow two years later.

Histories of teenage fashions in the 1960s rarely mention Pop Art (or pop-art); it gets subsumed within the broader description of the mod scene, but, like the floral shirts, it was one example of how mods in that decade never stood still, constantly seeking out subtle shifts in music and clothes, keeping one step beyond their more mainstream peers. What was common to all these young people was the forging of identity – social and personal. Unlike the majority of mods, *Citizen 63* had portrayed a group of young people with strong political and social views, but a number of members of that group – including Marion Knight – were also involved in the Portsmouth mod scene. Did their views alter? Were they still asking the same left-wing questions under the surface, but simply not a part of that new scene? Did some mods have political views that simply found no place for expression in that tribe, but developed in the following years? If mods were, at heart, more materialistic than other teenage subcultures, perhaps that was simply because the substantial majority in the busy years from 1963-1966 were working class – at a time when that label could mean frugal living, if not a degree of poverty, while they were increasingly bombarded by conspicuous consumption, insistent advertising on television and in magazines, and a swinging London that at its heart apparently demanded a degree of wealth.

In July 1957, Conservative Prime Minister Harold Macmillan had told "most" of us that we had never had it so good, but what did that mean? I have described my upbringing as lower middle-class which feels right, but economically it meant that not until the early 1960s, did my father earn a four-figure salary, and while my direct grant grammar school was fee-paying, even in my final year (1967/8) that amounted to just one hundred pounds per year. On returning from the war (RAF) my father had taken out his first mortgage on Festing Road at a reduced price because of slight bomb damage. It was a large three storey semi-detached house but in my earliest years it was shared with my father's brother and his young family, and after they moved to a smaller place in Teddington Road, we let off the top floor to the guest house next door. In 1961, we sold Festing Road and moved into the city, just south of Devonshire Square, to a terraced house that cost around £2,000 (again on a mortgage). There was no central heating, no wall-to-wall carpets, no telephone for the next two or three years, while my father never owned a car (I was the first qualified driver in my immediate family from the mid-1970s). Our holidays were always with relatives, mostly in Derbyshire, where we would explore the beautiful Peak District. Talking to friends from the Birdcage days, I know that our circumstances were relatively comfortable, but it was hardly luxurious in today's terms.

In terms of life more broadly in Britain, in late December 1962, *the Guardian* under the title "Verdict on the Bingo Age" reported from a government survey that "a strong flood of violence among youngsters has swept in since commercial television began", while the amount of gambling in the country had become "stupendous". The newspaper's Political Correspondent, Francis Boyd summed up the main social trends:

> More people will want to move into outer suburban life, buy cars, educate their children longer, suffer their surgical illnesses in private rooms of hospitals, spend their evenings staring at television, spend more, gamble more, buy more washing machines on hire purchase, take holidays in Italy, lay their own parquet floors and so on (19.12.1962)

In terms of entertainment and hobbies, almost two years previously, the same newspaper had reported on an "Average Family, 1961", from a new handbook by the Central Office of Information. This revealed that at least 25% of adults "play or watch sport", while 75% bet – mostly "occasionally for small stakes on football 'pools' or racing". Meanwhile, despite the threat of Bingo Halls, "cinema remains the most popular … outside the home", while "about five million go to a dance every week". But what was most popular overall? Probably gardening, with "4,000 horticultural societies, and 19 million spare-time gardeners" (*the Guardian* 10.1.1961). The latter included my dad, who loved his garden, especially his roses.

In Portsmouth, we generally trailed our London peers, often travelling there, to discover secrets of the new fashions in clothes, music, drugs and lifestyle. Nonetheless, we were living a life unlike anything that ordinary provincial kids had ever lived before, and every part of it left us not merely wanting but expecting more. Paul 'Oscar' Wild began a lifelong career cutting hair above the Smartwear boutique in Commercial Road, and recalls

> To have been a cog, small or big, in the 'mod' fashion scene still gives me that good feeling. How can one take away that electric feeling of being right at the front of the Birdcage and to see that so many people, especially the 'names' had had their hair styled in our 'studio', dancing away to Jimmy James & the Vagabonds, the Action, the Shevells etc.?

If what he describes and we were experiencing, does not count as the Sandbrook or Aaronovitch description of swinging, it demands an alternative term to describe how different it was from previous decades, and even from the majority of our peers in Portsmouth. In the provinces, the Sunday supplements, weekly music 'papers, television programmes like *Ready Steady Go!* or BBC's *Whole Scene Going,* and pirate radio stations, continued to play their part in disseminating the new fashions, sounds, attitudes and ideas, although cinema – with its long production times and need for mass audiences – rarely led the way. On the silver screen, not everything about swinging London was obviously as 'cool' as we were led to believe.

The tougher 'realist' British cinema of the late 1950s and early 1960s had much to commend it, with movies like *Saturday Night & Sunday Morning, the Loneliness of the Long-Distance Runner* or *This Sporting Life,* but the mid-1960s was perhaps rather less substantial. For example, following his fine quasi-documentary Beatles' film *Hard Day's Night,* director Richard Lester returned with the fairly daft offering, *The Knack*; Julie Christie in *Darling* (1965) swung in a pretty self-indulgent and ultimately pessimistic way, while David Warner as the hero of *Morgan a Suitable Case for Treatment* (1966) was a more interesting comedy/fantasy of the art world, politics and mental health; not exactly swinging but touching on that world and questioning the norms of middle-class comfort. Then in the spring of 1966 came Michael Caine as *Alfie,* which revealed the increasingly public, and often misogynistic preoccupation with sex, but offered a 'hero' who, had he added a handlebar moustache to his preferred RAF-coloured tie and double-breasted jacket with matching crest, might have been a veteran from the Battle of Britain, or recently 'demobbed' from National Service, rather than the heart of swinging London.

While the film is relatively innovative in its use of Alfie's speech to camera and a contemporary jazz soundtrack by tenor saxophone star Sonny Rollins, Alfie's one 'musical' night out (grey suit, striped tie) is in his local, entertained by a woman singer with a 1950s 'trad' band, and ends in a typical, geezers' punch-up. To a certain extent, *Alfie,* depicts a world of the past, not at all swinging, particularly for those he exploits and ultimately, despite his comeuppance and recognition of his errors, Alfie is neither funny nor clever. He ends by asking "what's it all about?" which leads us into Bacharach and David's challenging title song over the end credits – a black & white stills montage, which is as 'modern' and stylish as anything in the film itself.

By the summer of 1966, Italian director Michelangelo Antonioni had arrived in London to shoot *Blow-Up,* which despite (or perhaps because of) another noticeably misogynistic streak, came closest to a contemporary cinematic representation of swinging London, although it would be early 1967 before its London premiere. *Performance,* starring Mick Jagger, was delayed even longer and this remarkable if rather bleak depiction of the late sixties, actually ended up as a 1970s movie. One of the more interesting 'characters' associated with that film was Hollywood's rebel with any number of causes, Kenneth Anger, who made that fine 1963 film, *Scorpio Rising,* half-an-hour of gay 'biker', rock & roll montage magic. Before *Performance* finally made it to our screens, came the delights of watching *2001* 'spaced out', and the soundtrack album, like that from *Easy Rider,* became a regular on our turntables as the 1960s drew to a close.

The cinemas of the 1960s were not constantly showing movies of the swinging sixties of course, but whatever they showed, they found themselves under increasing commercial pressure. Hewison (1986) reported that from 1960-1975, about 50% of the original 3,034 cinemas closed, while "annual ticket sales shrank from 500 million to 116 million" (298). In addition, while an increasing proportion of films shown on British screens emanated from Hollywood, the Americans also increased involvement in British productions. One of the reasons was the expansion of television, with a third channel, BBC2 added in April 1964, and colour arriving in at the heart of the summer of love in 1967. Neither was it just a matter of an extra channel since, over the decade, there were more programmes and a later finish than BBC's 10.30pm on the first Monday of the 1960s. One of the most notable 'progressive' innovations of the BBC was the one-off Wednesday Play, which ran from October 1964 until 1970. Many fine writers and producers and directors worked on these productions, including Dennis Potter, Nell Dunn, David Mercer, Jim Allen, Tony Garnett, Ken Loach and even Samuel Beckett, while among the plays were *Up the Junction, Cathy Come Home, Stand Up Nigel Barton* and Beckett's *Eh Joe.* The average audience was around eight million and for *Cathy Come Home,* twelve million, while the BBC also dared to air a contentious yet popular comedy series, *Till Death Us Do Part* (Hewison, 32).

Back in Portsmouth, in late 1965, the Birdcage opened three or four nights each week with the excellent American 'girl' group Goldie & the Gingerbreads, the Vagabonds, John Mayall's Bluesbreakers, the Moody Blues, Cliff Bennett & the Rebel Rousers, the In Crowd, Herbie Goins, Georgie Fame, the T-Bones the Action, Steam Packet and from the USA, Lou Johnson ("Message to Martha"). A couple of months after arriving in Eastney, the club held its Official Opening Night on Thursday 21 October 1965. The two favourite regular Birdcage bands, Jimmy James & the Vagabonds and the Action were there, along with the Quotations while two other acts that were advertised, were probably considered superfluous by most Birdcage regulars; compere Jimmy Saville and top-of-the-bill Walker Brothers. The latter never showed up, but the excitement warranted a full page with photos in *Record Mirror* and 1,000 people were reputed to be there. One of the Walker Brothers was quoted as saying "we couldn't be bothered".

The Birdcage was still favouring soul, not least through 'Brady's' records but also other top club acts like Zoot Money's Big Roll Band, Herbie Goins & the Nightimers, Chris Farlowe & the Thunderbirds, organist Peter Bardens' Looners (Booker T-style, with Peter Green and Mick Fleetwood), and more American visitors, Ben E King (watched by Pete Townshend), Major Lance, and Wilson Pickett with the Links, plus his own guitarist who might have been Steve Cropper. Bo Diddley, booked and adver- tised, apologised for his non-appearance, although one of my great pals still swears he saw him there. There was also a fairly low-key Saturday night (30 October) with David Bowie & the Lower Third, and approach- ing Christmas, a relatively rare appearance by Geno Washington & the Ram Jam Band, plus the Action, the Clique, Alan Price, the VIPs, the Nite People, and a couple of popular local groups on Sunday nights, St Louis Checks who would reach the final of the *Melody Maker's* national compe- tition, and the one-time Roadrunners, Simon Dupree & the Big Sound. Alan Williams, then the drummer of St Louis Checks, recalls a heavily soul-influenced set typical of those days, including "Ain't Too Proud to Beg", "Dancing in the Street", "Midnight Hour", "Shotgun", "Road Runner", "Hold On I'm Coming", "First I Look at the Purse", "My Girl", "Heatwave", "Rescue Me", "See Saw" and "I'll Keep Holding On". On the Saturday before Christmas, the Who were back, at the Birdcage, while on New Year's Eve it was the Action again, and on the first day of 1966, Herbie Goins and the Nightimers.

Elsewhere in Portsmouth, the *Evening News* reported 100 teenagers in clashes in Southsea with a two hour "melee" in Osborne Road and lots of "noisy" scooters, while in late November 1965, there was another article warning about the "shock increase in cocaine and heroin addicts". The Searchers visited the Savoy, while the Kontiki on Hayling Island went back to traditional jazz and a smart dress code. Van Morrison's Them were at Thorngate, Gosport, followed by "zany comedy" from Dave Dee, Dozy, Beaky, Mick & Tich, and by contrast, America's Lost City Ramblers starred in a folk concert at the Oddfellows Hall. On that scene, Martin Carthy came to the Folkhouse (Talbot Hotel), while a new folk club at Kimbells booked Julie Felix, the Settlers, Diz Disley and Trevor Lucas (future Fotheringay). There was mainstream pop at the Guildhall in November with Lulu, Gene Pitney and the Rocking Berries, then Manfred Mann came with a new, augmented line-up (and Jack Bruce on bass) plus the Yardbirds. In the days before bands travelled with large PA systems, criticisms emerged about the quality of the Guildhall's in-house system, which had been designed mainly for speeches. At Christmas, the King's Theatre presented its annual pantomime, starring Dick Emery.

Mention of the scooters and the establishment of the Birdcage as the local 'home' of the mods brings me to a key distinction to be drawn and applied to many of the participants in that scene at the time. Nigel Grundy recalls leaving Portsmouth Grammar School (PGS) in 1964 and buying a scooter:

I bought a Lambretta, and then a parka jacket from Ben Grubb's ex-government store and started to spend my evenings in the Manhattan Coffee Bar. The people who went there were a fantastic crowd, Dockyard apprentices, shop workers, hard nuts from Leigh Park, office workers, hairdressing apprentices, homeless (even then), full-time pill poppers and mainline drug addicts etc. Among the Manhattan scooter mods, I was the only one who had been to Portsmouth Grammar School, but not one person referred to it or was derogatory about it; being an apprentice with Portsmouth Corporation may have given me some street credibility. I was just one of the crowd and we all got into mischief together, and went everywhere on our scooters, Southend, Brighton, the Shoreline at Bognor etc. I use the term 'scooter mods' because there were two distinct sets of Portsmouth mods, those of us of the parka jacketed scooter fraternity who spent all our money on our noisy two wheeled transport and those who were better turned-out and spent their money on good clothes every week.

When Rikki Farr opened the Birdcage at Kimbells it gave us all another place to meet and when he transferred it to Eastney it became even more popular – what a great music venue that was. A change in direction came for me in 1966 when a work colleague, who had a midnight blue mini-van that I envied, asked me if I wanted to buy it for £50. I didn't have £50, but that lunchtime I drove my Lambretta to a used car dealer in Copnor Road and sold it to him for £50. Back at work I swopped the money for the car keys. I enjoyed being a mod, but music and fashion was changing and so was I, and around that time many mods were swopping their scooters for cars.

The late autumn of 1965 saw three significant album releases as the longer format challenged the dominance of the cheaper 'single', giving the lie to banal suggestions that the extent to which the 1960s swung, can be measured simply by the quality of the chart-topping hit singles. Two of the albums were the Rolling Stones' *Out of Our Heads* and Bob Dylan's *Highway 61 Revisited*. The title track of the latter was certainly a rocker, there was a 'bluesy' feel to "It Takes a Lot to Laugh", and there was an organ and electric guitars, but still a folky feel – albeit amplified acoustic – on many tracks, including the mammoth "Desolation Row". The Stones were still covering Chuck Berry ("Talking About You") but despite their previous chart-topping success with the blues cover, "Little Red Rooster", they were now raiding more contemporary soul and rhythm & blues such as Otis Redding's "That's How Strong My Love Is", Marvin Gaye's "Hitch Hike", Don Covay's "Mercy Mercy", Solomon Burke's "Cry to Me" and Sam Cooke's "Good Times". There were also four original songs as their writing developed on the back of the success of their chart-topping single "(I Can't Get No) Satisfaction".

The third special release was the Beatles' *Rubber Soul* – out in time for the Christmas market, although *Melody Maker* suggested that it was "not their best on first hearing". They acknowledged that the group's sound had "matured" but felt it was also "more subdued", although the lyrics to tracks like "Nowhere Man" or "In My Life" certainly pointed to a new direction, away from the focus on typical boy/girl relationships in so many of the earliest Lennon/McCartney songs. There was folky guitar and a sitar on "Norwegian Wood", while their characteristic harmonies linked them to the sounds of American bands like the Byrds and Beach Boys, and simultaneously distinguished them from the Rolling Stones and the British rhythm & blues acts, most of whom featured a lead singer. The early Beatles performed some fine versions of rock & roll and rhythm & blues classics, not least covers of American girl groups like the Shirelles, Marvelettes and Donays, but their music had little or no obvious 'feel' for the 'deeper' blues or jazz, which perhaps freed them to explore a more British sound than the bands that started out rooted in jazz and blues recordings from black America.

Joe Boyd (2005) an American who worked extensively on the London scene of the late 1960s and 1970s, offers an interesting perspective on the differences between American and British pop/rock acts. The American acts, particularly say, Bob Dylan, the Byrds or most of the major psychedelic bands, were clearly rooted in pre-rock & roll American folk, blues and country music, whereas referring specifically to the success of Jimi Hendrix and the Who at the Monterey Pop Festival, Boyd suggests both performances "were part of a British tradition of artifice", with the British managers believing "everyone needed a gimmick" – at that time, apparently linked to the destruction of equipment (118).

In Portsmouth, 1966 opened with rumours that Rikki Farr had left the Birdcage to manage the Action, another British band that excelled in particular with original covers of Motown and other vocal groups. Rikki did take them on, with disappointing consequences, but if he ever left the club, he was soon back and it continued to feature soul/Motown acts like the Vagabonds, Ronnie Jones and Herbie Goins, plus guitar bands like the Action, and two others that would develop into interesting rock acts over the next year or two, the In Crowd (who became Tomorrow) and the VIPs (Spooky Tooth). On 22

January 1966, Southern ITV arrived to shoot a 30-minute documentary with Alan Price performing – sadly it seems no longer to exist – and the first month concluded with the Spencer Davis Group. While live bands still appeared on most evenings, a change of policy on Sunday nights saw the 'discotheque' replacing local bands.

In the history of British pop radio, the mid-1960s were the heyday of the pirate stations, such as Caroline, London, and 390, with the BBC's Light Programme seen as trailing behind. To some extent this perception was accurate, with the pirates focusing on (and sometimes creating) pop hits, while also introducing new sounds and, with the arrival of John Peel on Radio London in March 1967, *very* new sounds. By contrast, the Light Programme generally offered pretty dull fare, but it was often interspersed with special shows when, because of their policy of limiting 'needle' time, they would feature current acts playing live. A good example was *Pop Go the Beatles,* broadcast at 5pm on weekday evenings in 1963, and including guest acts, while the most obvious was *Saturday Club*, which ran for two hours on Saturday mornings from 1958-1969.

Saturday Club could be particularly interesting because, unlike the pirates, it featured live sessions and not necessarily versions of record releases. A very good example might be the Rolling Stones, who appeared on various occasions, and among their performances were "Memphis Tennessee", Roll Over Beethoven", "Beautiful Delilah" and "Don't Lie to Me" (Chuck Berry), "Down in the Bottom" (Howlin' Wolf) and "Fannie Mae" (Buster Brown), none of which appeared on their official releases. One of the most interesting if rather brief, series came around tea-time on Saturday evenings and was a perfect hour's preparation for the night to come. It had begun as *Jazz Club* but by 1966 was called *Jazz Beat* and each week featured two bands, almost always from the current London Club scene. Saturday 1 January 1966 for example, featured two bands that had appeared at the Birdcage, Georgie Fame & the Blue Flames and the Brian Auger Trinity, as did the following week's show with the Art Woods and the Mike Cotton Sound, then on 15 January, Chris Farlowe & the Thunderbirds and the Mark Leeman Five. With decent-length live sets from both acts, this was a quality show, which the pirates could not replicate. There were further appearances by acts like Herbie Goins, Alexis Korner, Jimmy Witherspoon, John Mayall & Eric Clapton, and Manfred Mann although sadly, within a few weeks, they reverted to traditional jazz with Sandy Brown, Kenny Ball, Acker Bilk, Chris Barber and others. The show ended in mid-May 1966, replaced by a weekly show of Scottish music. Ultimately, it is perhaps indicative of the Light Programme that the last record played before it split into Radios One & Two in September 1967 was by the Woody Herman Big Band.

The Spencer Davis Group had appeared at the Rendezvous and the Birdcage, and they came back to Portsmouth's Guildhall in February on a package tour with the Walker Brothers (who did turn up this time) and 'one hit wonder' Crispian St Peters. One week later, there was a rather different Anglo-American Folk Concert with Ian & Sylvia, Gordon Lightfoot, the Ian Campbell Group and Trevor Lucas. Attendance at the concert included a voucher to obtain a ticket to see Bob Dylan at the Royal Albert Hall in May 1966 – the (in)famous concert tour when Dylan played solo in the first half, and was then backed by the Hawks (later the Band) after the interval. That was the tour when, at Manchester, a heckler shouted "Judas" at the amplified Bob, but Bob did not believe him. Meanwhile, in Portsmouth, the mostly acoustic folk clubs were still attracting regular audiences.

By March 1966, Harold Wilson's Labour Government had a working majority of just one, so he went to the country and won a second election with a majority of 100, including Frank Judd who won Portsmouth West from the Conservatives. During their second period in Government, the Home Secretary Roy Jenkins introduced a range of liberal legislation dealing with issues including homosexuality, abortion and theatre censorship.

In California, from late November 1965, Ken Kesey and his Merry Pranksters organised a series of parties known as 'the Acid Tests', usually entertained by one of San Francisco's first psychedelic bands, the Grateful Dead, and continuing into 1966. A change was coming, although LSD was by now illegal in Britain, while across the year, convictions for possessing cannabis passed 1,000 for the first time. Within twelve months they reached 2,393.

During February 1966, American duo Charlie & Inez Foxx returned to the Birdcage and in addition to many of the regulars, there was a first visit by the Small Faces, but March was odd. It ended with the return of Alan Price and in the middle, the Who and the In Crowd were back again, but the club opened just two days each week, mostly with lesser-known bands like the Cat, Summer Set, the Nocturnal and the Green Onions. It seemed ominous, but April was back to normal, with 13 nights – all live bands – in four weeks, including two all-nighters and acts like Geno Washington, the Vagabonds, the Alan Bown Set, Graham Bond, Cliff Bennett, the Paramounts, Georgie Fame and from USA, Arthur Alexander ("You Better Move On", "Anna", "Shot of Rhythm & Blues" etc.). Briefly, everything seemed fine, but May fell away again, with an all-nighter each Saturday but only one other Friday opening, after which the club closed "for a re-vamp". During that month, there were a couple of less than successful nights back at Kimbells.

The problem was simply economic. The Birdcage was an independent club which over the years had a number of financial backers, but top bands were increasing their prices, and most of the Birdcage customers were appren-tices or school/college students. We could not all afford clothes, records and entrance fees two or three nights each week. Attendances were good for the bigger names and the popular regulars like the Action, Chris Farlowe or the Vagabonds, but not necessarily for the lesser known bands. There was also a growing diversity in styles with a group like the Summer Set from the Brighton area bringing harmonies and surfing sounds alongside the dominant soul and rhythm & blues. They were headliners too for the Art College dance at Kimbells, supported by locals the Third Dimension. Meanwhile in early July, came the first of the summer's Beat Cruises around the Solent with the St Louis Checks – these cruises soon attracted large audiences, and were extended through to mid-September.

One of the problems with trying to draw a broader, mainstream audience to the Birdcage was that by 1966, both the club, and mods in general, were attracting adverse media publicity for the Bank Holiday 'riots', drugs and everything associated with live music in late-night venues. After being closed for five weeks, the Birdcage opened again on 2 July with the Action and a new DJ 'Mad King Jerry', who was less cool and more manic than 'Brady' – rather like a Pompey version of Emperor Rosko. June had been quiet on the live scene but interesting for me in that I sang in rehearsal for the first time with a fully-fledged electric blues band, with some of whom I would enjoy exciting times in about eighteen months. For the time being Nick Hugg, of the Gosport musical family, got the gig, and they became the In-Pulse. It was coincidentally handy that there was less to do that month as I was taking my 'O' levels (GCSEs) but I did get to see the fine British modern jazz saxophonist Joe Harriott who appeared at Southsea's Cambridge Hotel, and a few weeks later in the same venue, jazz organist Alan Haven with drummer Tony Crombie. Elsewhere, traditional jazz died at Kimbells, with attendances often under 100, although Acker Bilk attracted a full crowd at South Parade Pier. The Guildhall began to book visiting jazz acts again and were advertising the Modern Jazz Quartet for mid-September, followed by older acts like Wingy Manone, Ed Hall and Bud Freeman. I saw the MJQ, which was well attended and very polished, if somewhat 'polite'; meanwhile those other nights incurred heavy losses with fewer than 500 people in the 2,000+ capacity.

Just prior to the release of their album *New Religion,* with sleeve notes and photos of the Birdcage (including my wife's pal Cilla on the cover), Jimmy James & the Vagabonds followed the Action to the re-vamped club, but there were also a number of bands appearing that suggested a declining interest in the classic organ/sax soul bands and a growing preference for guitars and a more pop-oriented sound. They included the Summer Set, the In Crowd, the Small Faces and the start of a popular residency by the Move. I suppose that all these years later, the Move are remembered as a lively pop group with a range of hit singles, before they metamorphosed into Roy Wood's Wizzard and imprinted themselves on every December with "I Wish It Could be Christmas Everyday", but in those early days they were always more than that, providing a link to the old soul stuff with covers of songs like "Watch Your Step" (Bobby Parker) or "Stop and Get a Hold of Myself" (Gladys Knight), to which they added show tunes like "Zing Went the Strings of My Heart" and Roy Wood's early compositions. Live they were exciting and I was glad many years later to find an endorsement of that view by Joe Boyd (2005). Perhaps they suited Portsmouth because, as Boyd suggested "they verged on psychedelia, but it was beer-drinker's psychedelia" as they "incorporated sounds coming up from the underground, magpie-like" (115). Boyd would take American visitors to see them at the Marquee and reported that Mike Bloomfield and John Sebastian agreed "it was the most amazing thing they had ever seen". For a while, we saw them most weeks.

Around then, there was also an appearance by a group called the Lovin' Kind that might have included Noel Redding and Neil Landon (the Flowerpot Men), plus nine record nights, and a visit from the Radio London Show. By August 1966 the club was announcing the Kinks as the start of a new 'pop' policy at the club and even threatening an appearance by Dave Dee's bunch. In the event neither came, and there was not much mainstream pop of any kind.

Following 'Big L', the Radio Caroline Show arrived there in August, the Move's residency continued, Jimmy James & the Vagabonds came again, and so too the Alan Bown Set. July and August were exciting elsewhere with Bob Dylan's new album *Blonde on Blonde*, early live appearances by the new 'supergroup' Cream, and Eric Clapton's farewell to John Mayall with the legendary *Bluesbreakers* album; described by Melody Maker as "a giant step for British music". Above all, however, came the release of the new Beatles album *Revolver* with one of the first recorded examples of British psychedelia. In Portsmouth's *Evening News*, 'Spinner' was "delighted with almost every track" but for him there was "one blot" on the "gem" with the "way-out electronic noise" of "Tomorrow Never Knows" which he said "fills me with horror". I guess not everyone got it, and in early November he was at it again, describing the Mothers of Invention's "It Can't Happen Here", as "mumblings, chantings, and toneless mutterings". He told us that other "freak groups" like the Velvet Underground and Blues Project were suffering a "total absence of airplay from discerning DJs". He did not necessarily reflect the most adventurous views around the city; Graham Laker recalls that when the first Velvet Underground album was released, his pal 'Jacko' bought it and they listened to it and eventually the follow-up album regularly.

Cream, with Eric Clapton leaving John Mayall, and Ginger Baker and Jack Bruce from the Graham Bond Organisation (and Bruce briefly with Manfred Mann) started rehearsing in late July 1966, and after one northern club gig, made their major debut at the annual Jazz & Blues Festival which had moved that year to the Racecourse at Windsor. Once again, the afternoons featured jazz sessions while in the evenings, the Spencer Davis Group, Geno Washington and the Small Faces headlined on Friday, the Who, Jimmy James & the Vagabonds, Chris Farlowe, the Move, the Summer Set on Saturday with the Yardbirds pulling out through illness and then on Sunday evening, the Cream, plus the Alan Bown Set, Action and then headliner Georgie Fame – as with the Animals in 1965, performing with a Big Band, in this case, that of Harry South. Every one of those acts except for Harry South's Band, appeared in Portsmouth and all but the Yardbirds, at the Birdcage – we were still regularly being offered the latest live acts.

The festival audience, paid £1 for advance weekend tickets and 20,000 watched Cream – surprisingly the largest crowd to which they ever performed. In the increasingly fashionable style, Eric Clapton and Jack Bruce played through (double) Marshall stacks while Ginger Baker matched them with two bass drums. Nobody would ever suggest that Bruce and Baker were cutting edge when it came to fashion, but Clapton was rather different. While most of the Yardbirds had sported long-hair, he dressed in the cropped hair, Ivy League suit style, then, moving to John Mayall's Bluesbreakers, briefly grew a moustache and adopted a beatnik look, more consistent with the serious bluesman. Now, in Cream, in the formative period of a shift from pop, rhythm & blues or soul towards 'rock', he appeared on stage in "white bell-bottom trousers and a striking silver jacket" with longish, carefully cut hair and large sideboards.

The band played a mostly blues-based set including "Train Time", "Spoonful" and their original "Sleepy Time, Time", plus Ginger Baker's showpiece "Toad". On the following night, they appeared at London's Cooks Ferry Inn, where their set also included "Hey Lawdy Mama", and "the First Time I Met the Blues". Despite these numbers, in an interview in early August, Eric Clapton told Richard Green of *Record Mirror* that Cream was not a blues group, "it's a pop group really" and identified just four British groups "who are developing their own directions – the Beatles and the Kinks and the Small Faces and the Who I suppose". Interestingly he omitted, or overlooked, the Rolling Stones. He was also sure he would "pack it in when I start to go downhill … maybe tomorrow, maybe when I'm 30". Or maybe not Eric? In December 2016, the 'forgotten' Rolling Stones released an album of blues covers, *Blue and Lonesome,* including a couple of tracks featuring Eric Clapton, now aged

71. On 7 November 1966, Cream came to Gosport's club, known as the New Spot at Thorngate Hall (Members 6/-, Guests 7/6d)

Since the early spring of 1965, the Birdcage Club, first at Kimbells then close to Bransbury Park, had been the sharpest venue in town, as the home of Portsmouth's mods. The club's summer of 1966 had been relatively quiet but on Sunday 25 September a coach party left there to travel to Soho's legendary Marquee Club to witness live performances by two of the Birdcage's favourite bands, Jimmy James & the Vagabonds and the Alan Bown Set. The evening was recorded and resulted in a live album on the Pye label which included a Birdcage logo on the front cover. We just could not stop 'swinging'.

In the following weeks, live performances at the Birdcage included those two Marquee acts plus the Move, Chris Farlowe & the Thunderbirds, Herbie Goins, the Action, the Birds, John Mayall's Bluesbreakers, Zoot Money's Big Roll Band, Ronnie Jones, Graham Bond, the Art Woods and a couple of hugely popular shows from visiting Americans. The first was Ike & Tina Turner on a Sunday afternoon that had all the life of a Saturday night, and then on Friday 25 November, the rock & roll legend Little Richard (12/6d). For once the mods had to concede prime viewing spots to the local Teddy boys who appeared in all their finery – but despite the tribal differences, it was trouble-free night, perhaps because of the wonderful music or possibly, as mod Ted Brooks suggests, because "they were mostly our older brothers!"

These then were entertaining times in the city but not everything was quite so positive. In the *Evening News*, a correspondent complained students "waste their grants on smokes, drinks and weekend orgies", while Southsea's hoteliers were concerned that South Parade Pier faced a "cash crisis" with debts of possibly £50k. Meanwhile the newspaper ran a major exposé of the local drug problem with two full-page articles (5/6.12.1966): "A City's Sinister Secret" and "Youth in Chains". Those two articles appeared on Monday and Tuesday, a couple of days after Cream appeared at the Birdcage (10/-), and while they gave a superb performance of their early blues-based material, the performance was truncated following the collapse of drummer Ginger Baker and the appearance of the local constabulary. The latter would arrive occasionally, accompanied by the sound of flushing toilets and with the house lights revealing a floor covered in non-prescribed medications.

It is probably an exaggeration to suggest that most people in the Birdcage were taking drugs at this point but there was a substantial minority, mostly using a variety of pills and powders to keep them awake and alive through the long weekend. There was also an increasing number beginning to use marijuana, which produced a rather different sensibility. John Boorman's first feature film, the Dave Clark Five vehicle, *Catch Us If You Can*, was released in April 1965 and included a beatnik sequence on Salisbury Plain in which there were clear references to drugs. Most of those teenage beatniks were not professional actors, but the social group from Portsmouth with Marion Knight, who had been filmed by Boorman two years previously, in his documentary for BBC Television, *Citizen '63*. Graham Laker remembered that one of the regular local haunts of those local beatniks was the Domino Café in Somers Road; also, that their appearance in the movie was marked by a centre page feature about them in *the Daily Mirror*. This generation was not the first to take illegal stimulants of course, but this was perhaps the start of that practice becoming more widespread, and beyond self-defining subcultures and discrete cultural tastes.

The American magazine *Time* had run its now-famous feature on swinging London in April 1966. It covered fashion, art galleries, cinema, theatre, the media, comedy, nightlife in the clubs and of course music – by which they meant principally a mixture of discotheques, plus the Beatles, Rolling Stones, and Animals with a dash of Sinatra and Fitzgerald. They quoted cultural commentator and academic Richard Hoggart, suggesting, "a new group of people is emerging into society, creating a kind of classlessness and a verve which has not been seen before". *The Guardian* felt that some parts of the "frenetic prose" were "overdrawn" but they believed the "vitality" was "unmistakable".

In terms of this publication, and its focus on Portsmouth, perhaps the key idea in the *Time* article was that "in fact, there is not one London scene but dozens" and also that "London is not keeping the good news to itself". The latter point was a reference to the global spread of the best (and worst?) of swinging London but that applied too, to the rest of the country – at least to the younger elements. Portsmouth was no more than a couple of hours travel from London, and a lot of young people made that journey in search of fashions, music, drugs and a broader range of cultural experiences. For example, my diary notes that on Wednesday 2 November 1966 my life-long pal Martin Richman and I had a day in London, visiting the Design Centre and National Gallery where we had lunch and spotted some beatniks in Trafalgar Square. Then we had a tour of King's Road where in the Chelsea Antique Market we admired the fur coats (£2 guineas) and colourful military jackets (£4). After returning to Soho, seeing but not visiting Tiles, the Marquee and Flamingo, we caught the 6.50pm train back to Pompey.

We were so taken by the fur coats that the next day Martin bought one in Lake Road for just ten bob (50p) but his father forbade him to wear it. Meanwhile, still at school (sixth form) and impoverished I sold my Sue Story album and bought a grey crew neck jumper in Commercial Road (Hym). In terms of the supposed purity and authenticity of the subcultural groups, these brief references to fashions illustrate one or two significant aspects of life as a teenager at the time. Martin and I had taken our 'O' levels in the summer of 1966, and while hardly high achievers in the academic sense, we were planning to follow college careers in the visual arts. We had been regular attenders at the city's Birdcage Club and more generally participants in the local mod scene in terms of fashions and musical preferences, without being in any sense at the heart of that scene – 'Faces' we were certainly not, although we knew enough to recognise those who were.

FROM BEATNIKS to MODS

(Standing left to right) Tom Powell who appeared with the
Portsmouth beatniks in Catch Us If You Can, Jim Lawrence, who
later ran 1980s Basins Club (with Chris Abbott), and Birdcage mod,
Bob Dunford. We have been unable to identify the young women
for sure although one might be Gill Beamish.

TURNING POINT

1966 offered a fascinating, transitional year, as popular culture began to develop in a number of interesting ways. In San Francisco, the Trips Festivals laid a foundation for 1967's summer of love, while in London the launch of, and launch party for, *International Times*, built on the Albert Hall poetry event of 1965, and led to the opening of the UFO Club. 1966 was also the year that the Beach Boys released the album *Pet Sounds* and the magnificent single "Good Vibrations", while the Beatles, like Brian Wilson, turned their backs on touring, and chose instead to explore the possibilities of the recording studio, beyond the creation of another pop hit. In Portsmouth meanwhile, it was the only complete twelve months of the mods' Birdcage Club, yet by the end of 1966 there were visible (and audible) signs that the high days of the mods were coming to an end.

In *1966: The Year the Decade Exploded*, Jon Savage suggested the year was one of "enormous ambition and serious engagement" when "music was no longer commenting on life but had become indivisible from life" (ix). For Savage, too, "1966 began in pop and ended in rock" and that would mean more than just a matter of sound, instrumentation and volume; it would concern what was being said, where, how, in what context and for what purpose. Not least among those leading the changes was Bob Dylan, with his amplified band which attracted scorn and praise. The times were changing and there was little time to look back.

Savage wrote with the benefit of hindsight, from the perspective of half-a-century. He said in his introduction that he was "attracted to 1966 because of the music" in which he could hear "ambition, acceleration and compression" and he focused on one particular track for each of the year's twelve months to develop a particular idea. While all the tracks came from 1966, one or two stretched a point, either because like "The Third Eye" by the Dovers or "A Quiet Explosion" by the Uglys, hardly anybody heard them then, or since – the latter was not even the 'A' side – or because like the choice for June, "I'll be Your Mirror" by Nico and the Velvet Underground, it would not be released until 1967. Other tracks ("In My Mind's Eye" and "Good Vibrations" for example) were certainly significant, reached the charts

Sergeant and Malcolm Price, while in North End, the Tia Juana Jazz Band offered a 'trad' night at the Oasis. Surfers the Castaways were at Thorngate, followed by former Small Face Jimmy Winston and then Bluesology on their 'New Spot' night. The latter may have included Elton John on keyboards, but these were not exactly 'cutting edge' events. Portsmouth's 1966 ended with old favourite Graham Bond, plus the In-Crowd and local band Wrong Direction in a late-nighter at the Birdcage (12/6d).

Now sixth formers but neither of us with any great interest in completing two-years of 'A' levels at school, Martin and I concentrated on art and we attended an evening class each Monday at the Art College. We became friendly with a couple of sixth form girls from the High School and would go after the class for coffee in Verrechias, Guildhall Square. We were simply friends through a common interest in art, but as in the clubs and youth clubs, mixing with the opposite sex made a refreshing change from school – I cannot recall any mixed secondary schools in Portsmouth in the 1960s, grammar, technical or secondary modern.

While happy to pursue my fondness for the blues with its roots in history, in the visual arts I was much more interested in contemporary and often experimental work. There were visits to exhibitions of kinetic and 'op' art, and surrealism, and I was thrilled by the large-scale abstraction that I saw around the Art College. There were also copies of *Studio International* in the art room at school which, beyond contemporary painting, introduced me to 'live' art, happenings, experimental film and other alternatives to traditional painting and drawing. This was all so new, and some of it paralleled what was shown at the Indica Gallery in London, which became such an important venue in the development of what was then usually described as the underground.

The *Melody Maker* continued to arrive every Thursday. There was always a pop focus to the 'paper but it had grown out of the dance band, big band and jazz eras, and stayed loyal to that following – or at least to jazz – whenever possible. Over the previous two or three years, it had also carried features and reviews of folk and blues, including the British scene. For example, they had profiled the leading figures and influences in the folk boom including Americans Woody Guthrie, Leadbelly, Judy Collins, Alan Lomax, and Pete Seeger plus, from the UK, Ewan MacColl, AL Lloyd, Louis Killen and the mysterious yet greatly admired Anne Briggs. They marked the visit of Doc Watson by describing him as the "real thing", and suggested that one of his achievements in the days of chart hits for Dylan, Donovan and others, was in uniting "the show biz moguls and the traditional purists in unqualified, unstinting praise". With regard to a fondness for the blues, a review of a Big Joe Williams album on Arhoolie suggested "these are expensive times for those addicted to blues listening", with albums now costing up to £2. What was a poor boy to do but listen to Mike Raven on Radio 390, on Sunday evening?

In late October 1966, *Melody Maker* anticipated Nik Cohn's theme with an article partly titled "The Great American Comeback" about the "New In Word" which happened to be "Psychedelic". They profiled six bands who might now seem surprising in terms of how we think of early psychedelia: the Monkees (who were yet to appear on British television), Count Five, the Left Banke, the Association, Question Mark & the Mysterians and Love. Only the last of those now trips lightly from the tongue in discussions of the genre. In passing they also mentioned the Young Rascals, Happenings, the McCoys, Positively Thirteen O'Clock, Five Stair Steps, the Fugs, Sidekicks and the Five Americans – the latter provided Portsmouth's Simon Dupree & the Big Sound with their first single, "I See the Light". There was also a mention for one of the legendary psychedelic bands, the 13th Floor Elevators from Texas. After a reference to American folk-rock predecessors like the Byrds, Lovin' Spoonful, and Mamas & Papas, there was praise for the "high priests of psychedelic happenings" – a strange judgement in retrospect – the Mothers of Invention, who "apparently" represented "the freak brigade". More accurately they suggested the band resembled, as much as anything, "a Charles Mingus group on one of its last chorus roar-ups".

Interestingly too, the article (by Chris Welch and Bob Dawbarn) noted that the word psychedelic was common in New York and Los Angeles (why not San Francisco?) while "without much apparent justification", it had appeared on the publicity for the new Yardbirds' single "Happenings Ten Years Time Ago". Graham Nash, still then in the Hollies, suggested musically "it's trying to create an LSD session without the use of drugs", adding "it's a question of trying to expand the consciousness to the limits". He described having seen Lothar & the Hand People who featured a theremin, while four projectors with different colours flickered on and off, creating a "pretty wild effect".

The only British group identified were the Fingers from Southend who warned about psychedelic rock that "the result too often tends to sound like distorted fuzz boxes". Maybe that is why they disappeared without a trace? The writers, struggling to take it all too seriously, observed about the term 'freaking out', "Cor blimey, don't remember the Troggs saying anything like that!", but all this was known about in London by then – the Beatles for example had played their last live gig in the home of psychedelia, San Francisco, at the Candlestick Park on 29 August 1966. The Beatles had had enough of the noise and the fuss of live gigs, and retired to the studio, but Paul McCartney in particular was engaged with the nascent underground in London, notably at the

Indica Gallery where John Lennon would meet Yoko Ono, at her one woman show. One week prior to *Melody Maker* publishing their psychedelic feature, came a major event at the Roundhouse celebrating the launch of Britain's first countercultural newspaper *International Times (IT)* with performances by Pink Floyd and Soft Machine. The event promised a 'Pop/Op/Costume/ Masque/Fantasy-Loon/Blowout/Drag Ball' and featured steel bands, strips, trips, happenings, movies. Green (1999) reported that for the two bands this was their first gig in a 'bigger' venue; Pink Floyd, with their lights, were paid £15 and Soft Machine (no lights) £12.50 (154). Jim Haynes recalled that "the launch party did make money, possibly £1000, and it launched the paper and launched the Roundhouse as a space" (Green 1998, 119)

International Times itself reported the event:

> 2,500 people dancing in that strange, giant round barn. Darkness, only flashing lights. People in masks, girls half naked. Other people standing about wondering what the hell was going on. Pot smoke. Now and again the sound of a bottle breaking. Somebody looks as if he might get violent. There was a lot of tension about (Hewison, 1986, 120).

Despite this uneasy beginning, and the scepticism of such as Cohn, Britain soon developed its own versions of psychedelia, the underground and the counterculture, with *International Times* as a leading contributor. That newspaper is often considered the first and longest lasting of Britain's journalist contribution to the underground, although Hewison (95) identified an intriguing group of predecessors, beginning in 1959 in Oxford, where Michael Horowitz launched *New Departures*. Six years later he would be one of the poets reading in the Albert Hall. Hewison cited 1,256 entries in a *Directory of British Alternative Periodicals 1965-1974* by John Noyce (95).

In the mainstream pop world, the *NME* maintained the capital's swinging image with a series about the newer boutiques like I Was Lord Kitchener's Valet, with its range of exotic army tunics and capes, plus clubs that catered for the 'show-biz' stars, like the Cromwellian, the Bag O' Nails, the Uppercut and the Speakeasy. Those clubs did largely fit the claim of those like Dominic Sandbrook, that only a limited number of people participated in the swinging sixties, but that ignores other clubs which were far more open and rather more 'cutting edge' musically – for example, the Scene, the Marquee and the Flamingo, where the sharpest new acts had appeared for some years. The next such venue, albeit very different from the mod rhythm & blues hangouts, would be the UFO club, established by record producer Joe Boyd and John 'Hoppy' Hopkins, photographer and leading light of the London underground.

UFO opened in Tottenham Court Road on 23 December 1966 – perhaps symbolically on the same day as the final broadcast of *Ready Steady Go!* It ran for about one year, and featured bands like Pink Floyd, Soft Machine, Tomorrow, Graham Bond, Zoot Money, Denny Laine, Aynsley Dunbar, Fairport Convention, the Crazy World of Arthur Brown the Move, Ten Years After, Family and the Bonzo Dog Doo Dah Band, all of whom appeared in Portsmouth around these years. UFO also featured lightshows, notably by artist Mark Boyle, poets, and some of the first screenings of American underground films, along with the Arts Lab and soon to be formed London Film-makers Co-op. Anticipating other late 1960s developments, there were signs of student protests at Mick Jagger's *alma mater*, the London School of Economics, while the first European protests against the war in Vietnam were held in Germany. Things were changing.

At the end of 1966, Portsmouth's *Evening News* ran its annual pop poll, with the top three visitors, the Vagabonds, the Action and the Alan Bown Set – three Motown/soul acts popular at the Birdcage. Similarly, the most popular local bands were both soul acts, Simon Dupree & the Big Sound and the Inspiration. The Alan Bown Set's popularity extended to local contacts too and one of their fans, Susan Hunt has an amusing story about their singer Jess Roden, her bedsit in Castle Road and the perils of Southsea seafront. It began with a day out with another friend Jeremy Ensor, a local student and subsequently a member of Principal Edwards Magic Theatre. Susan and Jeremy went to Slough to see the Alan Bown Set playing in a dance hall.

> After the gig, there was time to chat with the band, and it was then that I met Jess Roden, the lead vocalist. We kept in touch, and although they were a very busy band, when he got time off, he would come to visit me and stay for the weekend, much to the disapproval of my landlady!
>
> On one memorable weekend, Jess drove down from Ickenham in Middlesex, where he lived in the house of Bobby Pridden's parents. Bobby Pridden worked for the Who as a Road Manager and from 1969 as Sound Engineer.
>
> Jess drove an orange mini with very wide wheels, which certainly stood out parked in Castle Road. We were taking a walk along the seafront on this particular weekend, and Jess decided he would go down and touch the water's edge. There was a slope down to the sea, covered in green slime and unfortunately, his Cuban-heel boots afforded no grip – he gathered speed, and promptly ended

up in the Solent! I managed to haul him out but he was totally drenched.

We ran back to my bedsit across Southsea Common which had the grass cut recently, but as we ran, we kicked up grass clippings and from the knees down his green velvet trousers were covered. We made it back to my place and he changed into spare clothes he had brought, but unfortunately, the black velvet jacket he had borrowed from Bobby Pridden was ruined, and he also had a clutch of paper money – ten shilling notes and one pound notes – that were sodden, so we had to peel them apart and slap them down on the table to dry out. It looked like a counterfeit operation going on.

Many of the published and private stories from this time seem to emanate from the men so, as with the earlier memories from Donna, it is good to have recollections from a woman, although there might be more from the Portsmouth area. From elsewhere, there are some very interesting published accounts by women of that time, not least a beautifully presented photographic book by Lisa Law from the USA, while British contributions include Jenny Diski's *The Sixties*, Sheila Rowbotham's *Promise of a Dream: Remembering the Sixties,* and Sara Maitland's edited collection *Very Heaven: looking back at the 1960s*. The latter includes 22 separate chapters, some of which are recollections, some interviews, and a mixture of the well-known (Barbara Castle, Julie Christie, Leila Berg, Angela Carter) and the less well-known, including an interview about post-marital sex with 'Jane' who by the 1970s was living in Portsmouth. She had been born in 1938, married in 1959 and confessed she could not remember any popular songs from the 1960s "either because I was too old or because the decade passed in such a blur". She described the awkwardness of sex after marrying, two unexpected pregnancies and the sudden availability of the Pill which was "wonderful" and "changed my life". She recalled too the impact of

The Christine Keeler business and the Lady Chatterley case; suddenly you could talk about sex at dinner parties, because it was in the newspapers … ordinary, respectable, married women … could talk about it (1988, 151).

Sex was one issue; drugs another. In that first week of 1967, the *Evening News* reported that the National Union of Teachers had expressed "concern about school children taking drugs", while two days later their headline was "City Fears on Drug Taking in Schools", with Councillor EG Sheen reporting on a pupil "in a groggy condition in class". I was still a schoolboy in January 1967, albeit a sixth former, and had I ever taken any drugs? Not many, not at school and not regularly, but yes, I had started smoking 'joints'.

Graham Bond and the In Crowd welcomed 1967 at the Birdcage and the following weekend came three distinctly different evenings which indicated various strands on offer to the sharper teenagers in the city. Friday night was a records session called "Freak Out", Saturday night featured the Art Woods, one of the cult rhythm & blues bands including Ronnie Wood's brother Art, drummer Keef Hartley and organist Jon Lord (Deep Purple). Then on Sunday night, "Prince Bustup" was the first of a series of nights featuring ska records. The mods that followed that trend were still into suits and sporting pork pie hats, setting a fashion that would become a significant alternative to the colourful extravagances of the next few years. Nigel Grundy suggests "the mod movement was moving in two very polarized directions – the arty, psychedelic end had gone all hippy-trippy", whereas the "younger hard nuts from the council estates … shaved their nuts and sharpened their wardrobes". Paul 'Oscar' Wild, who by then was cutting hair, says

> It seemed to me that the skinhead fashion was for some people just an evolution from the college-boy, mod, fashion. The skinheads with a leaning to their mod roots tended to go for the compromise of the more moderate 'suede-head' haircut.

Graham Laker, who knew Nigel in those days and like him was from Southsea recalls

> Most of the mods I knew made the transition to Hippy – we were a group of mates ready for a change and, anyway, the new drugs and lifestyle looked like fun … I don't remember any from our group 'becoming' skinheads – this would have been a younger set.

It was a time of significant changes and contrasts. In the early weeks of 1967, as the first Jimi Hendrix single, "Hey Joe", moved up the UK charts, there was real variety at the Birdcage, with Charlie & Inez Foxx from the USA, soul regulars Geno Washington, a continuation of the weekly ska record sessions on Fridays or Sundays and a few of the newer sounding bands, including the In Crowd, the Real Thing, and the Syn. The latter included bass guitarist Chris Squire and Pete Banks (guitar) and is said to have anticipated the sound of Yes. The major event in January however, the event that for Portsmouth hinted at what would follow through the summer of love, came on Saturday 21 January when Pink Floyd arrived for the first time, with their lightshow.

Rob Chapman in his book about Syd Barrett, *A Very Irregular Head*, wrote about Pink Floyd beginning to tour the country around this time and the following extract was posted on my Blog, eliciting memories from those who were there:

> The gigs changed too. The Floyd left the sanctuary of the counter-culture and ventured out into Top Rank territory where their live set was often met with indifference or downright hostility. The Birdcage Dancehall, Portsmouth, the Top Spot Ross-on-Wye or the California Ballroom, Dunstable were not UFO or the Roundhouse. The Birdcage in Portsmouth was a mod stronghold and the audience greeted "Interstellar Overdrive" accordingly.

Few of the responses to this Blog post endorsed Chapman's version of events, although Chris Fosbrooke suggested that while the lightshow was "great" the band were less impressive, and drummer Terry Threadingham recalls that at the conclusion, Roger Waters thanked the crowd, saying "see you soon", to which one of the mods shouted back "fucking hope not!". That reaction might have been a one-off; the Birdcage was indeed "a mod stronghold" but bands like Cream, the Move, the Small Faces and the In Crowd had come before Pink Floyd, so innovation was not unheard of, and mods did not necessarily avoid listening to other styles – for example on pirate radio or new albums. One regular Blog correspondent Chris Abbot who in later years was an imaginative promoter in the city, said "I used to be surprised at all sorts of things in music. I was surprised when standing in the Birdcage dressed in my favourite mohair suit, I first clapped eyes on Pink Floyd, even though I was already into Hippy drugs!"

A couple of months before the Pink Floyd gig, *the Evening News* ran a story about those "hippy drugs", reporting a court case, in which an 18-year-old from Paulsgrove had been arrested outside the Birdcage, where Detective Constable David Hopkins had found 800 grains of cannabis in his scooter. Hopkins told the court that this was by far the biggest local haul, exceeding the previous highest of 135 grains. Apparently, a grain was "currently fetching one shilling" (5p) so that this amount would have been worth £40 – perhaps three weeks' wages in 1966. The young man admitted that for four months he had been buying the cannabis in London and bringing it back to Portsmouth.

Chris Abbott's pal and Birdcage regular Dave Pittard also remembered the

Pink Floyd gigs "very well" and had clear views about what Rob Chapman had written:

> It's very true to say that it was a mod stronghold and the mohair suits were still very much in evidence, but you must remember that the drug of choice had changed from speed to cannabis and therefore the band were well received in a 'couldn't quite believe our eyes' kind of way! (yours truly included). And as we all know that current incarnation of mod had had its day.

This confirms my recollections, I think initially we were somewhat bemused, but many of us were open to new experiences – that was the nature of the late 1960s. And if we had not liked Pink Floyd presumably, like a number of other newer bands, the Birdcage management would not have booked them back – but they did. About 10 weeks later, they returned and Dave Pittard was there again – although he doubts whether the author was:

> Mr Chapman was obviously not in attendance. I saw them both and what he describes is incorrect. Again, we get people telling us how it was, when it wasn't. I think he confuses himself in calling it The Birdcage Dancehall – It was a Club! Whoever called it a Dancehall? Nobody!

Dave Pittard went on to point out that around this time he and his pals were beginning to listen to American bands like Love, the Seeds and early Jefferson Airplane but added that this did not prevent them from "still listening to and loving the Motown, Atlantic and Stax records – and ska". Incidentally, not only was it not the "Birdcage Dance Hall", neither was it anything to do with Top Rank – it was an independent club modelled on the Flamingo and Marquee – indeed there was no Top Rank in Portsmouth.

Among the many chronicles of the first age of mod in the 1960s, Paul 'Smiler' Anderson's *Mods: The New Religion* is particularly relevant here because it explores the impact of mods outside London – including Portsmouth and the Birdcage Club, and his final chapter "It's All Too Beautiful", opens with the changes:

> As 1966 came to a close, mod had mutated into a completely different culture from how it had begun. The Scene Club had closed its doors and for many of its regulars it was the end of an era … Music was getting stranger too … Sounds from the American West Coast had begun to infiltrate the British airwaves (285)

'Smiler's' beautifully presented book draws heavily on oral histories of the time. Penny Reel from London remembers that by late summer 1966, in somewhere like the King's Road, there were "guys with coats down to their ankles, wearing floppy hats". She supposed they were "the first hippies, the first 'beautiful people'. They wore velvet, pink and purple". There is an important fashion point here. These days the archetypal image of a hippie is somewhat unkempt, smelly Afghan coat, straggly hair but when this change happened, it was not like that, because the mods who got into more flamboyant costumes were still smart and still clean. They did not iron creases into their Levis but Birdcage boy Ted Brooks might be right in preferring to describe these pioneers as 'heads' rather than hippies.

Changes in fashion gradually paralleled changes in listening habits. In late 2016, we learned of the death of Leonard Cohen, and in all the many tributes I did not come across one suggesting that the mods were necessarily big fans. But after noting his death on my Blog, the following discussion took place between Dave Pittard and his old pal Graham Laker, another Birdcage regular, indicating a shift in musical tastes, alongside the fashions:

> GL: I'm pretty sure we first heard of Leonard Cohen on the Judy Collins albums *In My Life* (released 1966 which included both 'Suzanne' and 'Dress Rehearsal Rag') and *Wildflowers* (1967, with 'Sisters of Mercy' and 'That's No Way to Say Goodbye'). We used to listen to these a lot at Bert's Sunday afternoon sessions. Leonard Cohen's first album wasn't released until December, '67.

> DP: Thanks, yes of course, it was through those Judy Collins albums that we first heard Leonard Cohen songs – round at Bert's Sunday afternoon sessions, along with an early foray into wine drinking – bottles of Graves I believe. How sophisticated was that? Ha!

Bert was one of those invaluable members of any young group in those days – the one who found out about all the latest releases, could afford to buy them regularly and willingly shared them with his friends, which in Bert's case was quite a number of people. Keith Dolan recalls that "he lived off Locksway Road, Milton, at his parents' house. He always had great, great music with which he entertained and, at times educated us boys, with the latest and rarest of musical offerings of the time, and times, even then, past." A couple of years later, Dave Pittard and I were in a band together with a roadie Davey Jones, who was a 'chippy', also lived at home (in Fratton) and he did the same for us. Through guys like Bert and Davey we heard the changing sounds pretty rapidly.

Until 1967, my wife Lou had lived mostly across the harbour in Gosport. She left school and home in 1966 and had a mod boyfriend with a scooter. They came across to the Birdcage and the Locarno in Arundel Street, and she went with school friends to occasional concerts at the Guildhall – the first one as a 14-year-old featuring Donovan & the Pretty Things. There were evening events at Thorngate in Gosport, or scooter trips to Southampton's Mecca and Bognor's Butlins. This was all very much a part of the provincial mod scene, and she recalls that it was her boyfriend, and the other boys with scooters, who mostly decided where they would go. Her sense of what was happening was informed partly too, by visits to London. She remembers a somewhat uncomfortable evening in Tiles, a location described somewhat negatively too by John Peel after a DJ gig there, but Lou tells too of the impact of a trip around the main streets of London, particularly the King's Road, and the newer boutiques like *Granny Takes a Trip, Hung On You,* and *Just Looking.* She too returned with a sense that things were changing.

One young man who had been photographed in an early magazine article on mods in London was Marc Feld who by now had changed his name to Marc Bolan and after a brief solo career playing acoustically, he had joined the early psychedelic band John's Children, who appeared at the Birdcage. Penny Reel told 'Smiler' Anderson, that previously "he was this really pugnacious hard nut; a roughneck Jewish boy who hung around Stamford Hill, devoted to mod", then by early 1967 he was transformed into "a beautiful hippie". His brother Harry has lived in Portsmouth for many years. Penny Reel recalled her fondness for literature, recounting how she would visit London's Better Books to read "Ginsberg and Corso ... loads of underground poetry. I was reading Orwell, Huxley and Sartre but still listening to black music". She added however, that suddenly "there was no time to be a mod".

The split among the committed mods and those who were attracted by new sounds and more flamboyant fashions was growing, and the Birdcage was no longer attracting sufficient numbers to remain viable. There were quite a few ska record nights and even a live performance by Prince Buster; the Who came again, plus favourites like the Vagabonds, Geno Washington, the In Crowd and the Action (who by now had started covering the Byrds on their way to becoming Mighty Baby). 'Brady' the man whose records had kept the place dancing for two years started experimenting with other sounds and environments, but he left in early February, following Robin Beste who had gone a couple of months earlier.

For three years, pretty well all the white and black acts appearing live at Portsmouth's two major clubs, the Rendezvous and the Birdcage, played music rooted in black American blues, rhythm & blues, jazz or soul, but now a distinct difference began to emerge between Jamaican ska (mainly on record) and soul on the one hand and white pop and rock on the other. The distinction was not absolute, of course, Jimi Hendrix had a huge white following, the new British blues bands were playing music rooted in black 1950s and 1960s Chicago, and in the next few years, the Temptations developed a psychedelic feel and Sly & the Family Stone emerged from San Francisco and were a success at Woodstock. But psychedelia in Britain and America increasingly offered itself as a 'hip', mostly white alternative to what had been the coolest black sounds.

During 1967, young people were causing their elders anxieties. Portsmouth's Licensing Committee heard that more young people than ever had been "convicted for drinking offences" although more than two-thirds of those misbehaving in the city were naval ratings. Then the *Evening News* front page on 18 February 1967 ran a "stark warning on dangers of drugs" with statistics showing prosecutions for possessing hemp had increased ten times in a decade and for heroin four times in one year. Five days later, the main headline ran "Too Easy to Get Drugs – Doctor" adding "Grave Concern about Young" and the next day we learned that local schoolteachers were "alert to drugs peril". In West Sussex, police raided Redlands, and charged Rolling Stones Keith Richard and Mick Jagger with possessing drugs. When they were (briefly) imprisoned a few months later, it caused an uproar among young people – and on 1 July 1967, William Rees-Mogg, editor of *The Times*, quoted Alexander Pope (1735), in heading his editorial "Who breaks a butterfly on a wheel?" The pair were soon released.

The live music scene in Portsmouth through the 1960s was often remarkable, and the quality of the bands at the Birdcage in particular had an impact on some local musicians. Rod Watts, a lifelong musician, was a guitarist in the Rivals in the early 1960s, appearing on Southern ITV, and supporting the Rolling Stones at the Savoy Ballroom. Rod then switched to organ, playing in one of a number of versions of the Soul Society before forming the Academy, something a local version of a 'supergroup', with guitarist Marc Tuddenham (Renegades, Dynamos future Cherry Smash), drummer Graham Hunt (J Crow Combo, Crow, future Aubrey Small), and bass guitarist Graham Barnes (Klimax, future Coconut Mushroom). They played mainly soul covers, some of which were relatively unusual among local bands, including, Billy Stewart's "Sitting in the Park", Don Covay's "Seesaw", Jesse Hill's "Ooh Pooh Pah Do", and the Capitol's "Cool Jerk". There was also a hint of things to come with "California Dreaming", and also James & Bobby Purify's "I'm Your

Puppet", which Rod and Marc still play today, in their current outfit Tuxedo Junction. Rod recalled

> As much as I loved the Savoy in my teens, the Birdcage was defi-
> nitely the place for some class acts as we approached and got into
> our twenties; it was a whole new world of music, artistes, atmos-
> phere, and it certainly made me realise this was what I wanted
> out of life, listening and learning from these wonderful musicians,
> trying (and sometimes failing) to emulate their style of playing.
> What a learning curve that was!

In late March, the Academy played an all-nighter at the Birdcage supporting Chris Farlowe & the Thunderbirds, an evening which came after a very
low-key period. The ska records sessions had been replaced by straight
records nights on Fridays and Sundays, with live bands booked mostly only
on Saturday evenings – and with a couple of late cancellations, only four
relatively minor acts, the In Crowd, Boz & the Boz Band, the Amboy Dukes
(UK) and the Knack, had appeared in the previous five weeks. Things were a
little livelier after that, but the club's future was far from secure.

The spring brought the return of Pink Floyd to the Birdcage on 'April Fool's
Day', then the Move, mixed in with Geno (again), the Soul Sisters, and Georgie
Fame's last Portsmouth visit with his Blue Flames. In June, the club re-invented
itself as 'the New Birdcage' but there were now more "Discotheque" nights
than live bands. July brought more familiar names, Herbie Goins, Graham
Bond and then Jimmy James & the Vagabonds for the penultimate of their
29 appearances which have become the stuff of local legends.

While some of the Birdcage mods (as elsewhere) stuck with the suits, the ska,
the soul and the dancing, their kid brothers and sisters became skinheads
and milked ska for all it was worth. But Ted Brooks was another Birdcage mod
who pursued the newer music and more exotic fashions. He explained this
other route to 'Smiler' Anderson, attributing it to "the drugs" and the fact
that at that age "you're always moving on through". Ted recalled:

> We met some girls from South London, on holiday in Hayling
> Island and they'd come down to the Birdcage Club. We made
> arrangements to go and see Geno Washington at the Mecca the
> next day. We went there and for want of a better word, I got bored.
> I suddenly felt it was all getting a bit 'samey'. I'd seen all the bands
> at least three or four times ... I suddenly wanted something new
> and to move on ... I couldn't just keep doing the same thing (293).

In 1966, for the only time in my life, I kept a day-to-day (*Melody Maker*) diary. It was pretty tiny, so not much room for anything but facts – I did this, I did that; I thought this, I thought that. Towards the end of the year I saw the Move who were "pretty good", Cream who were "great" (even adding a set list in the notes page), the Action – "not bad", Little Richard – "tremendous", but for Herbie Goins, and then the Vagabonds just "a drag". Did I mean the evening overall, or was this more specifically about the bands? I had never been a huge Herbie Goins fan but for some time I had *loved* both the Vagabonds and (especially) the Action. Perhaps I was recording much the same feelings as Ted. I had seen and heard so much, in such a short space of time and at 17 I was still on the lookout for the next thing. Nonetheless I retain many fond memories of the mod/soul days and still admire that first Vagabonds album, *New Religion*, while the Action, among the best of the live bands, were on the verge of significant changes.

Ted's lifelong pal Jim Lush, described to 'Smiler' a similar "natural progression" and again identified the change in drugs as a key factor, moving from 'speed' in the classic mod days, to "acid" and "smoking dope". Ted and Jim both began wearing more exotic clothes although Ted added "I'd never wear an Afghan coat" and while they looked different, he added, "one or two people got a misunderstanding … they thought (we) were hippies and it was all peace and love. We weren't at all. If you wanted to mix it, we'd mix it with you" – not at all untypical of Portsmouth at any time.

There is a very interesting account of the heady days of the Birdcage, written by one of its active participants, Ian Hebditch, as part of an assessment in his days as a fashion student. He called it "Weekend" and described a 'typical' Saturday of the afternoon in Commercial Road, the Action at the Birdcage and then a late-night trip to Bognor's all-nighter Shoreline Club. In it, he mentions a number of the Pompey mods, Fred Loveridge, Jim Lush, 'Jimmer' Smith, the girls who "beg lifts" on his scooter, and of course, Rikki Farr. Ian's piece can be found in a comprehensive mod anthology, edited by Paolo Hewitt (1999), and Ian also worked extensively on a history of the Action, *In the Lap of the Mods* (2012). Two members of the band, Mike Evans and Roger Powell collaborated on this and there are extensive references to the Birdcage, although very sadly Ian died before the project was completed, at which point his partner Jane Shepherd took it over. The final lavish slip-case publication did more than justice to those wonderful days and to Ian's memory – Jim Lush, Graham Laker and I went to a very enjoyable launch in London a couple of years ago.

In July 1967, 'Procul Harun' (their correct original name) were advertised at the Birdcage – they had visited quite often as the Paramounts, but this time they did not arrive. Two weeks later, Denny Laine's very interesting Electric

String Band presented a new sound with violins and cellos – a fascinating night. Denny was the singer and front man with the Moody Blues on my first visit to a rhythm & blues club almost three years previously, so it seems now, somewhat appropriate that his was the last act I saw at The Birdcage, and one that pointed to a very different future; even as I retained my deep fondness for the blues and still played it from time-to-time with Pete.

I will explain in a moment why this was my last visit to that beloved venue – at least as the Birdcage. The club did not last much longer. The Vagabonds came again in August but for the last two months the club opened only on Saturday nights. In August, we had two visits from the Joyce Bond Show and that was it; two-and-a-half years of magic, but now it was no more. By Christmas 1967, it was re-fashioned and re-opened as a nightclub the Brave New World and continued to offer cutting-edge rock acts alongside British jazz, folk, and cabaret. But it was never quite the same again – and neither were we.

FROM THE BIRDCAGE to the SUMMER of LOVE

Barry Thane, Dave Arney, who also appeared in Citizen '63,
and Lesley Cryer.

Photo courtesy of Chris Harris.

SUMMER of LOVE

Although I knew them only by sight in the Birdcage days, Ted Brooks and Jim Lush have both become life-long friends. Ted went to a secondary modern, worked in Billy Manning's funfair on Southsea seafront (featured with Ringo Starr and David Essex in *That'll Be the Day*) and after his apprenticeship became a painter & decorator. He's still doing it, particularly painting for the RNLI across the country. Jim went to the Technical High School, that imaginative third strand idea of the 1940s education reforms which rarely became reality, but did so in Portsmouth, probably because the local economy then was dominated by HM Dockyard. The dockyard is in decline now of course, but then it was the main employer of local men, and so many 1960s teenage boys like Jim Lush went there to do their apprenticeships. Dave Pittard, who was to become another lifelong friend, also went from secondary modern (including an extra specialist year) to his apprenticeship there. There were plenty of other Birdcage Dockyard apprentices.

Being a grammar school boy, suited me in one sense, since I preferred the humanities subjects (history, English), was hopeless at anything scientific or practical (unlike my dad, a frustrated craftsman) and pursued art, not because I was the most talented (above average maybe) but because it seemed to open up all kinds of possibilities of a broader social, philosophical and cultural kind. It excited my imagination and offered an escape from the potential boredom of an 'ordinary' provincial life – although I had no idea what I was actually going to 'do' with my life, in the sense of a job/career.

Nigel Grundy, who has published his account of those days in Portsmouth (2012) and heads up the Guildhall exhibition 'Portsmouth Music Experience' recalled his time at that same school, a couple of years ahead of me:

> Dave Allen, Paul 'Oscar' Wild and I were at Portsmouth Grammar School, and I think I know how they feel about the experience. As far as I am concerned, I struggled academically but look back on those years between 1959-1964 with fondness, though as I progressed things did become difficult because the school's views about music and society and my own were diverging.

We had music as a class subject but usually just sang traditional folk and shanty songs to a piano accompaniment. Some took violin and flute lessons but they were after-school activities, and if I remember correctly had to be paid for; instruments were expensive too, so it was a bit elitist. I can remember the excitement when it was announced that some pupils had formed a band and would be closing the annual school concert, I think I remember them playing Shadows hits. Paul Pond, who changed his name to Paul Jones, was a former pupil and those of us who were interested in the emerging R & B music scene thought Manfred Mann was a good band. Today a school would promote an ex-pupil's success, but back then the comment in, the school magazine, the *Portmuthian* was:

"Behind the tangled hirsute growth and the resonant harmonica of one of the Manfred Mann group, and in spite of its writhing body, many O.P.'s will have recognised the form of P.A. Pond, who was at school during the years 1950-1958. He plainly finds this form of occupation to be more lucrative than the continuance of his course of study at Cambridge University".

Maybe the school was right; he probably did find the 'occupation more lucrative'!

My friends and I were proud Paul had been a pupil at our school and looked at desk tops to see if he had carved his name on them. Manfred Mann had a residency at Kimbells on Thursday evenings; you could help them carry their equipment from the van to the stage and afterwards I would go to the Keyhole coffee bar in Osborne Road (now the Wave Maiden). The Keyhole was unusual because it was patronised by the last of the Beatniks, the motor cycle fraternity *and* the city's emerging mods in their Cuban heel boots, bell bottom jeans, high neck paisley, or blue with white collar shirts and a combat jacket or a PVC mac with a felt collar. There was occasional trouble between the groups, but the Keyhole was small and people were close together, especially round the juke box. I also went to the Delmonico in Osborne Road and the Manhattan coffee bar in Palmerston Road, Southsea

Nigel had left school by the time I spent one year in the sixth form (1966/7). I too had mostly "struggled academically" (I was certainly lazy), in comparison with our fast-tracked peers going to 'Oxbridge' or other universities.

One Saturday afternoon in July 1967, I left after an end-of-term cricket match, which was, with art, the other thing I really cared about. I had no idea what to do next, although I hoped to study Fine Art at some point in the near future.

I resisted seeking a job in that most interesting summer, and with another school pal, Steve Harley, set off to hitch to the west country. It was what people were doing, indeed what they had been doing for a few years, and while at the same time those travelling to San Francisco USA were advised to wear flowers in their hair, our trail was still rather more reminiscent of the beatnik years of jumpers, beards, and guitars – an attitude that had been established in the earlier years of the decade at the Beaulieu Jazz Festivals, CND marches and indeed down to Cornwall itself.

Steve and I saw lots of like-minded fellow travellers on the road, but we had little luck getting lifts, and after more than 24 hours, we turned left around Exeter and ended up in Paignton, Devon. This was not quite the plan but once there we had a rather fine time, probably because teenagers dossing on the beach were somewhat unexpected and we were generally left alone. We got to know a few locals including one or two pretty girls, hung out most days around the beach and frequented a café with a juke box although we relied on others to feed that machine, as we did not have much money.

Like most juke boxes back then, the records changed regularly, staying up-to-date. That meant mostly just the Top Twenty, but fortunately – and again, despite Nik Cohn's gloomy views – the summer of '67 was not too bad, with the early stirrings of psychedelic-pop reaching the UK charts, including "Whiter Shade of Pale, "All You Need is Love", "Strange Brew", "The Wind Cries Mary", "The Burning of the Midnight Lamp", "Paper Sun", "Groovin'", and "See Emily Play". Indeed, even Tamla Motown's Supremes were into "The Happening". Looming over all those songs, many of which have survived very nicely through the years, was the enigma that was Scott McKenzie's "San Francisco (Be Sure to Wear Some Flowers in Your Hair)". Any serious partici-pant in that particular city's 'real' summer of love loathed its exploitation of the scene, and its encouragement to hordes of young people to pack off to California in search of nirvana. In the end, flowers or not, overcrowding in Haight Ashbury was one of the most important reasons why things went wrong there so quickly.

There is no good reason to dissent from any scepticism about this LA-driven cashing-in on an intriguing scene, except that it is a not unpleasant, gentle singalong piece of pop of its time, it was on the radio and all the juke boxes back then, and however hard I try, I cannot escape the fact that since that extraordinary summer, it has become one of the triggers that remind me so much of many magic moments. It's not that I like it particularly – I never bought it – but, as pop can do, it sets certain wheels in motion; so, I'm stuck with you Scott. My only defence is that I was never fooled by the Flowerpot Men, who anyway did not arrive until September, appropriately late.

The 'real thing' was rather different of course. In San Francisco, the year began with the "Human Be-In" or "Gathering of the Tribes" in San Francisco's Golden Gate Park on Saturday 14 January 1967 – a date advised through consultation with a local Astrologer and sure enough blessed with a fine winter's day. On the previous day, the *Berkeley Barb* anticipating the event, proclaimed

> The spiritual revolution will be manifest and proven … Spiritual revolution to transform the materialistic bruted body and mind of America is NOW here, with the young budding.

The Be-In was the latest in a number of events emerging from the Haight Ashbury culture including the various Trips Festivals, the celebration of the Summer Solstice (June 1966), the Love Pageant rally (October) and the Now Day (December) all of which are described and illustrated by Anthony (1980).

Charles Perry (1977, 188) has suggested that for some people the Human Be-In was an event intended to "heal that conflict" between political Berkeley over the bridge, and hippie Haight Ashbury in the city. A large crowd came to this free afternoon event featuring Allen Ginsberg, Jerry Rubin, Timothy Leary, Dick Gregory, Rev Suzuki (San Francisco's Zen Temple), Quicksilver Messenger Service, Jefferson Airplane, Grateful Dead, Big Brother & the Holding Company, Country Joe & the Fish, Sir Douglas Quintet, and Loading Zone. Michael Bowen's poster simply promised "All SF Rock bands" as well as saints, banners, drums, incense, chimes, candles, flutes, families, animals, lovers and children. Rick Griffin listed some of the key individuals (Leary, Ginsberg etc.) on his poster but similarly added bottom left, "All San Francisco Rock Bands". The rock musicians were loved but not accorded star status in the Haight Ashbury of 1966 and 1967. The press release for the event suggested that "a new concept of human relations (is) being developed within the youthful underground", of which music was a key part, but this was no star-making machine.

In his later history of Haight Ashbury (1984), Charles Perry recalled that on that day, "some members of Country Joe & the Fish backed a folksinger named Pat Kilroy but others were too stoned to play at all" (126). Perry's other specific article on the event (1977) is accompanied by a large photograph of Joe and Kilroy on stage, and he described how

The press would go bananas in the next few days trying to figure out what this event was about. It would become one of the grand mythic elements of the Haight mystique, along with indiscriminate love and the anonymity of the Diggers – the notion of a meeting without any purpose other than to be. Together (1977, 192).

While the mainstream press went "bananas", the next month's *San Francisco Oracle* was their Aquarian Age issue (number 6) and included a photomontage and report of the event. The same issue included various artworks by Rick Griffin, an article entitled "LSD, Revolution and God" and features by or about Chester Anderson, John Sinclair, Paul Krassner and Alan Watts.

On that same Saturday in Portsmouth, the In Crowd were at the Birdcage so it is perhaps appropriate that they would soon move away from that mod name (and soul sound) and become Tomorrow, an early British psychedelic band. At one time, they were to have featured in the club guitar-smashing scene in Antonioni's movie, *Blow-Up*, which was released around this time, but they were dropped, and after he failed to get the Velvet Underground to fly in from America, the Director used the Yardbirds who were a bigger name. The In Crowd did at least record a song called "Blow Up", and the Pompey 'tribe' gathered on 14 January to see one of their last Birdcage gigs, and one of that tribe, Graham Laker recalled the impact of those changing times

By 1966 we had lost our propensity to shock. We were 18-year-old mods/stylists dressed in bespoke three-piece suits, cars had replaced scooters and alcohol had become the drug of choice. We still went to The Birdcage but as an end to the evening, rather than spending the whole time there. Imagine then hearing about this new mind-altering drug that was hot in San Francisco – that made you free, so that you could dress how you wanted, grow your hair again, and the music wasn't half bad either – Jefferson Airplane, Buffalo Springfield, Mothers of Invention (I particularly loved them when "It Can't Happen Here" was played on BBC's Juke Box Jury, and it was described as being recorded by a group of people on drugs!).

Ian Hebditch (2012) also recalled the split that was happening around Portsmouth at that time, describing the arrival at the Birdcage one evening of one of Portsmouth's original mods and "pharmaceutical adventurers" in an altered state, who looked around and rapidly rushed out again. Over the next few months, Ian recalls that in Portsmouth, "odd groups of mods ... tried acid", which tended to lead people to feel "different somehow, as if partly disengaging from the mod headset". Some were still mods however, and Ian suggests the Birdcage was

> Overrun by grey suits with massive vents. Everywhere you looked, they crowded in like a suffocating blanket; impeccably worn with clip on braces over fresh white shirts, the ties – spotted, striped or plain – with their perfect knots and shiny black brogues (125).

There is a suggestion here of mods moving towards a certain uniformity but Ian described his sartorial resistance in a period of what he called "transition mod", during which "everyone had their own interpretation", as "everything was changing" (126). He recorded how his pal Jim Lush began to wear increasingly 'exotic' versions of the mod look – not least because he "possessed a sophisticated design understanding", while alongside this came the new music – Jim is a life-long devotee of Frank Zappa for example – and those new drugs.

In San Francisco, following their celebratory January day, things became increasingly crowded through the year, and by high summer there was some concern about drugs – not so much marijuana and LSD, but harder drugs and the criminality that is often associated with it. On 3 August, acid dealer John Carter was brutally murdered and two days later a motorcycle racer was caught with Carter's money and possessions. On 6 August, another acid dealer 'Superspade' was also found murdered. Perry (1984) suggested:

> The vague disharmony between vision and reality had become a wrenching torture. Horror and ecstasy, two sides of a coin; a great drama being played out in these few city blocks with good and evil changing faces any moment. Would the experiment fail? (227)

On 20 August, San Francisco General Hospital reported that drug abuse victims had increased from 150 in February, to 750 in July. Nonetheless many (mostly young, mostly white) people had fun for a while and began to explore a host of new ideas and approaches to life. There was no 'road map', we were constructing it as we went along, while in 1967 there was of course, no internet. We did not really think of ourselves living 'globally' in the way we do today, but many of the latest issues, ideas and events crossed the Atlantic fairly rapidly, thanks not least to the free exchange of articles in the underground press. In Britain, *International Times* was appearing fortnightly and was available in some Portsmouth shops, then in February 1967, *Oz* followed. It had been published originally in Australia, but now in London it was, by contrast with the 'newspaper' format of *International Times*, more colourful, more psychedelic and in the future memoirs of editor Richard Neville, pursuing "Playpower". The two publications were different in their views of the counterculture too. Richard Neville (2009) later suggested, "while our rival *IT*, lauded the alternative world, *Oz* scratched its head in perpetual ambivalence" and quoted one of his 'supporters' David Widgery saying at the time, "the hippies in England represent about as powerful a challenge to the power of the state as the people who put foreign coins in gas meters." (92)

On the live music scene, UFO maintained its weekly sessions through the year, and at the end of April, a benefit event was held for *International Times* at Alexandra Palace, after the newspaper was busted by the police. It was called the "14-Hour Technicolour Dream" – to some degree London's indoor version of the Human Be-In, and featuring the usual suspects like Pink Floyd (with their new single "Arnold Lane"), Soft Machine, the Move, the Creation, John's Children, the Pretty Things, Graham Bond, Denny Laine's Electric String Band and the rebirth of the In Crowd as Tomorrow. Apart from Soft Machine who would not get to Portsmouth for a couple of years, we were seeing these bands in Portsmouth – most pretty regularly, although members of the Beatles and Rolling Stones were not there to check out what was happening, which they had been at Alexandra Palace. Neither was there much sign yet of lightshows, performance artists (including Yoko Ono), jugglers or underground movies, but they would come fairly soon. Incidentally the listings for the Birdcage, show the In Crowd playing there again that night. Perhaps they finished around 11pm, drove back to London and changed their name on the way? Nic Jones in the *Melody Maker* reported an attendance of about 7,000 in London, perhaps because "it was the first all-night rave in aid of freedom", adding "if they like the look of the underground movement that's surfacing, they will support it". The acoustics were poor – the high ceiling created too much echo, but he enjoyed it, and hoped there would be "more Technicolour Dreams".

The 14-Hour Technicolour Dream certainly attracted attention in England. The next event that is now seen as significant in this ever-changing world was the Pop Festival at Monterey in June 1967. I say 'seen as' to draw attention to the extent to which its historical importance owes so much to the success of the film, various books and three or four performances that have become legendary. If Woodstock is remembered as the 'high point' of the 1960s festivals, we must ask similarly, to what extent was that due particularly to the event being captured on film and seen in the cinemas of the UK as well as America? In the recent V&A exhibition in London, "You Say You Want a Revolution" a room was devoted to screening film extracts and exhibiting artefacts from Woodstock, but nothing of similar scale was offered for example with the festivals closer to home on the Isle of Wight from 1968-1970, the last of which was larger than Woodstock and had a line-up that was just as impressive. There was also the Bath Festival of Blues & Progressive Music in 1970 with a superb line-up from America and the UK, which was attended by Michael Eavis and led him to create the longest running major festival, Glastonbury.

Among the significant acts at Monterey were Jimi Hendrix, Janis Joplin and Otis Redding – plus perhaps the somewhat unexpected and lengthy Sunday afternoon with Ravi Shankar. Despite the spirit of peace and love, there were disputes afterwards about the whereabouts of the money, an issue pursued by the new magazine *Rolling Stone*, published then from San Francisco. They covered the tensions between those bands from the heart of Haight Ashbury, most of whom appeared at Monterey, and the LA acts who were 'in charge' (in particular John Phillips of the Mamas & Papas).

Because of another dispute over signing rights, some acts were never filmed, Perry (1984) noting that the San Francisco bands in particular "thought they smelled…a slick LA showbiz rat" (207). More broadly Selvin (1992) recorded "the tenuous accord between San Francisco and Los Angeles factions brought an underlying current of tension that ran from the festival's earliest planning stages right up to its final moments" (3). Hoskyns reports that one of the LA-based organisers Lou Adler admitted

> We were a business-minded industry. It wasn't a hobby. They called it slick, and I'd have to agree with them. We couldn't find the link. Every time John Phillips and I went up (to San Francisco), it was a fight – almost a physical fight on occasions. And that was right up to the opening day of the festival with the Dead – the Ungrateful Dead we called them – threatening to do an alternative festival (153).

The Grateful Dead never signed film rights, and because Janis Joplin's manager resisted on the Saturday, she had to perform a second time for her historic performance to be shown to the world. "Another band that didn't sign was Country Joe & the Fish. The reason for at least a couple of them was simple: STP. They were filmed anyway." (Perry, 207). Joe recalls that Owsley gave him one-and-a-half tabs of his new STP and he took it with another guy who did not really enjoy it at all. Joe eventually found himself on the beach where the dolphins were playing in the shallow surf. Joe remembers checking with them – "Hi how're you doing" – and later relating this to the audience although he is not sure that they understood. He particularly recalled an abstract pattern on a wall, as well as a moment when a freight train passed through his head!

Joel Selvin suggests that on Saturday night there were 8,500 people in the arena and around 35,000 in the fairgrounds. Perry thought more, suggesting that by midnight on Sunday there was a crowd estimated between 55,000 and 90,000 – "a huge, exhilarated gathering … uncharacteristically peaceful for its size and density" (1992, 209).

Scott McKenzie's hit song had been written by John Phillips, and during the Mamas and Papas' performance at the end of Sunday, they called on McKenzie to sing the song, which is still on the film's soundtrack. Selvin reports that Country Joe McDonald "still tripping, looked aghast" thinking "we've been had". Not entirely though – the amplifiers hired for the festival disappeared for a week, and were next seen at a free concert in Golden Gate Park, San Francisco. Selvin records how the Grateful Dead were contacted about this and in a contemptuous comment on the commercial opportunism of Scott McKenzie, their reply advised those coming to fetch them to "be sure to wear some flowers in your hair" (99-100).

In the run-up to the mid-1960s, the hip culture of San Francisco and the Bay area had been dominated by jazz, poetry, literature, theatre, folk music and the acoustic coffee house venues. One key figure, Kenneth Rexroth had moved to San Francisco in the late 1920s, and Campbell (1999) tells us that he was an "anarchist in politics and a champion of the radical and perverse in art" (159). He became a "father figure" to many younger poets including Allen Ginsberg, when the latter escaped from an east coast that he found repressive, and moved to San Francisco. Rexroth's performances included reading poetry to a jazz accompaniment and he was associated with a group that was interested in mysticism – both approaches may be seen as manifesting in the 1960s culture of Haight Ashbury as was the interest of these 1950s poets in moving away "from the formal … back to the vernacular" (160). The late 1950s folk revival brought a similar interest in the vernacular in music, albeit one rooted in a broader culture, and including a range of genres, 'poetic' songwriters, while providing a soundtrack for the Civil Rights and anti-war movements. These vernacular roots were apparent in the early recordings from San Francisco's psychedelic period by bands like the Charlatans or the Grateful Dead while the sound was extended by the possibilities of amplification, visual light/graphic innovation and social and political radicalism. Lyrically too, the writing of Robert Hunter, Joe McDonald and others probably reflected the importance of the written word in San Francisco's alternative scenes.

Poetry was always important in San Francisco. In 1953, Lawrence Ferlinghetti and Peter Martin opened the City Lights bookshop and three years later Ferlinghetti published Ginsberg's epic beat poem "Howl", subsequently the subject of an obscenity trial in which the publishers and poet were acquitted. This context and culture was gradually transformed from beat and beatnik in the 1950s, to hippie in the 1960s. In the transition, Ginsberg contributed significantly to the Haight Ashbury scene of the late 1960s and of course, to the start of London's late 1960s' counterculture as the leading participant at the Royal Albert Hall poetry 'event' in June 1965. While the mods and pop fans were 'dancing in the street' and the clubs, Britain's counterculture was sparked by a predominantly literary 'happening'. Given the centrality of music in the 1960s in the USA and Britain this is fascinating, for it indicates a certain willingness in the counterculture to construct alternative modes of entertainment, sometimes resisting the star-obsessed focus of the music industry.

To be a poet, of course, was to create something new with written and spoken language, and by the mid-1960s this was also happening increasingly with lyrics in popular music. The Beatles were important in the UK for writing and performing their own material, but while this was highly influential (and lucrative) there were precedents in some of their favourite American musicians such as Chuck Berry, Eddie Cochran, Buddy Holly and Smokey Robinson. While increasing numbers of young musicians enjoyed the creative opportunity to try writing their own material, the industry was also delighted to sign them to packages involving recording, agency *and publishing* deals for economic reasons, and therefore encouraged new writing.

During the Rendezvous and Birdcage days, very few of the British bands played 'original' material – the majority of rhythm & blues, soul and blues bands, covered American recordings for most of their set. John Mayall frequently wrote original lyrics but mainly in the form and style of the post-war 12-bar blues, Chris Farlowe's material included songs by contemporaries like Jagger & Richards but on the whole the range of acts, whether Downliners Sect, Graham Bond, Jimmy James & the Vagabonds, the Action, or Geno Washington, took their live material from others' records – even when, as with the Action, their arrangements and style brought something unique to the covers. The Who, like the Beatles, were an exception from their fairly early days with some fine Townshend-penned singles, and so too Ray Davies with the Kinks. Locally, very few Portsmouth bands were playing any original songs as 1967 arrived – they were generally expected to cover well-known material in whatever genre – but that would change quite soon, for some of them.

In terms of the major acts, when Cream appeared at the Birdcage in December 1966, they too mostly covered blues songs but with one or two originals, and in collaboration with poet Pete Brown, they would soon produce their own material more regularly. Pink Floyd had switched from rhythm & blues and wrote almost everything – notably Syd Barrett with his 'quirky' songs, some of which enjoyed chart success, plus longer, mostly instrumental numbers. Of the acts who began appearing from 1966 onwards, the Move and the Small Faces mixed covers with original songs and soon enjoyed chart success with self-penned material.

To a large extent, the mod years were characterised by a commitment to clothes first-and-foremost, then music and clubs, followed for some by scooters. For me, the music always came first, and I never owned a scooter, but beyond those things, in whichever order of preference, there was not much else. Being a mod never really implied or required a broader social, political or cultural commitment. But as the counterculture emerged through 1966/1967 it presented a far broader range of social, political and cultural options, which might have proved attractive to some of us simply because we were getting older, a shade more mature and interested in more than simply how we looked, where we hung out, (how we got there?) and what we danced to when we arrived.

During those years, I began to keep a somewhat random scrapbook of various newspaper and magazine cuttings and images, and early on, that included some pages from one of the Sunday magazines titled "Tom Wolfe's Britain". The American Wolfe was developing a new approach to factual writing called "the New Journalism" and the Tom Wolfe article I kept (number three in a series) was called "The Noonday Underground", about the young people who frequented the West End's Tiles Club in their lunchtimes. In the article, he wrote how teenagers, "girls especially", were able to find work in London which would allow them to live with others in a cheap flat around the West End where they enjoyed themselves: "within a very set style of life based largely on clothes music, hairdos and a … super cool outlook on the world".

In contrast to Sandbrook's subsequent claim that to participate in 'swinging London' required not just money but wealth, Wolfe, *at the time*, observed that it was that very "style of life" that made those young people "unique", not "money, power, position, talent (or) intelligence", and of course if that was the case, any young people willing to work at it hard enough could acquire that "style". In each generation, a few sought that, while most did not. Wolfe added a brief historical perspective covering the decade to date: "Just seven years ago all they had was the old Palais ballrooms with straight ballroom dancing, and then there was jazz, and then there were the soul clubs, but it was all derivative". Now "the mod thing" indicated how their lives might become less derivative, although as that began to develop, Wolfe was back in the USA and tracking Ken Kesey and his Merry Pranksters for his book about LSD, *The Electric Kool-Aid Acid Test.*

Also from around this time, I pasted-in reports from the *Guardian* about 1967's 'Legalise Pot Rally' in Hyde Park (we're still waiting), which was another event attended by Allen Ginsberg, and a warning from late 1966 that "The Fugs Are Coming …". There was also an account from one of the more 'sensational' Sunday 'papers about Britain's "First Hippy Wedding" with a picture looking distinctly summer of 1967, plus psychedelic colour photos of Pink Floyd and Cream, portraits of fashionable English 'Girls' and an article illustrated by Alan Aldridge, asking Paul McCartney "What Do the Beatles Mean?"

San Francisco, London and other hip centres of the western world celebrated their summer of love in 1967 after which we are told, things began to turn sour rather quickly, particularly in Haight Ashbury. During that summer, the writer and novelist Joan Didion visited Haight Ashbury to report on "the Hippie Generation" for the USA's *Saturday Evening Post* (23.9.1967). Her article was derived from a number of personal encounters and written to a large extent through description and dialogue – including reporting on the refusal of the San Francisco Police Department to speak with her. A hippie called Norris tried to persuade her to take acid, which she declined because she said she felt "unstable" and in response to his next question, she revealed she was (then) 32 years of age, to which he replied, "Don't worry … there's old hippies too". Didion described meeting runaways, hippies, artists, poets, the San Francisco Mime Troup, Chet Helms of the Avalon, yoga practitioners, macrobiotic diet followers, and a number of people who had been busted. She heard how people were moving rather rapidly from the recreational psychedelic drugs to other things, and poet Gerry told her, "your average Meth freak, once he's started putting the needle in his arm, it's not too hard to say, well, let's shoot a little smack". In the Panhandle, watching Big Brother & the Holding Company, she received a flyer which concluded in suggesting that if things did not change "by August, Haight Street will be a cemetery".

Didion described an apparently unpleasant encounter between the 'radical' Mime Troup, in blackface, and a group of "Negroes" who it seemed were being provoked by the Troup. As can be the way with this descriptive 'New Journalism', Didion revealed no resolution or conclusion to the event, and neither did she offer an analysis, other than a suggestion that it might have had "political overtones". She overheard a telephone conversation suggesting that people were not merely "sleeping in the streets" but "starving to death". It is not clear from all the various histories that this last claim was true, and the Diggers certainly did their best with the free food handouts, but there is no doubt that things became very difficult by the late summer. By the time of her visit, she reported the Diggers declining to speak with "media poisoners", which included Didion herself. Things continued to become complicated, and in early October, Haight Ashbury held a symbolic procession with a fake coffin marking "The Death of Hippie". At the same time, the Thelin brothers, Jay and Ron closed their landmark Psychedelic Shop on Haight Street and eventually moved out to Marin County. In 1976 Ron Thelin recalled

> After the Summer Solstice of 1968 people started to spread out to the country … The feeling was grow your own food, get to know your community, the system's gonna die … At one point, there were 25 or 30 people in here all the time (14).

In the same retrospective edition of *Rolling Stone,* Charles Perry (1976, 18) reported how Stephen Gaskin, ex-Marine, teacher and 'professional hippie', and a couple of hundred others left San Francisco around 1969/70 and moved to 'The Farm' in Tennessee. By the mid-1970s, their 1700 acre "totally self-sufficient" farm had over 800 residents and, among other things practised and promoted natural childbirth. Morgan Shipley in his book *Psychedelic Mysticism,* argued that just as critics were identifying the crises and disintegration of the counterculture around various high profile 'events' of the late 1960s, so Gaskin and the Farm began with less media coverage, and in very practical ways, to live more spiritually and more harmoniously. Gaskin died from natural causes in the summer of 2014, and an obituary published in the British *Daily Telegraph,* noted that the Farm was

> One of the longest running communes in America. When asked in old age why the community survived, Gaskin emphasised its practical approach. "We were hippies wanting to live together and we accepted the discipline it took to do that," he said". Utopia means nowhere. The Farm has a zip code. (www.telegraph.co.uk).

Things moved more slowly and less dramatically in Portsmouth, although we were close enough to London, attached not only by a reasonably quick rail/car journey but also the mass media that spread the news of the hippies, the 'underground' and the counterculture. The Haight Ashbury/London 'revolution' took a little longer to influence life on the south coast in any significant sense, although we need to remind ourselves constantly that even in San Francisco this was not how the majority of people lived their lives. In Portsmouth, it never threatened to resemble Haight Ashbury, but eventually it had an obvious impact on a number of teenagers and young adults, even if mainly through music and certain fashions.

One of the more notable, evenings at the Guildhall, occurred in the spring of 1967. A few years ago, the Guildhall's new Civic Trust asked some of us to suggest the five most notable gigs there over the years and via the Pompey Pop Blog, Chris Abbott nominated this one, featuring Nina Simone, black American comedian Dick Gregory and British jazz trio the Peddlars. Chris recalled the gig as "absolutely brilliant" and added

> It was at the height of the civil rights movement in the States and also the anti-Vietnam War protests. As a Dockyard 'Slinger' at the time, we used to meet a lot of American matelots on shore leave who wanted out, so we would share a joint in Victoria Park then into Verecchia's coffee bar in the Guildhall Square, a quick change out of uniform and they went over the road to the town station and hopefully onto Norway or wherever. That gig just seemed so relevant at the time and so for me very memorable – and then of course there was Nina!

Paul 'Oscar' Wild was there and agreed it was "great", describing the Peddlars as "superb". He added however, "the sad thing was the really poor attendance; a lot of people moved to the front from the cheaper seats". He can still remember some of Dick Gregory's socially relevant 'jokes' – I was there too, and the tale he told that has stayed with me was that in the stores in Chicago's Projects (the black 'Council' blocks) sales of tins of dog & cat food were particularly high, yet there was a rule against residents keeping pets. Simone has long had a reputation as a 'difficult' person, but her performance that night was superb, and a dramatic contrast to the guitar-based bands increasingly popular at the Birdcage and elsewhere.

In late July 1967, the hippies returned to Alexandra Palace for an all-night 'Love In Festival', starring Eric Burdon & the Animals, Pink Floyd, Brian Auger, Julie Driscoll & the Trinity, Arthur Brown, the Creation, Tomorrow, Blossom Toes, and Sam Gopal's Dream, plus lights, and flowers. As the summer moved on, Portsmouth's Guildhall presented jazz with a 'classical' feel from the Jacques Loussier Trio, American folk singer Julie Felix and Acker Bilk's outmoded 'trad' jazz – but no rock or pop. The King's Theatre meanwhile offered a week-long residency for Englebert Humperdinck and Joan Regan. Crooner Humperdinck's "Release Me" had famously kept the Beatles' great British psychedelic masterpiece "Strawberry Fields Forever" and "Penny Lane" off the singles number one spot.

On first glance then, late summer and autumn 1967 in Portsmouth appears to have been rather dull in comparison to the previous four or five years, but for a number of reasons it was not quite like that. Following the closure of the Birdcage Club, the really big club acts stopped coming to town, but they would soon return, and the leading local promoter Rikki Farr, after a few months' rest, would be as active as ever.

I have said that I missed the last month at the Birdcage in August 1967, for which there were three reasons. The first was travelling 'on the road' to the west country. That was fun when we got there but eventually Steve and I started to get short of money and in need of a bath rather than just a hand-basin wash in the seafront toilets, so we set of back home and another tortuous hitch-hike, which seemed far harder than anything experienced by Jack Kerouac and Neal Cassady.

We reached home on a Friday evening very tired, but after a night's rest I met up with another school pal and art student, Les Gerry who had a car, and we took off on the sixty-odd miles for Windsor, which this weekend was playing host to the first music festival I attended. It was, to give it its full title "The 7th National Jazz-Pop – Ballads & **Blues** Festival" organised by the National Jazz Federation and Soho's Marquee Club, sponsored by the London *Evening News*. Incidentally, the bold **Blues** is precisely how it was presented over that weekend of the 11-13 August 1967 for despite the popular image of the summer of love and the psychedelic records appearing then in the charts, the UK's club scene was enjoying its second blues boom, three or four years after the first.

Windsor 1967 kicked off on Friday evening with British pop psychedelia, including Tomorrow, the Move and headliners the Small Faces. Saturday afternoon, as usual, offered a mix of some fine UK and USA modern jazz – the latter including Yusef Lateef and Al Cohn & Zoot Sims. Then on Saturday evening came future Woodstock stars Ten Years After, and the Crazy World of Arthur Brown, while late in the evening the programme promised the Pink Floyd. Sadly, however, they did not make it, because Syd was already struggling on live gigs and they were replaced by the Nice who were there principally to back American soul singer PP Arnold – a refugee from the Ikettes. They were well-received in the penultimate slot on Saturday night, unlike the headliner, Portsmouth's Paul Jones, who had departed Manfred Mann and was given a poor reception, leaving the stage before his set was finished. Ike Ginn was in the audience and enjoyed "helping to boo him off stage".

Another correspondent on the Festival website, Stephen J Chibnall, was in for something of a surprise at the festival. He described himself as a mod from Bedford and remembered seeing his "first hippies at the London station" and more "bizarrely-dressed people walking through Windsor", even before he got to the festival with its smells of joss sticks and, he suspected, grass.

He bought himself a psychedelic poster of Arthur Brown and particularly enjoyed Cream who he had seen previously at Bedford Corn Exchange, and the Nice ("the real discovery for me"). He decided against staying on-site in case "the sound of bells would keep me awake"!

Sunday afternoon was appropriately gentle with folk singer Al Stewart, the veteran British blues 'Goddess' Ottilie Patterson and Donovan. He was two years on from the impact of his first appearance on *Ready Steady Go!* and his first hit single "Catch the Wind", since when there had been further success with "Colours", "Mellow Yellow" and "Sunshine Superman" as he became more amplified and perhaps more 'trippy'. There was a break then until the evening's show which started around 7pm and headed for the strict curfew at 11.30pm – and equally a limit on decibels level which led to some adverse comments from the punters about the general sound quality.

With my great fondness for the blues – and back then, especially, anything that drew upon the post-war amplified sound of the black Chicago bands – I was thrilled to see and hear the debut live performance by Peter Green's Fleetwood Mac. I have long thought Peter Green to have been the finest of British blues singer/guitarists, and here he was with Jeremy 'Elmore' Spencer, Mick Fleetwood plus a 'temp', schoolteacher, Bob Brunning, on bass guitar, since John McVie was not yet free to leave John Mayall's band and join them. Mayall (with McVie) played later that evening with Mick Taylor on guitar, while the third 'guitar hero' of the Bluesbreakers, Eric Clapton topped the bill with Cream. Since the Jeff Beck Group featuring Rod Stewart, Aynsley Dunbar and Ronnie Wood also appeared, it was quite a night for guitar and British blues fans, especially as Fleetwood Mac, Ten Years After and Chicken Shack all played in the smaller marquee, the only other stage at this festival.

Other than those predominantly blues-based electric guitar-led bands, the evening was significantly enhanced by the folk/jazz ensemble Pentangle with acoustic guitar masters Bert Jansch and John Renbourn. A couple of mod favourites, the Alan Bown Set and PP Arnold & the Nice were there, and a third act that had appeared at Portsmouth's Birdcage Club Denny Laine, brought his Electric String Band. It was a relatively short-lived band but they enjoyed some success with the song "Say You Don't Mind", which would be a bigger hit for the Zombie's singer Colin Blunstone five years later. A good example of their string sound can be found on "Why Did You Come? and it has obvious links to the use of strings by George Martin and the Beatles on recordings like "Eleanor Rigby".

I do not have a clear memory of the end of the evening except that we drove back to Portsmouth. I remember throwing up before we left (no, not drugs or drink) but also that Les must have had a car radio because we listened in a somewhat melancholy mood to the last show by John Peel on Radio London. On the following day, the Government's Bill would come into effect, outlawing the pirates.

In his final "Perfumed Garden" show on Radio London that night, John Peel mixed the Mothers of Invention with Moby Grape, Tyrannosaurus Rex with Howlin' Wolf, a reading from Winnie the Pooh with Al Kooper's Blues Project, Simon & Garfunkel with Canned Heat, the Misunderstood with the Electric Prunes and the Seeds with Elmore James. Other British acts included the Attack, the Syn, John's Children, Orange Bicycle and Jimi Hendrix Experience, while among a number of singer-songwriters were Tim Hardin, Donovan and Judy Collins.

He played a number of tracks from the Beatles' new album of course, and others from the UK included Pink Floyd, Donovan, the Incredible String Band and Traffic. From Haight Ashbury, we heard Country Joe & the Fish, Jefferson Airplane, the Grateful Dead and Janis Joplin, and from elsewhere in the USA, the Velvet Underground, the Misunderstood, Tim Buckley, Captain Beefheart, the Mothers of Invention and Bob Dylan. The popular story is that *Sgt Pepper* revolutionized music in that period, but many of us listened regularly to John Peel, so the 'loveable mop tops' album was simply one among many, breaking new ground – and not necessarily everyone's favourite example of the new music either. A few weeks after the generally unpopular legislation was enacted, on 30 September 1967, the BBC launched Radio One and John Peel reappeared with similar choices on a BBC show called *Top Gear*.

Les and I got home from Windsor in the early hours and the following day I was sick again, the doctor was called and I was confined to bed with, for the only time in my life, a (quite severe) attack of tonsillitis. From mid-August, that rather stuffed the rest of my summer of love and meant that I missed the dying days of the Birdcage.

While that legendary venue had closed, other venues and institutions offered alternative opportunities to see and hear live music. In 1967, there was no University in Portsmouth, not even a Polytechnic, which came into being in 1969, but there was a College of Technology. It was much smaller than today's huge institution, concentrating mainly on science and technology courses, albeit with a growing number of social science/history courses, and the stirrings of what would become one of the first Cultural Studies degrees in the country. There was also the very lively independent Art College (now the Eldon building) with its main course in Fine Art, and regional diplomas in subjects like Graphics and Fashion. The boys' and girls' Grammar Schools had their own sixth forms, while Highbury Technical College ran various courses, mixing day-release for the local apprentices who had usually left school at 15, full-time courses in skills like hairdressing and 'A' levels for those who wished to study in a more relaxed atmosphere. All these post-school institutions had begun to get involved in organizing their own entertainment on a regular basis through the 1960s and in the next few years, the College circuit would become very active in the city.

Nigel Grundy, who participated very fully in the local mod and coffee bar scene has some clear memories of the transitional period with the closure of the Birdcage in 1967 and the emergence of a hippie and college scene in the following years

> In 1966/67, I found the emerging London and West Coast psyche-
> delic music and fashion scenes exciting. The clothes were more
> colourful and free form, it was even ok to make your own, and the
> music was more adventurous, experimental and less restricted
> in form. London had UFO and the Middle Earth clubs, but the
> hippy scene in Portsmouth was quite small and didn't have a
> major focus point like the mods had at the Birdcage. 'Psychedelic'
> bands like Pink Floyd and the Move etc. appeared at the Birdcage
> but I don't remember queues of Hippies stretching down Eastney
> Road, as there had been queues of mods a year or two before.
> Locally I have a photograph of a small group of us sitting at
> Speakers Corner by the Rock Gardens listening to the Salvation
> Army Band one sunny summer afternoon. Although Kimbells
> had the more experimental bands, I think it was the College of
> Technology/Polytechnic students who saved the day with the
> gigs they put on at the South Parade Pier and the Guildhall, but
> as now, the student population and the locals didn't mix much at
> 'dances', as we used to call them. I went because I was involved
> with music photography, and they were good evenings, but as
> I remember it, the number of local people in the audience who
> were not students was small.

> So, local gigs, unless student-organised, were full of Portsmouth
> teenagers who mostly knew each other, but there was an
> exception when different groups of people would meet and that
> was on the Beat Cruises. A ferry with a couple of bands would
> leave Southsea, call in to Ryde on the Isle of Wight and then cruise
> up and down the Solent before returning their Brickwood's Beer-
> fuelled passengers to catch the last bus home. They were great
> fun and I can't remember any trouble, though I do recall a chap
> being pursued through the boat for nicking a handbag as we

were approaching Ryde Pier. He made it to the top deck before leaping into the sea and striking out for the pier, resulting in the ferry having to tie up for an hour or so while a police and lifeboat search was made for the thief.

By 1966, the students were running their own regular folk club at the Talbot Hotel in Goldsmith Avenue or the Star in Lake Road, where their main acts included the Incredible String Band, Al Stewart, the Strawberry Hill Boys (Strawbs), Louis Killeen, the Young Tradition, and Pete Stanley & 'Wizz' Jones (bluegrass). There were also student dances featuring the 'British' Amboy Dukes at Clarence Pier, while the main hall at Highbury hosted Sounds Incorporated, the Paramounts and Sons of Man and a short while later, Unit 4 + 2 and Herbie Goins. The only disappointment was a lunchtime jazz club which closed through very poor attendances. For the main 'STWEEK' rag week event in 1966, the students booked Manfred Mann and three local bands Sons of Man, the Klimax, and the Tea-Pots (soon to become the Wrong Direction) at South Parade Pier.

During 1967, the Students' Union began moving into the old 'Stables' ('K' Block) opposite Park Building and the south side of the Guildhall. It would be the site of some interesting events in the near future, although it is now long-gone. There was a students' Film Club showing varied and often challenging movies like Antonioni's *Red Desert*, Godard's *Tous Les Garcons*, Strick's *Savage Eye*, historic early silent reels by the Lumiére Brothers, and from the 1920s the quasi-surrealist *Seashell & the Clergyman* by Germaine Dulac. In the spring of 1967, the charity week 'STWEEK' returned with a folk concert at the Savoy with Dorris Henderson, Johnny Silvo and the Three City 4, plus a bluesy STWEEK Ball with John Mayall's Blues Breakers, Alexis Korner and Zoot Money. The 'STWEEKOTHEQUE' in an empty shop in the Guildhall Square featured DJs, although in future years it would host local bands and a coffee bar, every day for a week.

For the slightly younger audiences around the city, there were also lots of church and youth club venues for discos and live bands and this, added to the brief disappearance of the bigger club scene, encouraged local musicians. There was something of an explosion in local bands at this time, although there had always been a busy post-war local scene. In the autumn, Portsmouth's own Simon Dupree & the Big Sound, would hit the UK Top Ten with the pseudo-psychedelic, oriental sounding "Kites". It was said they were not fond of the song but it would become their biggest success, and in April of the following year, 'Simon Dupree' (Derek Shulman) told Spinner that he was "surprised" that it sold so well:

It taught us the lesson that you have got to think commercially all the time. It's no use being musical, you have got to be as commercial as possible. It established us as a hit parade group … (4.4.1968)

Despite the success of that record, he described their first single "I See the Light" as their "best record … because we were so enthusiastic", and added, from those days, "I loved the Indigo Vat crowd … if we had audiences like that everywhere, it would be beautiful".

With the demise of the Birdcage, the Indigo Vat (in Hampshire Terrace; now Scandals) was one of the important live venues in the city and others included the Savoy, Kimbells, and the Parlour on North End Junction, while others would begin to open (and sometimes close) over the next couple of years. In addition, even without lots of major gigs to go to for a few months, there was a Southsea scene, which centred around certain pubs like the Palmerston (now Owens), the Osborne (Kingsleys), the Portland (One Eyed Dog) and the Cambridge Hotel (at the back of Debenhams, now demolished), plus a number of coffee bars including the Manhattan, Le Bistro and Delmonico which had a dancing club upstairs. On Elm Grove, there was the Esperanto (now Rosie's). These were places to hang out and some of the jukeboxes offered interesting contemporary choices. They were also places to find drugs.

In the spring of 1967, the *Evening News* reported the city's first prosecution for possession of LSD after a 'tripping' youth was arrested in hospital, having "stripped off his clothing and jumped through a first-floor window". The city developed a strategy for addressing problems with drugs including pamphlets to be made available to all school pupils over the age of 12. The newspaper suggested that the drug taking shown in a party scene in Antonioni's newly-released movie, *Blow-Up*, was "a close but distorted look at the swinging scene". The film was concerned principally with the fashion scene and the central character, a photographer (David Hemmings) probably based loosely around David Bailey. Where fashion was concerned, if clothes were bought in Portsmouth, as opposed to trips to London, it was most likely to be Commercial Road which contained most of the boutiques – at least until Rikki Farr opened his "Apache" boutique on the corner of Marmion Road.

During the summer of love, local beat group Travis Raymar reformed, naming themselves Tangerine Slyde, and telling the *Evening News* they hoped "to please with pure psychedelia", and the possibility of an increasingly fashionable light show. In 1969, I would enjoy a wonderful time playing with three members of the band, guitarist Steve Farrow, keyboard player Brian Grice and bass guitarist Mick Legg whose recollections of how they got to the psychedelic sound make interesting reading.

Mick was working for the council with Bob Beard, a Pompey character involved in the early days of the Birdcage, and Bob could access American Forces Radio, through which Mick first heard bands like the Association, still one of his great favourites. Before Tangerine Slyde, Mick played locally in the Poor People and then Morgan's Camel Train (with future Coconut Mushroom guitarist John Clark) and in the mid-1960s began playing covers of the Association (Pandora's Golden Heebie Jeebies", "Along Comes Mary"), the Lovin' Spoonful ("Do You Believe in Magic", "You Didn't Have to be So Nice", "Did You Ever have to make Up Your Mind") mixed in with some soul (James Brown, Wilson Pickett) and rock & roll numbers.

In the early days of Tangerine Slyde, Mick Legg recalls

> We just did standard stuff, because Steve Farrow and I were more interested in how far we could push sound – from chaos comes order, so we would rub our guitars together, making amazing sounds or I would play my bass guitar with a violin bow. We would do harmonic feedback, with Steve getting a certain pitch, then I would set the bass strings vibrating and we would let it build up.

Eventually Mick recalls, they "tired of that, and got down to serious rehearsing" with some of those songs listed above, plus others by the Byrds ("My Back Pages", "Eight Miles High", "Mr Spaceman", "Turn, Turn, Turn"), Love ("Alone Again Or", "Red Telephone", "Bummer in the Summer"), Moby Grape ("Hey Grandma", "Omaha"), the Creation ("Painter Man", "Makin' Time"), John's Children ("Desdemona") and the Move ("Night of Fear"). From that period, and the new approaches, he remembers Coconut Mushroom as a "good band" with a more "style and satin shirts" approach to the west coast sounds, while Tangerine Slyde had "more passion than looks" and were perhaps "a bit more inventive". Overall, he describes the era as "unforgettable" and wishes he could find a band playing some of that music today, although I heard from him early in 2017 that he had started rehearsing some Byrds numbers with another couple of musicians on the Isle of Wight, where he has lived for many years.

During the summer of 1967, Jimi Hendrix released his first album, and locally that sound influenced the Fruits of Love, as well as my pal Pete Gurd, who was in the early stages of playing with the band that became Harlem Speakeasy. Although called the Harlem Soul Band, they played a number of tracks from the first Jimi Hendrix album and Pete, on lead guitar, developed a visual appearance almost as exotic as Jimi's!

Peace and love was on trial as the *Evening News* led its front page with "The

Agony of Seeing Your Idols Jailed" (30 June 1967) followed by "Rolling Stones' Appeal Starts" – a reference to the drugs trial of Mick Jagger and Keith Richard just up the A27 in Chichester. The Beatles performed "All You Need is Love" on the "Our World" television satellite broadcast experiment at the end of June, and in the *Evening News* weekly pop column, 'Spinner' reported the British release of USA Elektra albums, advising us to watch out for Love and the Doors both from Los Angeles.

He reported also that popular local soul band the Inspiration had re-formed as Coconut Mushroom with a repertoire based on what at that time were generally known as the west coast bands. They planned to "present the city's first home-grown attempt at a fully-fledged light show and psyche-delic 'happening' at the Parlour". The photograph accompanying the piece showed the first version of the band who also appeared on one of the regular, popular Beat Cruises around the Solent, where "their lights wouldn't work … but their black, red & white face paint did".

Before the summer of 1967 was over, the hippies had another fun weekend out at Woburn Abbey's Festival of the Flower Children". Nigel Grundy went to both Windsor and Woburn, and while he does not recall that many hippies at the former, they were certainly there at the Abbey to see a number of British bands, again most of whom had appeared in Portsmouth. The headliners were the Small Faces, the Move, the Bee Gees, Eric Burdon, Jeff Beck, Denny Laine, Alan Price, Marmalade and Zoot Money – plus of course, Tomorrow. There were nightly fireworks, free flowers and sparklers and weekend tickets cost 30/(£1.50). The *NME* was critical, however, calling it "WOE-BORE", while the *Daily Telegraph* reported that the event had raised a profit of £20,000. Apparently, the Duchess of Bedford disappeared for the weekend thinking it was going to be a bit like the Chelsea Flower Show. Nigel recalls

> I used to go to London at weekends and in August 1967, I also went to the Windsor Jazz and Blues Festival and a few days later, the Festival of the Flower Children at Woburn Abbey, sometimes referred to as the first of the new music festivals. While there I met some Hippies from London – we were a colourful crowd that attracted the press and they wouldn't leave us alone, so as a joke we staged 'the first Hippy wedding in the UK' and the press fell for it; the next day we were all over the papers and national TV.

If, as the *NME* suggested, Woburn was exploiting the 'real' thing, that might have contributed to the apparently sudden decline in flower power; or perhaps it was simply a consequence of the shorter, colder days of autumn and winter. By October, with the 'Death of Hippie' ceremony taking place in

Haight Ashbury, *Melody Maker* was asking "Who Killed Flower Power?" – not you note, the death of the underground or counterculture, but of "flower power", which as a 'look', rather like the flowers themselves, was mostly pretty ephemeral. The piece (by Nick Jones) was stimulated principally by the closure of London's UFO Club, which in part was a victim of its own success – six months after opening it was attracting crowds of such a size that not everyone got in; then the more lurid newspapers and police started to create pressures, forcing it to move from Tottenham Court Road to the Roundhouse, where the rent was higher, local skinheads menaced the hippies, and the increasingly popular bands increased their fees, even for the club that had helped to nurture them. That was rather different from the situation in San Francisco. Meanwhile, *Melody Maker* reported that "flower power" as a visual fashion at least, was now being "mass produced" and ridiculed in newspaper cartoons, but, as one of the originators of UFO, Joe Boyd told them, "UFO was just a surface manifestation like the clothes, the beads and bells". A new version of the club would resurface in late 1967, named Middle Earth after the increasing fashion for Tolkien's stories of hobbits, wizards and orcs, and in the heart of the then very active Covent Garden market.

I mentioned previously, Nik Cohn's views of these developments, and how as a relatively contemporary chronicler of events he found himself suddenly out of sympathy with much that was going on as he looked back fondly to the first post-Elvis decade of relative innocence, that was now coming to a conclusion. One of the attitudes he reported, common at least to most post-war social groups, was how one age group (hardly a generation) would look with contempt at those just a couple of years younger, who followed. For example, in the *Observer* magazine of 27 August 1967, coincidentally the Sunday of the Woburn Festival, Cohn wrote an article "Ready, Steady Gone" (later re-worked as "Today There Are No Gentlemen" in *Ball the Wall*) which reprinted a famous photograph of Marc Feld (Bolan) from *Time* magazine in 1962, when, in his early teens, he was one of the original, 'original' mods. Feld revealed he would go home "and literally pray to become a Mod", at the time when "clothes were all that Mod was about", because "the music and dancing and pills and scooters came after".

Portsmouth had its own leading mods but that would not have satisfied Marc Feld who went from being one of a really exclusive minority in north London to part of a much wider movement, marked by *Ready, Steady Go!* publicity in the press and media, and the Carnaby Street phenomenon. He said that from around 1962, "Mod suddenly started to get out of hand. The new Mods were completely uncool and I wouldn't even speak to them". Cohn found one of these 'new' mods, Chris Covill from Shepherds Bush, who described his life as a mod – "uncool" in Feld's eyes – before adding in much the same vein, "a lot of false mods came along, just ordinary kids who weren't dedicated. They wanted to be cool, but there was violence in them, and they couldn't change".

The violence had erupted most noticeably of course in the seaside clashes with the rockers in 1964 and 1965 – depicted 15 years later in *Quadrophenia* – and Paolo Hewitt, another chronicler of those times, although too young to have been there, has followed Feld's lead in dismissing that group – mostly just a couple of years younger, as "Sods" not mods. The original commitment to the right look mattered sufficiently to someone like Marc Feld that he recalled

> I didn't think at all. The only thought I ever had was 'Oh I just bought one suit this week and I should have bought three'. That was all. I was completely knocked out by my own image, by the idea of Marc Feld. I was regarded as very cool very fast.

By the autumn of 1967, Marc Bolan seemed to have transformed himself in to something very different – poet, folk singer, member of John's Children, about to launch the elfin duo Tyrannosaurus Rex. And in Portsmouth? After a couple of quiet autumn months, those who were interested in the new music and fashions were offered a remarkable bill at Portsmouth Guildhall on 22 November 1967, featured the Jimi Hendrix Experience, the Pink Floyd, the Nice, the Move, Amen Corner and Eire Apparent. The tour ended with a series of gigs in London, as Hendrix became increasingly popular. Elsewhere, the Savoy presented The Alan Bown! Marmalade and the Nite People, while the Guildhall hosted a student dance with Arthur Brown. Spinner reported that he was "dazzling" but that some of his stage comments were "distasteful".

Locally, the Bryan Hug Group had a song on the soundtrack of the contemporary London movie *Up the Junction*. They re-named themselves Cherry Smash and released "Songs of Love" on 29 December. There were "light shows and old time movies at Thorngate's Thursday sessions", while Tangerine Slyde were now heavily west coast influenced and also featuring go-go dancers. By contrast, the *Evening News* printed a stage photograph of St Louis Checks' singer Chris West in 1920s 'gangster' clothes as the film *Bonnie & Clyde* made a fashion impact, while picking up on the same theme, the Harlem Soul Band moved away from imitating Jimi Hendrix and became a six-piece, re-named Harlem Speakeasy, with a short residency at the Brave New World on the Sundays before Christmas.

I said it was not really the dullest time – the genie had been out of the bottle for a few years, and magic was afoot, not least in my life. While I continued to study somewhat fitfully at Highbury College, the sixth member of Harlem Speakeasy, the new boy, was me.

GOING UNDERGROUND

During the legendary summer of '67, I left school for the last time, hitched to the west country, attended my first festival and then recovered from illness, mainly at my aunt's house in Petersfield, as my parents had taken their first-ever holiday abroad. I had a girlfriend, Jenny, who kindly visited me quite regularly, otherwise I spent most of the late summer indoors, reading and listening to the radio – with the pirates outlawed, that meant the often-dull BBC Light Programme. Despite the very sore throat, it seemed for the first time in my life there was no one around telling me to get a haircut, or what I should be doing.

When my folks got back from holiday, we agreed I would try for the Art College during the year, and in the meantime, my dad pressed me to get a job. With his help, I spent two days on the front desk of the city's Education Department in Western Parade but it was dull, and when they told me I needed a haircut I left. I got a job in a boutique but they sacked me after one day – I was not born to be a salesman. I had no idea what to do, so in the autumn I signed on for one year to complete my 'A' levels in the far more relaxed atmosphere of Highbury Technical College, where I studied Art with one of those rare 'great' teachers, Doug Everitt. Years later Doug moved to the Eldon full-time, but for now I was also doing a part-time course with him at the Art College and it was there that I first begun to understand and be excited by the possibilities of abstraction.

With Doug's guidance, I became increasingly interested in contemporary art. Fortunately I had my pal Martin to share that with, and he and I, in very different ways, both pursued careers in that subject. During my 'A' level years in the Sixth Form and then at Highbury, I had access to whatever the newspapers, television and Sunday magazines were saying, as well the more specialist *Studio International,* through which I discovered a great deal about the latest abstraction, including the shaped canvases of Jeremy Moon and Richard Smith and colourful abstract sculpture, led by Anthony Caro. I enjoyed most Pop Art, and read of Richard Hamilton's involvement with the work and ideas of Duchamp which would shortly have such an impact on the late 1960s/early 1970s conceptual work. Around then I discovered Robert

Rauschenberg through a Sunday magazine and, alongside his paintings and sculptures, learned of his multi-media work and his collaborations with composer John Cage and dancer Merce Cunningham, in their performances. It would eventually suggest possibilities for extending more conventional musical performances.

Another example of that came in the October 1966 edition of *Studio International* which carried a written profile of Mark Boyle who, in addition to his earth/street sculptures, was a leading figure in the lightshows at clubs like UFO. Eleven months later came another article, with photos of his light/performance work ("Son et Lumiere for Bodily Functions and Fluids") and of his street and beach hanging pieces. I read too of "Happenings" and how an event in Prague in 1966, just two years before the 'Prague Spring' revolution of Dubcek, was a response to the London symposium on Destruction of Art, with Townshend's 'mentor' Gustave Metzger. *Studio International* suggested these eastern European Happenings with "political overtones", compared favourably with recent events in New York which "seemed to have lost much of their spontaneity and to have become formalized into sequences reminiscent of vaudeville" (210, 10/66). In the month of my 17th birthday, I was new to happenings, but certainly intrigued by them. I was fascinated too by the fashion for kinetic art, which filled the pages of *Studio International* in February 1967, anticipating an exhibition at the Brighton Festival, which Martin and I visited that spring. Also in Brighton was Hornsey College of Art's "Light/Sound Workshop, profiled in the magazine in April 1967. Light/sound was very much of the future, particularly for Martin, and if the kinetic art proved something of a cul-de-sac for contemporary art, in those days it was another signal that there was more to that world than painting and drawing.

There was much more of course, and to some extent it was a matter of letting this stuff seep in and work its way into my thinking, and my art work, over the years. During 1967, Martin and I were selected to attend classes at the Art College for the most able school students in the city. The activities there anticipated those typical of Foundation Courses at the time and we loved them, even more because they were held on Saturday mornings when, unlike other local schools, we were timetabled for classes. The activities and the work were thrilling, but it soon became clear that in comparison with the other students, our art education at the 'posh' grammar school was somewhat unimaginative – almost entirely painting 'realist' compositions on sugar paper, or pencil drawings of a still life or figure. The classes were a revelation for me, as through 1967/8, were those at Highbury College and more Art College evening classes. Over the years, I suppose I was the nearest thing to an Art (College) student who never attended full-time.

Within a few years, that range of experiences would pay off significantly, but I realise now that I was not yet ready to engage fully – and anyway music was calling.

In September 1967, Martin went to the college full-time to study graphics and I kept in touch with him and his classmates, particularly another Birdcage boy Geoff Allman who had come from the Southern (state) Grammar School. The three of us and others became good pals and we had some good friends on the fashion course, a group of 'girls' who seemed extraordinarily stylish. When one, Lesley, became my girlfriend in that autumn it did wonders for my fashion sense and my previously very limited sex life, and overall this shifting between Highbury and the Art College introduced a whole new dimension to my life. I could see no problem that the slightly uniform world of clothes and music that was mod, had become more expansive, more open to a wider variety of practices and ideas.

It still seems entirely natural to me. In 1967, Cohn described the "generation war" having been reduced to a "two-year cycle". The dismissal of succeeding generations by Marc Feld, Chris Covill and others, is easy enough to do and if it is limited to a criticism of people who merely imitate and then get stuck, it has a certain point, although for some people that might be sufficient. But one essential feature of 1960s' mod, alongside visual style and a good taste in music, was the ability to engage imaginatively and creatively with culture in its broadest sense. It is also obviously the case that people are different at 17 or 18 than they were at 14 or 15. At that younger age, concerned principally with self-image, it was enough to care about the clothes and the music, although this liking was less ephemeral than some might suppose. At 14 I fell in love with black music, specifically the blues and to a large extent that is still true, just as mod fashion tastes still most obviously inform how I dress; but as things changed and we moved on, we could take the best of all that, develop it and learn new things.

Of course, in some cases, where we moved towards involved some pretentious, superficial and plain stupid stuff. There is nothing so remarkable in that; we were teenagers and, in comparison with previous generations, we were offered a bewildering array of choices, so it was a matter of exercising intelligence, acquiring some experience and hoping things would work out. I find it sad that a fine writer like Nik Cohn decided at such a young age that (almost) everything had been great and (now) everything was not, particularly since, in describing the late 1960s, he depended so much on generalisations that do not hold much water, even in the provincial city where I was growing up. For example, in a 1969 chapter called simply "Love" he told us:

> In America acid really mattered. Over here, it never got beyond
> being a one-shot curiosity and only a few thousand people ever
> used it … It moved in very limited circles and it wasn't believed
> in as magic (223)

It took perhaps a year or two for acid to become relatively widespread among
those most likely in Portsmouth, but Cohn's views here do not fit with my
experiences at all and the details of our story will follow. Maybe he is right
about London, but I doubt it, and in Portsmouth, for a while at least, among
a specific group of people, acid "mattered" and had quite an impact. But poor
old Nik did not like what was happening:

> All over the world, kids walked around in rainbow robes and
> wore beads, bells, flowers in their hair but it was all down to play-
> acting now, it was only a new toy … The next step was transcen-
> dental meditation … a craze that blossomed one day after the
> Beatles took it up and dropped dead exactly one day after they
> abandoned it again (230/1).

Of course, for those motivated only by the current fashions, that was broadly
true, as it would always be, even with the music and fashions that Cohn
seemed to love so much. I hope to suggest through the remainder of this
book, however, that Cohn was wrong in so many respects with regard to
where all this led – and that Joe Boyd was much closer to the truth in describing UFO and the clothes, beads and bells as "just a surface manifestation" of
something more significant. For many people, it was and still is, rather more
than merely a matter of extravagant decoration, and lasted longer than the
latest trend.

Gradually I became more aware of what was called London's underground
scene, influenced for sure by what was happening in San Francisco and
elsewhere in the USA, but, also developing its own character and characters
in Britain. Among the key figures in London were John Hopkins, Barry Miles,
Joe Boyd and John Dunbar who through 1967 were involved variously in
the publication of *International Times*, the establishment of the UFO Club
and the Indica Gallery and bookshop – with the latter eventually moving to
separate premises.

Within a couple of years, examples of the musical underground were finding
their way into the mass media so that, for example, in the early summer of
1967, Pink Floyd appeared in a full-length BBC television programme performing tracks like "Astronomy Domine" in glorious black & white psychedelia.
John Peel, was now a regular on Radio One, including the bonus of live

performances, and was also writing regularly for *International Times* which helped us to discover more about the new American bands, particularly from San Francisco. It also put into context some of the claims made for the Beatles' *Sgt Pepper* which often seems in retrospect to have dominated the first summer of love. We soon realized that there were a number of American bands making equally interesting music, who had often released their first albums prior to the release of *Sgt Pepper*.

To date my focus has been on music and fashion, but the counterculture introduced a broad range of other ideas, often reflected in the pages of *International Times* and *Oz*. Looking again at the early pages of my scrapbook of cuttings and images from those days, there are two pages already mentioned, from our *Evening News*, about Portsmouth's drug problems, followed by some intriguing articles from the *Guardian* published on 11 & 12 October 1967. The second of those days was my 18th birthday, and I was enjoying the relaxed atmosphere of the college, I was playing in a band, and now, at an age similar to that of my elders in *Citizen 63*, I was ready to explore a world beyond music, fashion and sex. It was quite thrilling, and I woke pretty much every morning, wondering what the day might offer.

On those two days, the *Guardian* published Margaret Drabble's article "The Sexual Revolution", an interview with Scott McKenzie, a list of 17 "Priests and Prophets of Permissiveness", Geoffrey Moorhouse on RD Laing, the "Psychiatrist of Liberation", and poet Adrian Mitchell's "Guide to the Underground". It was a variety of topics and approaches, some of it too new yet for me to comprehend, but I must have felt them worth retaining, for I still have them.

"Adrian Mitchell's Guide to the Underground" began with "three rousing psychedelic ho-hums for the permissive society" and continued in a fairly tongue-in-cheek vein, drawing attention to the restricted availability of the Victorian pornographic novel *Fanny Hill* or the nuclear holocaust film *The War Game*, which you could only see if you were a media-defence correspondent, but not if you were merely a film critic or a member of the public; the Government and BBC were 'protecting us' from such fictional horrors. For Mitchell, permission "implies the wisdom of an officially appointed elder brother" satisfying "only the powerful … and the timid", while the permissive society "is only a stage in the real, long, bloody struggle for freedom". But the permissive society is not quite the same thing as the underground – many people who pursued permissiveness and freedom had no direct connection with what was known as the underground.

Mitchell traced a history of the latter back to the 1950s and CND, the Aldermaston marches and a growing willingness to challenge authority more broadly. He identified the "current tendency … for radicals to move in small specialist groups" which is interesting since that has often been identified by the media as a much more recent tendency as people grow disenchanted with party politics. For Mitchell, these groups were a part of the underground, which he defined as "an anti-commercial, anti-war, anti-police collection of people, some good, some bad, some phoney, some real."

Of particular relevance to this publication, and a long way from the mods, was his observation that "many of the underground … are moving now towards mysticism of many kinds". In respect of drug-use, he suggested that "nobody in the underground doubts that pot will become legal" but wisely he put no date on that, although he declared too, a strong dislike of heroin as "a particularly horrific way of suicide". He wrote of LSD, sex, and the prejudice against certain forms of dress and hair, adding, "very few of the boutique owners are anything to do with the Underground".

Mitchell wrote on behalf of all writers about the challenge of censorship, suggesting that, unlike America, for twenty years the post-war arts in Britain had been fighting the "disease" of "a compulsion to stay small … to take no major risks", and for this reason "the strong American influence on the British underground should be welcomed". The article concluded with warnings about people "cashing in" on the idea of the underground and "too much vagueness" around political questions, but praised its "gentleness", its "willingness to experiment … its generosity and gaiety". It was not by any means a definitive version of the underground, but it was of its time and by someone involved in an aspect of it.

The 20 "Priests and Prophets of Permissiveness" (including four Beatles), were all male and all white, except for Cuban leader Fidel Castro, which probably caused little comment at the time but certainly would today. With William Blake, Sigmund Freud, and Lenny Bruce included, they were not all still alive, and some others pre-dated the hippies, flower children and nascent underground, including Dr. Alex Comfort ("poet and prophet, anarchist and pacifist"), the philosopher and CND champion Bertrand Russell, Dr. Benjamin Spock, and Castro. Others were rather more of the time, including Allen Ginsberg, Bob Dylan, Peter Cook, John Hopkins and Jim Haynes – "now founding an Arts Laboratory in Covent Garden". The others from the arts world were poet Mike Horowitz, playwright John Arden, theatre director Roland Muldoon, artist and poet Jeff Nuttall.

Around the same time and possibly from the *Daily Mirror*, I pasted a large feature on "The Young Outsiders" about beatnik drop-outs in Trafalgar Square. One of them was known as 'the Artful Dodger', who, "like a surprising number of outsiders … went to public school and did well.

Four 'A' levels. At Oxford, he got bored with physics and opted out for 'the drug scene'."

In the *Observer*, John Crosby wrote a whole column called "The King's Road Grenadiers", about the growing fashion for colourful, historic army and navy uniforms – not only in Chelsea, but in Portobello Road too. Shortly after, there was a longer, illustrated piece in the *Observer Magazine* by Gillian Strickland on the same topic. The young people shown wearing the full regalia, including top hats, looked pretty middle class and not quite the hippest, a thought confirmed by the inclusion of Jimmy Saville looking like an extra from *Mutiny on the Bounty* – plus Mick Jagger in a red and yellow Grenadier Guards jacket. On the lines of latest fashions, but not necessarily the more challenging ideas of the underground, I included a photo of a young woman loading bags into her convertible Triumph Herald outside Mary Quant's shop Bazaar in the Brompton Road.

While the focus of my interest was becoming broader than just the music and fashion of the mods, that focus was on theoretical and cultural interests rather than explicitly on politics or spirituality – both of which would become key elements of the counterculture in the late 1960s and beyond. There is a recent publication by music and countercultural American journalist Richard Goldstein, who recalls that as a young man in New York in the 1960s the impact of the Civil Rights movement was significant for someone who was "itching for something to believe in, as passionately as I didn't believe in myself" (2015, 17). Goldstein, five years older than me, wrote for the Village Voice from 1966, when he produced his first book *1 in 7: Drugs on Campus*. Americans of his generation had three major issues that stimulated those of a radical persuasion: Kennedy and the Cold War, the Vietnam War, and Civil Rights. In Britain, we had CND, but its broad impact on the generation of *Citizen 63* – the same age as Goldstein – had dissipated somewhat by the late 1960s. We had a Labour Government whose Home Secretary Roy Jenkins argued that permissive really meant "civilized", and while his government contributed to important legislation around various issues, Prime Minister Harold Wilson was not wholly convinced of all these initiatives, but nonetheless, while he gave notional support to Lyndon Johnson, he refused to send British troops to Vietnam.

In this broadly 'liberal' context, and with high employment, there was a brief period when it was not always obvious which cause(s) the young British radical might support. In broad terms the initial answer was probably authority in general, and the established institutions in particular. In its first edition (October 1966), *International Times* identified a couple of political issues, but neither the Vietnam War nor the Dutch 'Provos' with their white bicycles were British. Similarly, edition 4 carried an interview with black American radical Dick Gregory, and by 1967 they were calling for the arrest of the Home Secretary. They also featured articles on Buddhism (by Gary Snyder), Hare Krishna and the Age of Aquarius by John Michell who would become a regular writer for them, and in the UK, more broadly on Glastonbury, mysticism and esoteric topics.

Edition 13 in late May 1967 was dominated by popular music, although there were articles about the 'Provos' and Malcolm X, plus the question "is British protest getting stuck in a Psychedelic rut?" By mid-summer 1967, the publication found its local causes, first when Indica Books and *International Times* itself were raided by the police, then as 'Hoppy', John Hopkins, one of the leading figures in the new underground and a member of its editorial board, was tried for possession of cannabis, and, unlike Mick Jagger and Keith Richard, imprisoned. Edition 14 (2 June 1967) carried the Headline "All Human Life for Sale", with a box inset "Free Hoppy" after his sentencing to nine months. The topic continued to be a key issue with the police, judiciary and establishment in general in the line of fire. *International Times* edition 19 in October 1967, celebrated the 'paper's first birthday with lots of rock & roll, some drugs plus John Michell on "Centres and Lines of the Latent Power in Britain", and another piece on Aleister Crowley – the "proto hippie".

I doubt whether I saw the first two editions of the other notable under-ground magazine *Oz*, which appeared in the UK from late January 1967 but I remember number 3 (also May 1967) with a psychedelic Mona Lisa on the cover. *International Times* had a somewhat serious feel, but true to Richard Neville's enthusiasm for 'Playpower', the colourful graphics of the delightful Martin Sharp and others, enhanced articles about Ken Kesey & his Merry Pranksters and Timothy Leary, the 'real' Frodo Baggins, cartoons and photographs for two competitions – beautiful breasts and boys' nice tight bottoms. In the letters section, a correspondent suggested that the 1966 *Time* publication about swinging London had "imposed an image on the city which simply didn't fit" but he praised various individuals (David Bailey, Peter Watkins, Ken Loach, Ronan O'Rahilly etc.) and offered a broader view that

> For the first time, anywhere, young people, in the prime of their talents, have had a proper chance to make their impressions on culture, business and commerce while they are still young, and before they are battered into conformity by their elders.

It was the spirit of those times. There was a photograph of a naked young woman sitting on a toilet over the Houses of Parliament with the caption "Why politics is giving everyone the …", although it was (typically) another opportunity to reveal a pair of tits; it led into the main political issue, an address to politicians and their "phony, ill-written, unutterably boring, lying, arse-licking speeches". There was a savaging of the quality of pop music on the BBC, and an attack on the anti-pirates' legislation and the current laws on abortion, plus from 'Outsider' Colin MacInnes, "In Praise of Ugliness". *Oz* always seemed to be having fun – the colour here was psychedelic pink and blue and not everything was easy to read; the two publications complemented each other very well.

International Times and *Oz* were from and by the counterculture, aimed mostly at young people, but the impact of these new ways was becoming more widespread, and on Sunday 3 December 1967, the *Observer* magazine had as its font cover and main focus "The New Society" which led with the observation

> If you are over 25, you feel uncomfortably aware that Pop is not just music; Something Is Going On Underground. If you are under 25 you are certain that It's All Happening. A curious alliance has been struck between teenagers, the hippies, commercial pop, and the young intellectuals. Somehow all have crystallised into a separate society or 'scene'.

Unsurprisingly, for all its "new" vision, the scene that they described was London-centred, predominantly male and predominantly white, but for my parents, around 50, and others like them, it would still have been an unfamiliar and probably fairly astonishing tale.

On the opening pages, there were biographies, and photos of the 16 people who comprised "Who's Who in the Underground" in Britain, including Caroline Coon (age 22) the co-ordinator of the drug advice/support centre Release and two more women (and two men) in the Dutch design co-operative the Fool. The other groups were the Beatles, three of whom were 25 or over and the two members of designers and musicians Hapshash & the Coloured Coat. Otherwise, of the 12 individual men, only singer Arthur Brown and 'Miles' (Barry Miles), gallery owner, editor of *International Times* and subsequently chronicler of those times, were under 25. The elders included Jim Haynes of the Arts Laboratory, photographer and founder of the UFO club John Hopkins, artist and light show man Mark Boyle, *Oz* editor Richard Neville, poet Pete Brown, accountant Michael Henshawe, Steve Abrams who was Director of the USA's Society of Mental Awareness (SOMA), Ravi Shankar the Indian sitar maestro, Joe Boyd pop manager and producer, and 28-year-old Radio One DJ John Peel, who suggested that "the BBC's main problem is that it has to experiment in public". Other than Shankar, they were all white.

In the same edition, the *Observer's* grumpy pop critic, Tony Hall, ignored San Francisco entirely in reviewing the year's ten "most surprising" LPs. He did not like them very much, although he praised Cream ("the only pop group who improvise"), while suggesting that *Sgt Pepper* was not "the perfect record, sycophants lead us to believe". Of the other eight, six were British: Scott Walker ("mostly self-pitying love dirges"), the Bee Gees ("self-indulgent wailing"), Eric Burdon & the Animals ("unintelligent, mostly unintelligible"), the Rolling Stones ("disappointing"), Pink Floyd ("others have developed, the Pink Floyd haven't") and Jimi Hendrix whose first album was "mostly out of tune and probably out of time". The two American albums were by the Monkees who produced "the Lowest Common Denominator of trendy, gear pop music" and *Absolutely Free* by the Mothers of Invention, which was "a giant send-up of a sick culture – ours" – although he passed no judgement on it. Palmer was then 26, so perhaps he was too old to get it?

There was an article "Inside the Underground", also called the New Society, the counterculture, or the Flower Power scene – which had started with poets who were still playing a significant role. It described the "several thousand people … who have their own vocabulary, dress, stimulants, entertainments, communications network, posters and shops". This New Society contained a variety of people:

> Pot-smokers and transcendental meditators; kids who like to dress up at the weekend, as well as full-time drop-out hippies; sensation-seekers and seekers after truth … those who foster the revolt of youth against its elders and those who try to bring the generations together … those who flirt with Black Power and those who fail to see what Black Power has in common with Flower Power.

There was also an article about "Poster Power" featuring Martin Sharp's Bob Dylan 'Urine' image and a large photo of a range of posters in front of which was a jeep in which were seated seven very colourful, exotically dressed and crucially neat, clean hippies. Whether they had been mods I cannot be sure, but they were perpetuating the principle of "clean living", whether under difficult circumstances or not, and there was a profile of the Fool with their cosmically, medieval fashions. On music, there was a feature on Jimi Hendrix, again dressed exotically, colourfully (and neatly), as well as two articles about pop promoters with smart suits and neat hair. A glossary defined money as "bread", police as "fuzz" and "Zowie" as imported from San Francisco and apparently meaning "hippy language". I've no memory of anyone using that one. Opposite the glossary was an image of a drinks session prior to a formal dinner at a very posh 'white tie' event, advertising White Horse whiskey. The contrast was vivid, whereas a page or two later, Murphy televisions were sympathetically 'tuned in', advertising a "revolutionary set" which naturally was "painted red". There was a half-serious, half tongue-in-cheek article by the chef Clement Freud, "Freud's Freakout", which offered one serious recipe, one daft one for "stoned porpoise" and a basic introduction to macrobiotics and yin and yang, the "antagonistic but complementary forces". Esther Ronay considered the antecedents of hippie art and suggested we had reached a time when children exercise "absolute powers over parents" and finally, David Widgerey explained his understanding of hippie philosophy, before we were informed of the imminence of colour arriving on our television screens.

That magazine reveals the extent to which the mainstream media were intrigued by what was happening – and even if that was principally in London, such articles, plus a BBC television feature on Pink Floyd, the controversy surrounding the jailing of the Stones, John Peel on Radio One and the underground publications, were all heard about or available in Portsmouth, endorsed by the visits to the city over the next couple of years by most of the more interesting musicians and bands. Then, as we learned more about UFO and its successor Middle Earth, Indica, Better Books, the Arts Laboratory and the London Film-Makers Co-op and other new initiatives, we could, and did, travel easily enough to London to sample the 'cutting edge'. When appropriate, we brought some of those styles, ideas and practices back to Portsmouth.

COCONUT MUSHROOM:

At the Indigo Vat Club.

Photo: Nigel Grundy

SING, SING, SING

In addition to all this general excitement, I was now playing regularly in a 'proper' band, Harlem Speakeasy. It had been fun to meet up with some old schoolmates when I went to Highbury College, but I was surprised when they asked me to join them, because the band was a classic five piece – singer, guitar, bass, drums, organ – now focusing on Motown and contemporary soul. I was effectively the second singer, a luxury that perhaps a local band could afford, but otherwise not essential, even given the fact that we were performing covers of tracks by duos and vocal groups like Sam & Dave or the Temptations. Nonetheless, it meant teaming up with Pete again, and I was thrilled to be asked, so in the autumn of 1967, I appeared with them for the first time, on stage at a club gig in Guildford.

In terms of local musicians, we were the new generation of course. Some of our elders (and betters) were still playing, while others like Colin Wood were married now, sorting out a home, having kids and no longer playing. Guitarist Pete White continued to play but did not experience much of what was happening on the late 1960s' scene, recalling, "by that time I was married and commuting to Brighton each day to work, plus playing on the weekends, so I missed all that."

Having added me as a sixth member, Harlem Speakeasy went on expanding. By January Pete Gurd had switched from guitar to trumpet, which he taught himself with his usual flair and we found a tenor sax player, Phil Jones. I added a bit of pretty hopeless baritone sax and we were an eight-piece now, a real soul/pop act, a bit like Amen Corner I guess, but modelling ourselves rather more on the post-soul sound of the renamed Birdcage favourites, the Alan Bown!

In Portsmouth, the main gig each year for local bands was the Lord Mayor's Charity Dance, usually at the Guildhall, which in 1968 took place on 30 April, and featured Machine, Harlem Speakeasy, Blackout, Lace, Coconut Mushroom, and dancers Crimson Ballet – it is the only time I have ever played the main stage at the Guildhall, and I remember being astonished by how huge it was. The evening ran from 8pm – 1am, and tickets cost 5/6d (27.5p). In his review, Spinner mentioned the "creditable light show at the Guildhall", which had been created at the Art College by my pals Geoff Allman and Martin Richman and was called Light Emporium. They were paid 10/- for their efforts and their success led to a light show residency at the newly opened Paradise Found Club at the Foresters Hall in Fratton Road. Geoff Allman's diary of the Guildhall gig records the Harlem Speakeasy set list, which is indicative of the kinds of numbers covered by local soul bands at that time. There were songs by the Impressions, Junior Walker, the Temptations, Otis Redding, Edwin Starr, a medley of older rock & roll songs and another by Stevie Wonder. There was a hint of newer styles in our cover of "All Along the Watchtower", although the set ended with popular soul crowd pleasers, "Sock it to 'em JB" and "Land of 1000 Dances".

In May, Harlem Speakeasy and Light Emporium appeared together locally for the last time at Copnor's Red Door, as the band were turning professional after we signed with a London agent Richard Cowley (Chrysalis) and Polydor Records. The story of how we landed a top record label and agency deal is worth telling for what it reveals about the pop world at that time, although it had little to do with the growing counterculture.

We were an ambitious band, probably ambitious beyond our ability at that point. Early in 1968 we took ourselves off at our own expense to perform in a hall in Romford High Street at a public audition (advertised in *Melody Maker*) and organised by the notorious agent Don Arden. He filled the hall with young pop fans who thought we were rather good, so he invited us back a couple of weeks later, still auditioning, but promising to bring hit record producer Mickie Most to check us out. This time we drew a crowd who had remembered us, Arden pocketed some dough, and Mickie apparently "loved" us, but had to leave early and would like one more look.

So, we went again. My memory is that this time we were probably advertised, that the hall was full again, that Arden could not be there personally, and that Mickie 'left' again without any contact between us. By this stage, we were pretty clear what was happening, but what occurred next was a combination of insanity and fate. Our 'roadie', who was in reality a pal and more like a personal manager, Richie Anderson (later to work with Mott the Hoople), could appear fairly fearsome, and he took Pete and me (the biggest two) up to London on Monday morning, suitably armed just in case, to confront Mr Arden. Given his reputation, we must have been bonkers, and to be honest, I'm a Lover not a Fighter. We saw the man with a 'pal' or two of his in attendance, and we were probably fortunate to escape with nothing more than a "fuck off and don't come back". He had screwed us, and that was an end to it.

Frustrated, we departed for a coffee in a Denmark Street musicians' café. As I have said, we were rather taken by Alan Bown's band and to some extent our performing style and set was derived from theirs. We sat there with the coffee, cursing and considering out options and were overheard by a guy, sitting on his own in the next cubicle. He came to talk to us and astonishingly revealed that (a) he was a roadie with the Alan Bown! (b) they had just moved management/agency from a Soho-based team, Richard Cowley and Kenny Bell and (c) Richard and Kenny were looking to sign similar acts, because they had a recording deal with Polydor. These days, "you couldn't make it up" is a bit of a cliché – but you couldn't, could you? Yet it happened exactly like that.

The coincidence now strikes me as something quite extraordinary – or even something more than that, and beyond rational explanation. It did not finish there either, as we contacted Richard Cowley and Kenny Bell, visited them and they arranged an audition for us at the famous Speakeasy Club, which would have been a tough test. Then, the night before we were due to appear there, in the spring of 1968, the club was hit by a fire. So instead of performing at a pretty demanding London venue, we went to Richard's flat, took just basic equipment and auditioned, semi-acoustically offering no clear sense of our live sound or performing style. On that basis, we signed the deals and in the spring of 1968, about six months after joining my first proper band, I signed a contract naming me as a "professional musician" and moved into a flat in Fratton Road where the whole group lived together. I dropped out of college without taking my 'A' levels, and turned down the offer of a college place in Leeds, that autumn. My folks were bewildered and not a bit delighted, but typically very tolerant.

The first time we met anyone linked to Polydor was the day before recording our first single. Our producer Chris Brough (son of Peter – and Archie Andrews) worked with us in a rehearsal studio on a cover of a Drifters' song called "Aretha" that we had chosen, and we had responded to the demand that we should write the 'B' side with a song called "Sights of Pegasus". Keith Shilcock (guitar) and John Lytle (organ) wrote the chords, including a middle eight and I wrote the lyrics/final melody influenced by the title at least of Cream's "Tales of Brave Ulysses". Remembering as a kid, the mythological tales I read in *the Wonder Book* and *Tanglewood Tales*, I took the tale of Bellerophon and Pegasus, the mythical hero on the winged horse, but wrote it ambiguously, as a kind of love song. That sounds a bit smart-arsed, and the lyrics are pretty simple, but it was deliberately done like that, and you can still find it on YouTube on the red Polydor label and with our three surnames in brackets as the writers. For me there would never be another one, but it is a very special thing in my life.

Back in Portsmouth, we took a month out before the release of the record and then went on the road. *Melody Maker* said "Aretha" was "quite fun", comparing it with "Concrete and Clay", *NME* described its "captivating Latin flavour" and Radio One liked it enough to play it on their new release show. The following week it reached number 10 in the charts – but only in Portsmouth. I think it sold about 500 copies and although we each had a contract and prepared a new single, a few months later, Polydor told us to bugger off.

With the first single just released, we started travelling up-and-down the country from July 1968, but there was another surprise as Richard Cowley and Kenny Bell amalgamated with the Ellis-Wright Agency to create a considerably larger project, the Chrysalis Agency, which would soon add a relationship with the progressive Island Records label. Suddenly we were on the books alongside Jethro Tull, Ten Years After and all the other new-sounding bands, and as a pop-soul act we got booked more modestly. There were however, some enjoyable nights, including a gig in Chester with the hilarious Champion Jack Dupree and the Keef Hartley Band (destined for Woodstock), the Nottingham Boathouses alongside Rory Gallagher's Taste on one side and Duster Bennett on the other, a soulful all-nighter at Manchester's Twisted Wheel which was like a trip back in a time machine, and on Monday 29 July at Cheshford Grange near Coventry, a support spot to the Equals around the time of their number one record, "Baby Come Back". This was probably our great triumph as the large, young and predominantly female audience consisted mostly of pop fans who rather liked us. Had we stuck with that sound, that approach, that audience and type of venue, we might have gone further, but while most of us found playing "Ain't Too Proud to Beg" or "See Saw" acceptable, by now we had added "Simon Says" which was a stage too far in pursuit of commercial success. We started adding covers from the Byrds' *Younger than Yesterday* and the Rascals, and fairly soon promoters, expecting a mainstream soul act, began complaining to the agency that our style was somewhat 'mixed'.

It was also insanely tough at times. We would often leave Portsmouth on a Friday morning – nine of us plus all the (mostly WEM) gear in one Ford Transit – and drive back on Monday or Tuesday morning as the sun was rising after three or four consecutive gigs. Only occasionally did we have the money to book into a B&B and we often slept in the van and the motorway services. We did not eat very well and were often too tired to play well after four nights in, say, Birmingham, Walsall, Wolverhampton and back to Birmingham – or maybe a long weekend in Norfolk where we played regularly. On one occasion, we played a Saturday night in Oxford, where two or three of our microphones packed up, messing up harmonies and the brass/reed section. The next day we were in Derby, which on a Sunday in 1968 was the deadest place in the world. With no way of repairing or replacing the equipment, we bodged our way through a second night, the crowd mostly ignored us, the promoter was unsympathetic and we were deflated. We were a very decent local band, promoted at that time beyond the level of our competence and without the resources to develop. We had been signed by a big London agent and record label, but no-one from either organisation *ever* came to see us play, or offered any advice. We were between 16-18 and entirely on our own. We had no Brian Epstein or Andrew Loog-Oldham to guide us, although perhaps we did not really warrant one.

As things got tougher, almost inevitably we began squabbling. We had no idea how to handle what was happening, made personnel changes and in November after just four months on the road, Kenny Bell wrote to us, saying that because of some poor reports from venues and the "constant" changes in the band, it was all over. He did offer to talk again in three months if things were resolved, but on Friday 13 December, what remained of Speakeasy (no longer Harlem) performed for the last time at Portsmouth's Manor Court Club and we went our separate ways to new ventures – of which more later.

Despite the disappointment and the fact that I was now in a somewhat uncertain situation, I would not have missed it for the world. I had now experienced pretty fully, London's pop entertainment world at first hand, and I had grown up very rapidly from a naive grammar school/college kid, although I was so preoccupied with living that particular life to the full, that I missed much of what went on through 1968, in terms of culture, music and in particular politics. I was just the right age and inclination for a taste of that street-fighting man stuff, but much of it simply passed me by.

Talking of 'street-fighting men', during that summer, my old favourites, the Rolling Stones recorded *Beggars Banquet* and that album provides me with an intriguing tale from the time that we recorded our single, which was done in the Olympic Studios in Barnes. After Abbey Road, it was probably the biggest in town and we arrived there late one sunny afternoon in the spring of 1968 and carried our gear from the van into the studio, through a group of teenage girls who seemed entirely uninterested in us. As we were loading in-and-out, and up the stairs, a posh motor (Daimler? Bentley?) with darkened windows arrived and out stepped Keith Richard who was apparently more to their taste. Once inside, we discovered the Stones were working on *Beggars Banquet* in one studio, Donovan was downstairs in another studio, while we were in the third. At one point, we met Charlie on the stairs and he was a delight, handing out the fags and chatting about what we were doing. During our recording session, Mick Jagger walked in with a kitten on his shoulder to listen to us covering a Drifters' song (as he had once done) but we were too overawed to speak to him, although we chatted later to Donovan. We discovered from Jimmy Miller that Brian Jones was missing and by that time often worked separately, dubbing his parts when the other guys were not there. Jimmy also revealed that despite the considerable hourly rate at Olympic – of which we were constantly reminded – the Stones had recorded nothing that evening. Eventually however the album arrived and was well received, in comparison with their psychedelic *Satanic Majesties Request*. There was also a movie, of sorts.

I have to confess that while we were at Olympic there was no sign of a film crew, but during that spring and early summer, the Stones were filmed working there on a new song, "Sympathy for the Devil", which began rather like a slow blues but ended in a more up-tempo, percussive style. The film ended with two titles, one of which was the same as the song and years later, in the *Observer,* Andrew Hussey described it as "a rock film which has all the immediacy of reportage from a distant war-zone" (21.5.2006). It is a pretty astonishing film, although less surprisingly so since it was directed by the master of the French 'New Wave' and later radical Maoist cinema, Jean-Luc Godard. It is not an easy film to watch for fans of rock music, with an unsettling montage, cutting-in fictional extracts including Black Power activists assaulting and killing young white women, a bookshop selling a selection of strange material, a young woman wandering about on a beach and voice-overs about the assassination of the Kennedy brothers and Marxist readings. Despite this construction, Hussey also suggested the film is "a snapshot of a far-off, lost world where rock music is still a redemptive and revolutionary force". Perhaps it was once?

The film was released in the UK as *Sympathy for the Devil*, at which Godard was furious. He is reputed to have fought with the producer at the premiere because he wanted it to be called *One Plus One* – a reference to the significance of modernist montage where one meaning, juxtaposed with another, produces a third (1+1=3). As I have said, I did not witness any filming and, preoccupied with my life as a neophyte pop star for a few months, I certainly did not see the film on release. Indeed, I think I did not see it for some time, none of which would mean much, except that within a decade or so I was studying avant-garde and experimental cinema as a significant part of my postgraduate research, and subsequently my Ph.D. and by the late 1990s, I was teaching about much of it, including Godard's work. If anyone had suggested that was my future in the spring of 1968, I would have thought they were completely barmy.

The key point with the song "Sympathy for the Devil" and Godard's film, is that they were in their differing ways a part of what is so often described as 1968's shift from flower power and the summer of love in the previous year, to twelve months of unrest and 'revolution'. This was partly transitional and partly a matter of approach and attitude. Hill (2016, 199) has quoted Marc Arno as pointing out that in the USA "if it was political it wasn't hippie, it was yippie. Hippies could not, *could not,* be political, they had to be apolitical".

In the USA, in particular however, specific situations drove young people towards the political – most obviously of course centred on opposition to the Vietnam War. Elsewhere there were the May 'events' in Paris, where students and workers took to the streets; in Czechoslovakia, there was the Prague spring, with their own hippies (yippies?) on the streets with guitars until the Russian tanks rolled in; while back in the USA, the assassinations of Martin Luther King and Robert Kennedy led to an upsurge in Black protests, plus mayhem at the Democratic Party Convention in Chicago.

All these events and more, explain why 1968 is characterised as it is, but we have already seen that *International Times* and *Oz* were carrying political articles at the height of the summer of 67, alongside sex, drugs, rock & roll and psychedelic images, while the latter were still there during the turbulent months of 1968. It is a convenient simplification to explain the late-1960s in terms of '67: Peace and Love; '68 Revolution; and '69: The End – but once we move beyond such generalisations, the reality is always more complex.

It is partly so, because there has been a tendency for these histories to be driven by two things. The first of those is the popular representations, which emphasise some events and ignore others. As I have suggested, they tend to imply, for example, that the Woodstock Festival was far more significant than the second and third Isle of Wight Festivals, principally because of the impact of the feature film. But it was the Isle of Wight that got Dylan in 1969, and in 1970 a bigger crowd than Woodstock, as well as some 'interesting' political protests. The other issue is chronological, so that when the histories are told of the counterculture they are driven mostly by when things happened 'first' – whether in San Francisco, London or elsewhere – and initially at least it tended to be written by the people who were there at the time.

For example, in a profile of (Barry) Miles, one of the leading figures in London's mid-1960s underground, *the Guardian Review* (20.03.2010) cited Jonathan Green, suggesting that through Miles' door "everyone who was going to be anyone passed or claimed to have passed". Green was there at the time and so his claim is unsurprising, but if he is right about "anyone who was going to be anyone" then down in the provinces, I guess we were 'nobodies'. Certainly, Green's two interesting books are built upon interviews with the generally acknowledged key figures, while there are few 'ordinary' participants to be heard – and almost certainly reflecting the 'balance of power' of those days, 82 of his 101 correspondents are male.

As with the matter of originality and authenticity among the mods, anything that came along a year or two later, or from somewhere else, tends to be dismissed as mere copying, denying the significance of specific experiences for particular individuals and groups, in particular contexts. How does anyone know that those of us in the provinces were *merely* imitating those who preceded us, or that we had nothing interesting to offer or say for ourselves? Was anyone asking? Perhaps there can be some value in starting out as a follower, and subsequently finding ways of engaging with and developing these new ideas over longer periods beyond the point at which a specific social movement, say the mods or the counterculture, is deemed to have ended? That is a key argument in this account of life in the provinces. It may be that those who were born to follow make little contribution to the grand events of the time, but how useful is the experience in terms of their personal, intellectual and emotional development? That is not something that can be judged so easily by others. What do Jonathan Green or Miles think of my experiences or those of my peers back then, or how those experiences impacted subsequently on the way we lived? The answer, of course, is they think nothing, because they know nothing about us.

Here is one simple example which draws a longer picture of the consequences of those days. We know from the early Trips Festivals in 1966 that alongside the newer rock groups, people started experimenting with lights, which developed into the rather grand projections in San Francisco's dance hall light shows with the top west coast bands, while in London, artist Mark Boyle was one of those developing similar illuminations at UFO through 1967. In Portsmouth, most lighting at live gigs through 1967 was traditionally theatrical but I have related how, early in 1968, my pals Geoff Allman and Martin Richman started developing their own light show with melting colours and slide projections. Initially they worked regularly with Harlem Speakeasy until we went on the road as professionals, by which time they were appearing in a number of other local clubs. Eventually they were taken on by the College of Technology/Polytechnic/Art College students, and separately by Rikki Farr and other promoters for the bigger local gigs, particularly in the beautiful old ballroom on South Parade Pier. Over the next few years, they worked locally with a variety of top bands including Iron Butterfly, Traffic, Velvet Underground, Black Sabbath and Yes, while Geoff was actively involved in the Students' Union and produced a number of posters for gigs, happenings and other events at the college. After leaving college, Geoff went to Manchester where he still runs his successful graphic design company Spoken Image; Martin worked for some years around the world as a fully professional lighting man with a number of top acts, before going back to college, and completing a Fine Art degree at St Martin's. Since then he has worked professionally on many visual art projects across the western world – many of which feature lighting prominently (www.martinrichman. com). It seems entirely irrelevant to that later success that his lightshow, or Geoff's graphics 'followed' those in San Francisco and London.

We know that the 'revolutionaries' of 1968 – always a significant if vocal minority – were mostly middle-class and/or educated and there was a student presence of sorts in Portsmouth then, albeit mostly engineers and scientists who were perhaps less likely to be at the barricades. We know too that across Britain there were not that many students – the Robbins Report of 1963 revealed that in the USA, 20% of young people went into higher education, with 8% in France, 6% in USSR and just 4.6% in Britain, and given that Portsmouth has always been below the national average, we can see that relatively few Portsmouth teenagers went away to university. The national figure incidentally is now about ten times that number – it is a very different time for young people. Brenda Marshall, was the first woman elected as President of the College of Technology's Students' Union in 1966, although it is not clear at this distance how deliberate that was. Nonetheless the University's Archives carry reports about a 'Radical Women's Group' at the College from at least 1968 and there were also a number of demonstrations around issues like Anti-Apartheid, Chile and Government Education Policy as well as student grants, fees and general cuts, although in fact there were more student 'demos' and 'sit ins' in the 1970s.

There were at this time debates about the organisation and curriculum in higher education, and in Britain in 1968, that included the London School of Economics and Hornsey College of Art. One of the participants, Tickner (2008) has documented the latter, which commenced with an occupation in late May, just three weeks after the start of 'the Events' involving students and workers, in Paris. At Hornsey, it followed proposals in 1967 to merge the independent college with others to form one of the proposed new Polytechnics which came about in 1969 (including Portsmouth). By May 1968, the occupation crystallised around demands for student autonomy and representation on college management structures. One of the Hornsey students, Kim Howells was also actively involved in the Vietnam Protest movement in this country and later became a Labour MP. At the conclusion of her account, Tickner acknowledged that the "authorities seemed to win" but more positively proposed an "open verdict" with the action being "essentially hybrid and ambiguous", and the experience being carried by participants into the future.

The various events in May were already a couple of months after the first major rally against the Vietnam War in central London, focused on the American Embassy in Grosvenor Square and London's underground publications kept a focus on that and other issues. Sheila Rowbotham, in a fine memoir of the 1960s, recounted her participation in the rally of 17 March 1968, and contrasting it with the earlier CND events, suggested that the new protesters were "more angry than good, and far less passive than was customary on British CND demonstrations" (170). Rowbotham also wrote intelligently and honestly about the stirrings of feminism in 1967:

> Women I decided did have a culture, (which) … took various forms, depending on your class … Yet feminism did not interest me, I knew it only as the suffrage movement of years ago or as a lobby of professional women for advancement at work … Adamant that I didn't want to be like a man, the evident contradictions in how to be a woman kept making me question my own emotions and relationships (158/9).

Some months later, Sunday 27 October 1968, saw the second major London demonstration against the Vietnam War with an attendance of 100,000, and while the front page of the old *Guardian* was too large to get into my scrapbook I still have the whole newspaper. The three front-page photographs showed the police "under attack", carrying away a demonstrator and "helping a colleague" who seems to have sustained some damage. The main headline read "A peaceful march – except in Grosvenor Square and the 'paper reported "39 arrests and six policemen injured". Other pieces carried a variety of headings: "Violence flares but the cordon holds", "A calm kind of control", "Politics of action heralded", and "Anarchists use banner poles as spears".

The Guardian reported how, in the USA, the out-going President Lyndon B Johnson, backed fellow democrat Hubert Humphrey against Republican Richard Nixon, suggesting the latter was "the man from the past" – although it was a past that would come to haunt the future. Inside the back page was a report from the final day of the Mexico Olympic Games which is remembered partly for the two Black Power rostrum salutes by Tommie Smith and John Carlos, just a few months after the assassination of Martin Luther King (April 1968). There were more photographs and reports of demonstrators on the back page and two reports from Higher Education: at Cambridge Enoch Powell came to speak to the University's Conservative Association and gave the slip to "several hundred left-wing" objectors, while the students who had been occupying the LSE, left the building.

All of these stories were appearing a national daily newspaper, while radicals like Tariq Ali were producing a more overtly political magazine *Black Dwarf* alongside *Oz* and *International Times*. The new arrival announced it would "not pick quarrels" with fellow left-wingers "but with our principal enemy, Capitalism". At the start of 1969 they published an edition called "1969: The Year of the Militant Woman?" although the design treatment caused the 'sisters' some dismay. Even in the counter culture it was generally a man's world.

During the early months of 1968, I had been increasingly preoccupied with being a musician, while also enjoying my art classes with Doug Everitt, but barely engaging with and rarely attending the 'A' level classes in History and English Literature. There is little evidence from my scrapbook or my memory that I was deeply interested in the politics informing these street demonstrations, and the College of Technology students did not seem much engaged with the ordinary people of Portsmouth, although I enjoyed hanging out with my close friends at the independent Art College. By 1969, that link would be increasingly significant, but in the meantime, there were two significant student-led *cultural* interventions in Portsmouth that drew upon examples from London's counterculture and had a significant impact on my life beyond that of being a mere pop singer.

The "Dance of Words" was a unique event for the city that took place in Portsmouth Guildhall on Monday 27 May 1968, using the main auditorium, without the seats, plus two side rooms with smaller stages. There was no headline 'star' but a variety of different acts appeared throughout the evening as the audience ambled between the rooms, sat on the floor or danced when appropriate. Fairport Convention made one of their first public appearances with Sandy Denny, Free came to back Alexis Korner, poets Brian Patten and Michael Horowitz who had been at the famous Royal Albert Hall event in 1965, read work, Principal Edward's Magic Theatre impressed compere John Peel sufficiently that he would sign them to his new Dandelion label – although he subsequently regretted that, when they proved difficult to work with. King Idas' Watch Chain came from Newcastle with music and poetry, and Cream's lyricist Pete Brown appeared with his First Real Poetry Band. Local art lecturer Ray Selden brought his modern jazz group who performed with other poets, while the Portsmouth rock scene was represented by the west coast-sounding Coconut Mushroom and their two young women dancers, Crimson Ballet.

Students Guff Putowski and his friend Jerry Ensor (who would later join Principal Edwards) were the main organisers. They produced a simply duplicated and stapled programme, which offered the following opening statement about the 'underground' (not yet generally called the counterculture). Since I do not believe it has ever been reproduced, the 'philosophical' part is here in full:

The underground has existed for many years, since before the 1930s, however it is from this period that many of today's activities may be directly traced. The fusion of poetry, music and drama then is being continued, and consciously and unconsciously many of the techniques of pre-World War II avant-garde drama are undergoing a new lease of life.

This does not mean that today's British underground is unorigi- nal but it does introduce an element of continuity in a portion of society that frowns upon what it considers to be wrong with the Wider Society. In spite of much of the underground's desire to opt out of the mainstream of British Society, it is sad to reflect that many members of the underground invariably conform or perish. Perhaps their work may last as a norm of a wider society, in which case the originator agrees to conform by the very acceptance of his work. The alternative to this is often censure and ostracisation from the Main Society, and sometimes ridicule from the newer underground members, as the artist's avant-garde work ceases to be regarded as avant-garde.

In "The Dance of Words" we have tried to combine the very best of the current British underground.

It is interesting to note that even in provincial Portsmouth, by 1968 they were identifying "many members of the underground (who) invariably conform or perish". Such is the impatience of youth, although it is consistent with many of the subsequent histories.

Following the "Dance of Words", I pasted in my scrapbook the full page of reports, plus six photographs of the event from the *Evening News*. It is inter- esting to note that one of those pictures was of a uniformed security guard with Alsatian dog with a caption which began "The potential was there for a 'riot'". In truth, I have rarely attended a more peaceful event, but that is the media for you, and the report did acknowledge that actually he had "little to do". The other five photographs were all of the local members of the audience, sitting and listening, or dancing and mostly resembling neophyte hippies. The various performing poets and musicians were important to the event but the new way of engaging with such presentations was just as significant, and the photographic representation got that right.

We had seen Pink Floyd at the Birdcage, twelve months before, but this was the first major event in the city linked explicitly to the broader under- ground. As such, it is probably no coincidence that it was a student event, and, in May 1968 that places it about two years 'behind' Haight Ashbury and about 18 months behind London's *International Times* launch event at the Roundhouse. Nonetheless, it had a considerable impact in the city. The *Evening News* reported that over 1,000 people had attended and that "the general policy was to do just whatever one felt like doing". The crowd certainly included undergraduates, as well as 'graduates' from the Birdcage, although the hair was longer and the clothes looser, more colourful and more varied, while Guff Putowski described it as "something more than just an ordinary dance or concert".

In addition, around this time, the notion that Portsmouth was what Spinner described in his weekly column as a leading "progressive centre", owed something to the establishment that year of the "Portsmouth Arts Workshop" – one of a network of such venues around the country. Their main influence was the recently opened Arts Lab (by Jim Haynes) in London's Drury Lane. There were three organisers in Portsmouth – all architecture students at the College of Technology: Stefan Szczelkun, Peter Jones and Mel Croucher (who still lives in Southsea). The Arts Workshop was generally held in the new (and temporary) home of the students' union, K Block and former stables (since destroyed). The varied guest acts who appeared there included Roland Miller, the Exploding Galaxy, John Stevens, the Liverpool Poets, the People Show, bluesmen Alexis Korner and American Spider John Koerner, and Marc Bolan who arrived with DJ John Peel and his Tyrannosaurus Rex partner Steve Peregrine Took. This was around the time that the elfin duo played the first Hyde Park free concert in London with Jethro Tull, Roy Harper and Pink Floyd, which I attended with a number of friends from Portsmouth.

Yoko Ono, booked for our workshop, never arrived, but she contributed material for the weekly booklet of poems. The students operated with the support of their department and produced experimental films and even video – a rarity in 1968. Environments were created using plastic and other found materials and on occasions the participants created street theatre in the city centre. Years later in his Ph. D. thesis, Szczelkun recalled the events as "a celebration of everyone's creativity". He believed that they were "radically challenging culture, society and ourselves" in what constituted the beginnings of the "counterculture" and a "new alternative society". He added "our efforts were imbued with tremendous hope, optimism and utopian zeal". Like the Dance of Words, they offered me ideas about how I might resolve some of the contradictions I was experiencing between my interest in contemporary, broadly experimental art practices and the commercial world of 'pop' music. The latter beckoned as much as anything because it offered the chance of sufficient economic stability to try more adventurous ideas and practices – in the end, it was not to be.

It was however all rather thrilling, and in this sense 1968 might perhaps be identified culturally as Portsmouth's '1967', or perhaps simply *one* of our summers of love. Elsewhere in and around the city, local bands Coconut Mushroom and Tangerine Slyde continued to play new sounds, albeit mostly covers, while Brother Bung from just along the coast appeared quite regularly in the city with an approach that mixed Hendrix and contemporary blues. They included Bob Pearce who would be a leading figure on the British blues scene for many decades. Terry Threadingham was the original drummer with Tangerine Slyde before switching to Coconut Mushroom, during a reorganisation, after the original Coconut Mushroom had proved to be a rather short-lived development from soul band the Inspiration. Singer Colin Carter was the common factor, and Terry Threadingham recalls

> There was a brief time when the Inspiration changed to Coconut Mushroom, they apparently did one set of soul and Motown, and the next set psychedelia. At the same time, I left Tangerine Slyde to form a band with Rod Watts, Graham Barnes and John Clark, to do a 'Vanilla Fudge', but without Rod, we ended up somehow forming a new version of Coconut Mushroom, adding Roger Giffin on 12-string guitar. I remember getting bad receptions from soul venues at that time, which was difficult, and that's why we loved playing at colleges.

On 1968's live music scene in Portsmouth, the Who came to the Brave New World, while Coconut Mushroom played at London's 100 Club and then reported further "offers of London club work". Shortly after, they (like Jon Isherwood) signed with the Beatles' Apple label, although the band would produce no records with them. In 2010, two late-1960s tracks by the band appeared on a compilation CD album: *Look at the Sun: Precious Seconds thought gone from the British Underground 1967-1970*. They were part of a number of recordings for Decca producer Mike Berry, in this case, the original "Without Her" and a cover of the Who's "Call Me Lightning", Other acts on the album include Elmer Gantry's Velvet Opera, Kaleidoscope, and the Fleur de Lys.

In the spirit of the times, soul band St Louis Checks changed their name to the Magic Roundabout, although despite the shift towards the newer American sounds, there was also "vintage" rock & roll at Fratton's Railway Hotel with Southern Sounds & Apex Four. On 12 January 1968, the *Evening News* featured a major story "LSD Danger to Unborn Innocents" under the regular by-line "Civic Commentary" by VG Pafford, *Evening News'* Chief Reporter. He reported information from USA, via Portsmouth's Senior Officer for Mental Health that the "horror drug… LSD, can have similar dread effects on the babies…as those of thalidomide". It was not true.

The folk scene was not quite so busy as it had been, but the Guildhall offered the Dubliners in January, then Jon Isherwood, Pat Nelson, Diz Dizley and the Strawberry Hill Boys, while Bert Jansch appeared solo at Havant's Jug of Punch in February. There was also a March concert at the Oddfellows Hall starring Sandy Denny and the return of the Strawberry Hill Boys. Folk-blues performer Gerry Lockran was at the Railway Hotel, followed in May, by Roy Harper and Diz Disley, while Shirley Collins and the Tinkers appeared at the Jug of Punch. Duke Ellington's Band had brought stardust to the Guildhall in 1967 but big jazz events were becoming increasingly rare, although Maynard Ferguson's Big Band came from the USA to the Guildhall.

At Highbury Technical College, the students booked Amen Corner who failed to arrive. The Pretty Things substituted but Skip Bifferty stole the show and Harlem Speakeasy also appeared. Rikki Farr's Brave New World opened a licensed bar and took an increasing eclectic approach; the club featured the Amboy Dukes, the Herd and Ten Years After; invited Jon Isherwood to run Sunday folk nights and offered jazz acts like Dakota Staton, Stan Tracey and Tubby Hayes. The club also booked more soulful Birdcage-type performers like the Vagabonds, the Carl Douglas Stampede and Chris Farlowe. Some of us who had been regulars in the classic days were turning away from the mod fashions and musical genres, but there were others who stuck with the danceable soul and ska and suits – one of their favourite venues became the Marina (formerly Ricky's Club) on Goldsmith Avenue.

The variety at the Brave New World continued. The *Evening News* carried an advertisement in early April 1968 for the club, now including "Papa Joe's Speakeasy Bar" – the Birdcage was not licensed – with free entry on Thursday for the DJ now known as 'Pete Brady', and on Friday for Errol Bruce; two guys who seemed to come-and-go somewhat. The next three nights carried an admission charge: on Saturday, pop/rock with Lace, Sunday's Folk Night with Jon Isherwood presenting the Singing Postman, and Monday night's Modern Jazz with Humphrey Lyttleton and singer Elkie Brooks, after which Tuesday was closed and Wednesday was again free entry for "Rikki Farr's Off Night". It was very mixed and no longer offered the clear identity of the Birdcage, although a notable residency would begin on the following Thursday with the arrival in Portsmouth of Leicester's finest, Family. They are remembered with great affection around the city. Other acts of that kind that came to the new club included John Peel as compere for Blossom Toes and Gary Farr, Spooky Tooth, and Julie Driscoll and Brian Auger. The latter two acts and Zoot Money also played the Guildhall, and in April so did the Bee Gees with Grapefruit and Dave Dee, Dozy, Beaky, Mick & Tich. It was a strong period for mainstream pop for concerts there, including Gene Pitney with Don Partridge, Status Quo and Simon Dupree & the Big Sound, then the Four Freshmen and Scaffold followed by Englebert Humperdinck and one-man-band Don Partridge. At the end of April, Duane Eddy came with the Chantelles, and in early May, Johnny Cash and June Carter, the Statler Brothers and Carl Perkins. Two weeks later saw the Seekers and Russ Conway, while Julie Felix, Manfred Mann and Lace entertained students from Milton's College of Education at Clarence Pier.

The 'new' Indigo Vat revived in Hampshire Terrace and was listed among local clubs by the *Evening News* along with the (no longer Soul) Parlour, the Incredible Black Cat, Paradise Found, Manor Court Youth Club in Drayton and the Locarno. Coconut Mushroom appeared at the Brave New World where "jazz & folk look like folding" and the club's application for a late licence was rejected. Light Emporium appeared at the Parlour with Blossom Toes (Friday) and Fire (Sunday) who – like Coconut Mushroom – were said to have signed to Apple. Chris Ryder and Mick Gill of Cherry Smash joined England who "aimed to play west coast music". A month later Spinner suggested that England were "going down extremely well with student audiences (who) seem to appreciate west coast sounds more than most fans". Meanwhile their former vocalist Chris West was rehearsing with Tangerine Slyde. Julie Felix returned to the Guildhall on the first day of June, and locally, the debut by local blues band Chicago's Insolence at the Incredible Black Cat was well received. The Savoy promoted a Charity night on Thursday 13 June featuring no less than twelve groups and two lightshows. The main acts were RCA recording band Skip Bifferty, the Mojos and the (British) Amboy Dukes.

Spinner previewed Rikki Farr's Apache promotion, with Traffic, Family and Spooky Tooth in the open air at the end of South Parade Pier, promising a contribution from Martin & Geoff's Light Emporium to provide "off-beat atmospheres". The tickets were 10/- (50p) and Spinner subsequently praised the "success of (this) experimental show which attracted a gate of 2,500" despite the fact that for various safety reasons the main pier lights had to remain on and the lightshow could not operate effectively – many of us have fond memories of that very fine evening. Spooky Tooth soon returned with Fairport Convention, Skip Bifferty and England at the Guildhall, while Glass Menagerie and Terry Reid appeared at the Brave New World, as DJ Erroll Bruce departed.

August opened with a variety of visiting acts visiting the city including Amen

Corner at the Locarno, Blossom Toes and Elmer Gantry's Velvet Opera at the Parlour, and ska band the Skatalites with the Motives on the Solent Beat Cruise. Despite some interesting acts booked, the Brave New World never emulated the success of the Birdcage and finally closed in late September 1968, to become briefly a mainstream nightclub, renamed the Pack; I would play there with my new band in 1969, partly as support to a transvestite drag act! Rikki Farr, with the Foulk Brothers, shifted his attention to the first and smallest of the three Isle of Wight Festivals, entitled "The Great South Coast Bank Holiday Pop Festivity", which ran from 6pm on 31 August until the following morning, and featured Jefferson Airplane, the Move, Arthur Brown, Plastic Penny, the Pretty Things, Tyrannosaurus Rex, Fairport Convention, Aynsley Dunbar Retaliation and others. The *Evening News* described it as "the Festival that became a fiasco", criticising poor refreshments and toilets, technical "breakdowns" – notably the Move's speakers and Airplane's light show – and boredom, while adding "experimental sounds in pop are laudable but 16 hours of the same sound can prove tedious". The *NME* ran the headline "It really was Hell at times at Godshill: But Jefferson got big reception". Sadly, I missed the first visit of a San Francisco band to this part of the world as I was with Harlem Speakeasy on a weekend of gigs around Manchester and Stockport.

Spinner updated local readers with the news that "after three months of constant rehearsal, a new group, Heaven, makes its debut at the weekend", playing "uncommercial material…(which) can be vaguely described as that of Blood, Sweat & Tears crossed with Electric Flag". They included former members of the Inspiration, Soul Society and Universal Trash band and would soon be described as "Portsmouth's home-grown Family", becoming one of the finest of the new-style bands around the city. Other visitors to Portsmouth in September, were Skip Bifferty (the Parlour), the Small Faces, Simon Dupree & Big Sound, and Madeline Bell with two shows at the Guildhall, plus the Nice, Family and Pretty Things (Rikki Farr's Apache Promotions) at the same venue, tickets 10/- (50p). In early October, Free, were at the Parlour – their first club gig in the city. Sadly, when "many fans turned up" for Pink Floyd and the Deviants at Highbury College, neither group arrived, so Coconut Mushroom and Tangerine Slyde entertained the students instead.

In mid-November 1968, a couple of months after the closure of his Brave New World, Rikki Farr opened a new Sunday night 'Blues' Club at Kimbells with Pete Bardens' Village. The club was advertised as "all very freaky" with Irish band Taste the following week. Even more 'freaky' was an *Evening News* report on 21 November 1968, that "a youth and a girl walked in the roadway in Elm Grove, Southsea. Later the girl and group of youths…waved their arms and shouted 'this is a freak-out man' and 'we love the fuzz'" The girl was charged with obstructing the highway.

During the summer months, Harlem Speakeasy got to be pals with Tangerine Slyde who had the good fortune to secure a number of appearances at Covent Garden's Middle Earth, which had succeeded UFO as the club at the heart of the London's counterculture. Our double-wheel-base Ford Transit was posher than their old van and on a couple of occasions they used ours to go to London and I accompanied Richie and acted with him, as a roadie. On another (rare) free Saturday, Martin and I hitched up to the club, but sadly, while I enjoyed going there, the only act I recall seeing was the musical version of Hapshash & the Coloured Coat – as a band, they were very good designers. Mick Legg, however, reminded me that we went on the night they supported Tim Buckley and Roy Harper too, but I certainly missed the Slyde's support spot to Captain Beefheart which on the whole they were not fond of, but I am sure I would have loved. Five years later I saw him in the most magnificent form at Southampton University. I have mentioned another occasion when I certainly saw Roy Harper which was the first free concert in Hyde Park. The weather was perfect and the line-up very interesting with Harper, plus early Jethro Tull (*This Was*) who impressed me with their (then) jazz/blues feel, the elfin duo Tyrannosaurus Rex and Dave Gilmour, fairly early in his time with Pink Floyd. The latter seemed perfect for a summer's afternoon in the park.

In my scrapbook, I kept an *Observer* article "The Grand Tour Turn On" about the young travellers taking the 'hippie trail' to the east. It was never a possibility for me while I was committed to my bands, although in truth I doubt I would have enjoyed it, but my pals Jim & Liz Lush and Harry Odey went, I think in 1970, and we waved them goodbye on Portsmouth & Southsea station. In part, the article was interesting for its references to Zen and other eastern religions which were becoming one important, if gentler and more reflective aspect of the counterculture. There was a mystical soundtrack of sorts from a couple of new albums that most of us listened to, Pink Floyd's *A Saucerful of Secrets* and the (new) Moody Blues' *In Search of a Lost Chord* including the mantra "Om". *Melody Maker*, unconvinced by all this, suggested another approach to enlightenment was to "down eight pints of draught cider", adding that they did not want the Moody Blues to take themselves "too seriously". The Yardbirds split, leaving guitarist Jimmy Page to start a new band that would fairly soon shift the focus away from the more meditative side of things, while another fine guitarist Jimi Hendrix and his Experience released the new album *Electric Ladyland*. The Rolling Stones, after working 'for' Jean-Luc Godard took more control of their moving images for their television *Rock & Roll Circus*, the last time Brian Jones appeared with the band.

They were not satisfied with their performance however, and it was never screened at the time, although it is now available on DVD. Some women singers had notable releases around this time, including Aretha Franklin with her hit single "I Say a Little Prayer" and two white singers who modelled themselves somewhat on that sound, Dusty Springfield with her American recording, "Son of a Preacher Man" and Janis Joplin with her band Big Brother & the Holding Company and the album *Cheap Thrills*; sporting a cartoon cover, courtesy of the underground's master illustrator Robert Crumb.

As with the first Isle of Wight Festival, I was gigging elsewhere in the country when the two Californian bands, the Doors and Jefferson Airplane appeared in a Middle Earth promoted gig at the Roundhouse in September, but my pal Martin went around his 19th birthday, and came back with tales of enjoying the whole thing, and in particular the theatrical performances by Jim Morrison of songs like "The Unknown Soldier" and "the End". In *NME,* Nick Logan praised the Airplane's "cleverly layered" sound, adding "the famous lightshow ... deserves star billing of its own".

There was much that was positive and enriching in this new world, but not everything was sweetness and light. At the end of October 1968, *International Times* published their second birthday edition and announced that with "frayed tempers and a rather sick-looking bank account" they had "moved to new headquarters" but could not afford to continue publishing 24 pages. At around the same time, Middle Earth was struggling to survive and suffering from police raids which led it to threaten that *any* drug use – even by registered addicts – or drug-dealing "will be reported to the police". There was also a report of a falling out between artist/writer Jeff Nuttall and those organizing a celebration of Apollinaire at the ICA over whether Nuttall should be permitted to exhibit a bucket of shit. There was of course still room for tits on page 3 of *International Times* (belonging to a naked, pregnant woman), while DJ Simon Stable urged people to reject the October anti-Vietnam demo and go instead to a free Blackhill concert.

As 1968 and (no longer 'Harlem') Speakeasy approached their last days, a variety of recording acts appeared in the city including Blonde on Blonde at the Parlour, hit recording trio the Gun (with Speakeasy) at Kimbells, and singer-songwriter Al Stewart at the Railway Hotel Folk Club. There was a second Lord Mayor's Charity Dance at Kimbells featuring Elmer Gantry's Velvet Opera, with local acts Heaven, Gold Dust, and Virgin Circle, while Alan Bown! Fairport Convention and the Idle Race played at South Parade Pier, and Free were at the Parlour again with Chalk Farm, by now more often known as the Oasis, and Manor Court's Christmas Dance in the school hall featured a return for Alan Bown! the (reformed) Inspiration, and DJ Steve Hamilton.

Family appeared at the Kimbells Blues Club on 22 December and on the following night there was acoustic blues at the Railway with Gerry Lockran and Cliff Aungier. The Jug of Punch would start 1969 in similar vein with west country folk-blues player Mike Cooper.

The publication of Spinner's Annual Pop Poll reflected the variety of styles on Portsmouth's live scene and the relative demise of the previously dominant soul acts, with (in order) the most popular visitors being: 1-Family, 2-Amen Corner, 3-Alan Bown! 4-Gun, 5-Blossom Toes. It seemed that like the Birdcage, the Vagabonds and Action had disappeared.

PINK FLOYD

In the dressing rooms at South Parade Pier.

Photo: Nigel Grundy

I SEE THE LIGHTS

I n March 1968, *International Times* (number 27) published a "Special Pop Supplement", in which they described Berkeley's finest, Country Joe & the Fish, as

> The most evocative of all the West Coast groups, with two worthwhile albums … Distinguished by imagination of lyrics and simplicity of sound. Listen to "Eastern Jam" and "Porpoise Mouth".

Country Joe & the Fish would arrive in Portsmouth twelve months later and strange as it might seem, again in the early 21ˢᵗ century, as they began an interesting longer relationship with the city. Among other American bands in the article, the Byrds were called the "original West Coast acid-rock group", the vocals on the first Big Brother & the Holding Company's LP were "shrill to the point of ludicracy (*sic*)", the Butterfield Blues Band were "certainly the best white blues group in the world", Clear Light were "slightly second rate", the Fugs were "the most outrageous group in the world", Jefferson Airplane were "the West Coast sound personified", whereas Love were "probably the best West Coast group". West coast was then a particularly popular generic term, covering quite a variety of music, including as we have seen, one or two of Portsmouth's groups. In the supplement, Moby Grape's hyped launch (five singles released simultaneously) "wasn't worth it", the Misunderstood "definitely were", and the Mothers of Invention were, after the Beatles, "probably the world's most experimental and progressive group". We could now read about these bands and we could obtain the records, as well as hearing them through John Peel on Radio One. The choice was ours.

There were mentions for other American bands, the Doors and – briefly – Pearls Before Swine, Quicksilver Messenger Service, Vanilla Fudge, the "eerie" Velvet Underground and the West Coast Pop Art Experimental Art band who it was suggested veered between Bartok, with "very original" statements and "a state dangerously near psychedelic muzak". Others mentioned included a number of amplified blues guitarists/singers Albert King, Alexis Korner, BB King, Buddy Guy, soul man Otis Redding, and a range of singer-song-writers: Arlo Guthrie, Bob Dylan, Donovan, the Incredible String Band, Janis

Ian, Mimi & Richard Farina, Simon & Garfunkel, and the three 'Tims' – Hardin, Rose and Buckley – with the latter praised for his album *Goodbye and Hello* and its "wonderful arrangements, well produced, well sung".

The British bands mentioned were Arthur Brown, Aynsley Dunbar Retaliation, Beatles, Bee Gees, Bonzo Dog, Chicken Shack, Cream, Dantalian's Chariot, Deviants, Fairport Convention, Fleetwood Mac, Grapefrut, Jimi Hendrix, John Mayall, the Move, the Nice, Pink Floyd, Procul Harum, Rolling Stones, Spencer Davis Group, Soft Machine, Tintern Abbey, Tomorrow, Traffic and the Who. The Beatles and Stones both came to Portsmouth in 1963/4, and virtually all the other acts appeared in Portsmouth between 1967-1969 – mostly at the Birdcage, Brave New World or Kimbells, and a few in concert. Some including Fairport Convention, the Move, Pink Floyd, Tomorrow and the Who visited on a number of occasions, and the Who returned to film *Tommy* in the city in 1974.

Meanwhile the two other American acts listed are particularly significant. The Grateful Dead were described as "the leading San Francisco Acid-Rock group (and)... very much part of the Hippie community", although *International Times* suggested their first album (released March 1967) "falls somewhat short of making it". It was an album of songs, with their own treatment, mostly taken straight from the old acoustic blues, jug band and country songs of the Mississippi Sheiks, Gus Cannon's Jug Stompers, the first Sonny Boy Williamson and Obray Ramsey. More than any other American psychedelic album, this one illustrates very clearly the origins of the new music in something old enough to be pre-rock & roll, or what Greil Marcus called the "Old Weird America".

These days it is possible to find suggestions that in a musical context, the term psychedelic was coined by Roky Erickson of the 13th Floor Elevators rather than by someone in San Francisco. Whether it is true or not (does it matter?) it became an increasingly common term following the summer of love. In the supplement, it was just one of a number of terms used in an attempt to describe the new music. The various, often interchangeable terms, and representative acts were identified as:

> West Coast: Big Brother & Holding Company, Byrds, Clear Light, Country Joe & the Fish, Jefferson Airplane, Love, Richard & Mimi Farina
> Acid-Rock: Byrds, Grateful Dead
> Psychedelic: Dantalian's Chariot, Pink Floyd
> Underground: Deviants, Soft Machine,
> Folk-Rock: Fairport Convention, Simon & Garfunkel
> Progressive: The Gods, Mothers of Invention, Tintern Abbey
> UFO-type Club Group: Tomorrow

Presumably the last of those descriptions was limited to British bands – and it seems that was the case also with underground, which was a term used mostly on this side of the Atlantic. It is quite a range of terms beyond say, pop or beat group or perhaps (still) rock & roll, although there was no attempt to define the terms. Presumably it was assumed that anyone reading the piece would understand, and if they did not there was relatively little point in reading it in the first place.

In the same edition of *International Times*, the "New Deviants" announced in a "Mean and Filthy" management advert, that they had formed from the breakup of the old Social Deviants. With front man Mick Farren involved in *International Times,* and in 1970 in Worthing's "Phun City Festival" and the assault on the fences at the third Isle of Wight Festival there was unsurprisingly a 'political' edge to the band and both they and Soft Machine were regulars at the UFO Club. There again, so were the Pink Floyd, although they were rarely seen in those days of Syd Barrett as overtly political – but was there a distinction implied in this article, between their Pink Floyd's psychedelia and the "Acid-Rock" of the Grateful Dead? We cannot know for sure.

I became very fond of much of this music, and while I retained my commitment to the blues and jazz, this was perhaps the one period in my life where I paid greater attention to music that was predominantly white and contemporary – and British as well as American. My fondness for much of it has stayed with me, even when I revert to my life-long love of black American sounds and styles.

If parts of 1968's revolutionary spirit somewhat passed me by, other events such as Portsmouth's Dance of Words, and Arts Workshop or the Hyde Park Free Concert, planted the seeds of ideas that would resonate with me over the years. The national and local music and social scene was changing rapidly through 1968, although with regard to politics, I have found little evidence of any significant local emulation of the activism in other parts of the world – which is not to say that people from Portsmouth did not travel to London and elsewhere to participate in whatever might be happening. On the whole however, even the local students were pretty restrained – for example in February 1969, the College of Technology's Students' Union voted "overwhelmingly" against 'sit-ins' or marches in support of the action at the LSE. Some students involved in that meeting reported that the Civil Engineering students had deliberately "invaded" it, "acting like storm troopers" and opposing any action. In the same month by contrast, 100 student protesters in the city disrupted a speech by right-wing MP, Patrick Wall which had been organized by the College of Technology's Conservative Association.

While we were on the road in 1968, there were some days when we could barely afford to eat properly, so as far as I can recall I was only buying magazines occasionally. I am pretty sure that I saw *Oz* most regularly when Martin, by then studying graphics, bought it; certainly, the online archive reveals some familiar covers and articles through its first three years. My preference for *International Times* was, I think, to do with the range of articles and ideas, and after the first five editions, a greater focus on music – *Oz* did not seem quite so committed to the latter.

I still have the *International Times'* music 'special' of March 1968. The cover has a stoned Mickey Mouse grinning and holding a smoking joint, while page three offered not one, but two pairs of tits – eat your heart out Mr Murdoch. On the same page (Barry) Miles' column declared that "the age of 'economic man' draws to a close" and described America as "a society in the last death throes of its existence". Perhaps, someone should tell Trump. There was a full page on the uprisings in Paris and other European undergrounds, while (after more tits) the centre spread was like an embryonic *Time Out*. As well as the supplement, there were lots of adverts for new albums and singles, while another for London's One Stop Records began with a quote from the *I Ching*

> The beginnings of all things, lies still in the beyond
> In the form of ideas that have yet to become real

I am still not sure which new releases that was all about, but around this time I began to be intrigued by the increasing, and more serious coverage of what might best be described as 'eastern philosophies', although like many others, in those early days of discovery, I skipped about between such as Zen and the Tao, the *Bhagavad Gita,* Herman Hesse, Aldous Huxley and Jung. While *International Times* took a few editions to embrace popular music with anything much more than adverts, from the outset it was happy to mix politics and spirituality. The first edition of 1967 (number 6) offered Norman Mailer on the Vietnam War, Allen Ginsberg on the cerebral cortex and Paul McCartney interviewed about fame, spirituality, drugs and electronic music. In the next edition (30 January 1967) John Michell wrote about Flying Saucers and the coming of the Aquarian Age, while the headlines called for the arrest of the Home Secretary; in mid-February, Allen Ginsberg offered "Reflections on the Mantra", Gary Snyder on "Buddhism and the Coming Revolution" and editor Tom McGrath on "Racism in Cuba" – all alongside an interview with Pete Townshend. While I retained my loyalty to *Melody Maker* as a source of information about music, this mixture was all rather new and exciting.

With respect to these spiritual and 'New Age' ideas, I understood very little initially but I was starting out on something that has stayed with me and become increasingly significant in my life. At some point in 1969 I bought the classic Richard Willhelm translation of the *I Ching* (introduction by Carl Jung) – probably the only version then available in Britain, from somewhere in London. I doubt if it was on sale in Portsmouth, even though back then we had more bookshops then than we do now; despite a massive increase over those years in student numbers. I still have that copy of the *I Ching*, and now many other versions alongside it, and I still make use of them quite regularly.

In the March, *International Times,* John Peel who had recently joined Radio London, wrote in his column about some noisy new bands, Blue Cheer and Steppenwolf, and ended sadly by reporting the death of his hamster, concluding "remember, Dandelion loved you too". Did the punks ever know about this? On the back page, the subscription form wanted £3 per year. There was a report about a police raid on Middle Earth but also an advert for forthcoming gigs there with Fleetwood Mac, Alexis Korner, Jeff Beck, Tyrannosaurus Rex, Fusion, Family, Juniors Eyes and Pink Floyd.

I have another copy from August 1968 with Fidel Castro on the cover ("Happy Birthday Revolution"), in which page 3 carried a full-page reader's questionnaire ("Head Quest") about drug use. Opposite that was a news item about a lacto-vegetarian community and the Vegan Communities Movement, including newsletters from both groups. There was too an advert for Notting Hill's "Macrobiotic Restaurant" with "meals from 3/6d cooked according to the Zen principles of Yin & Yang", the Bardic and Druid Order was alerting people to a celebration of the Festival of LUGHNASADH, while a Surreal pantomime was being prepared for a North Devon beach. There was an article about travelling to Kathmandu, and various advertising sections included "In the Sticks" with events in Manchester, Hastings, Brighton and the Sunbury Festival – which had moved from the earlier years in Richmond and Windsor – but sadly nothing in Portsmouth. Reviews included *Saucerful of Secrets* and the third Country Joe & the Fish album, *Together,* plus William Burrough's *The Soft Machine* and a book of poems by Leonard Cohen. The back page proposed that *"The Yellow Submarine* marks a real milestone in the development of the British cinema". Did it?

In October 1968, around my 19th birthday, I could read articles in the latest edition by a sexologist, another about Black Power, plus the new 'hippie' musical *Hair,* which had arrived in Shaftesbury Avenue from the USA. In addition, on page 2 of the edition from 4-17 October was a short piece about Portsmouth:

> PORTSMOUTH artswork coordinates, promotes, explores, emanating mainly from the college. There have been several

mixed media occurrences of varying size and success in the past six months. Planned for the coming months are The People Show; an underground film festival with Bob Cobbing; revolutionary dialogue/provocation; and Exploding Galaxy exploration and localized events".

"Help and participation was invited" and the address given, 111 High Street, Old Portsmouth, was then the location of the School of Architecture and down the road from my old school. Since it was October 1968, it is perhaps unsurprising that there was much talk of 'revolution', including "Tariq Ali's crowd calling for a demonstration", and Norman Mailer on the Chicago Democratic Convention. Jolly John Peel noticed that although "the sky is overcast … the clouds are leaving my thoughts. Let us exchange sunshine soon. It is good to be a part of you". I am not sure that the Fall ever made use of that.

Another underground DJ, Simon Stable, offered a column plus a 'Top Ten' of "Underground Albums", headed by Simon & Garfunkel's *Bookends,* followed by Cream, Canned Heat, Moody Blues, Fleetwood Mac, John Mayall, Ten Years After, Doors, the Nice, and Pink Floyd. The criteria were not clear (sales from his shop perhaps?) but if the list meant anything, then it was more British than American, and more (white) blues than psychedelic. That edition also carried a profile of the delightful Jo-Ann Kelly, the woman with "the most powerful female blues voice in the country", who visited Portsmouth's folk clubs on a number of occasions (and the Guildhall once). Meanwhile, Middle Earth was advertising its move from Covent Garden to the Roundhouse, with a selection of bands, including the Grateful Dead on my birthday. I was not there, because Harlem Speakeasy got one of those (theoretically) prestigious gigs at the legendary Flamingo in Soho. We got there to discover it was now wholly a Black club and for entirely understandable reasons they hated us. We had to disappear out the back door at the interval, and return in the early hours for our gear. I was frightened.

In the last weeks of Speakeasy, with various personnel changes, I became the sole (but no longer soul) singer, and we started working on covers of very different material by bands like Family and Spooky Tooth. By the end of 1968, even provincial Britain had experienced 18 months of versions of psychedelia in the charts, thanks to the Beatles, Procul Harum and the rest, and some of us were growing familiar with the original thing from San Francisco. There was now clearly a strong group of British bands playing regularly in the hipper venues and on the London club scene, most were playing their own material or covers of relatively obscure stuff and they were getting plays on John Peel – none of which identified them as strictly psychedelic, by which I mean simply, that their recordings either invoke the sense of 'tripping' or had been made under those conditions – or perhaps both

Over the years, I have come to the somewhat unadventurous conclusion that my three favourite psychedelic albums are all by classic Haight Ashbury bands: *Electric Music for the Mind & Body* by Country Joe & the Fish, *Aoxomoxoa* by the Grateful Dead and *After Bathing at Baxters* by Jefferson Airplane. There are others of course, and sometimes they are just individual tracks such as "Third Stone from the Sun" by Jimi Hendrix or "Cloud Song" by the United States of America, and there are even a few British albums – for example, Steve Hillage's *Rainbow Dome Music* – but while there was a great deal of exciting and challenging new music from this country at that time, there is not that much British music that I think of as clearly psychedelic. Incidentally it does not necessarily follow that because I define the recordings in that way, they are my favourite albums or even the best offerings by those artists – in the case of *Aoxomoxoa,* for example, however much I like it, that is not the case.

I have a real fondness for music that I consider psychedelic but I realise it is not to everyone's taste, and there were other bands and recordings at the time that began to shift popular music a long way, without being or wishing to be considered psychedelic. In Britain, these were for example the early Fairport Convention and Jethro Tull, Family, Traffic, Spooky Tooth and others who for convenience might be defined as the first generation of British 'rock' bands – assuming of course that we feel the need to define them by genre at all. Perhaps one of the strengths of that period is that the best of these bands defied any *precise* categorization, although that does not suit the record labels, stores and marketing men. For a brief period, these bands were defined as underground which is all very well until they become popular ('overground'?). Even rock seems a misleading label if we are to include Fairport from *Unhalfbricking* days, Pentangle, the Incredible String Band or the awesome Van Morrison album, *Astral Weeks*. With the exception of some of the popular British blues bands, it was innovative however, and even in that more 'rooted' world, John Mayall increasingly wrote his own songs, while my favourite British blues band, the original Fleetwood Mac, soon moved away from their 'Thames Delta' sound into more adventurous things.

In this context, Harlem Speakeasy had played mostly tried and tested live material, and although having our roots in black American music was not essentially different from the starting points of members of Traffic, Pink Floyd, Jethro Tull or many of the other most popular live bands of that time, we were playing catch up with these older, more experienced guys. Despite including a number of very talented musicians, we were not yet sufficiently mature musically to challenge for recognition in the new world. Apart from the flip-side of our single and our never-to-be-released second record, all we played were covers, which was no longer the case with most of the major bands.

Around Portsmouth in 1967, probably the main influences on what were called the first local west coast bands were Love, and the Byrds – in particular tracks from their third and fourth albums *Fifth Dimension* (1966) and *Younger than Yesterday* (1967). The latter, had what we would now recognize as psychedelic sounds and lyrics and its release in February pre-dates *Sgt Pepper's Lonely Hearts Club Band* by some months. Interestingly too, *Jefferson Airplane Takes Off* appeared in 1966 and their first with the classic line-up, *Surrealistic Pillow* also in February 1967, the Grateful Dead's first, eponymous, album appeared in March 1967, and the first Country Joe & the Fish album in May 1967 – followed by the Beatles' contribution in June, alongside the first from Moby Grape. Outside any strict definition of psychedelia – or indeed pop – there was also that extraordinary first album by the Velvet Underground and Nico. In America, fanned somewhat by Ralph Gleason in *Rolling Stone,* there seemed to be a creative tension between the style of the Velvet Underground and Gleason's beloved San Francisco bands, but in Britain we were less concerned with those regional rivalries and embraced anything of interest – and the Velvet Underground were most certainly that. We heard the first 'Banana' album fairly quickly, not least via John Peel – it is a myth that nobody heard it back then; indeed, in late 1969, my next band, Rosemary, would spend some time recording tapes with a visiting young woman from America, who was singing her version of "Pale Blue Eyes", from the Velvet Underground's third, eponymous album (released March 1969).

Among the other American influences on local bands in those earlier psychedelic days were the Lovin' Spoonful (notably with Sons of Man who were shifting from rhythm & blues in their later days), the Doors, whose first album appeared in January 1967, and a number of harmony acts including the Beach Boys, the Lemon Pipers ("Green Tambourine"), the Turtles and the Association – particularly admired by Tangerine Slyde. There were however, very few examples of the core San Francisco bands providing material for their counterparts in Portsmouth, but there was a general move away from the previous focus on black American R&B and soul, and in some cases, it led to bands developing a rather more 'English' sound.

Among other influences, in early 1968, CBS released the first rock sampler album, *The Rock Machine Turns You On*. Alongside tracks by acts familiar to British audiences such as Bob Dylan, the Byrds, the Zombies, Moby Grape and Simon & Garfunkel, were a number of newer names, all with their own albums including Spirit, Peanut Butter Conspiracy, the bluesy Taj Mahal, two examples of the new jazz-rock sound of Blood Sweat & Tears and Electric Flag, singer-songwriters Leonard Cohen, Roy Harper and Tim Rose, plus the electronic experiments of the United States of America. The final track "Flames" was by Elmer Gantry's Velvet Opera – a short-lived British outfit who enjoyed some good nights playing live in Portsmouth. Pretty well everybody on the Portsmouth scene bought this sampler or knew someone who did, so again we got to hear these new acts and often someone would then buy the whole album by that artist (which was the idea of course). Given my blues bias I loved Taj Mahal, but I can recall pals owning albums by Spirit, Moby Grape and the United States of America among others.

The arrival of such records provided material for local bands to cover, but for them to seek to progress beyond local recognition, it became increasingly important to begin writing. To do that was also an interesting challenge that offered a considerable degree of aesthetic pleasure to the bands, although it required audiences to engage with unfamiliar material. From 1968, this began to happen more regularly in Portsmouth, with one of the first examples, Heaven, playing songs written by the band – especially the very talented Brian Kemp, previously a keyboard player in the Inspiration, but now lead singer and bass guitarist.

Harlem Speakeasy split after that 13 December gig, by which time our bass player was Mick Legg, also of Tangerine Slyde, and he was active in bringing together members of the two bands, and adding drummer Dave Pittard – one time very stylish Birdcage mod, but now rather more resembling a cross between Gandalf and Buffalo Bill. He would be a significant influence on the musical direction of the band and a mate for life. John Lytle (keyboards, guitar) and I came from Speakeasy – two-thirds of that band's songwriters, while our new band's approach, encouraged Steve Farrow (lead guitar) to start writing too. We called ourselves Rosemary – I've always wanted to claim it was after the Grateful Dead track but I believe it was probably a simpler reason closer to home, and it was a name that suited the pastoral tendencies of those times. In addition to the guys mentioned, Brian Grice had come with Steve from Tangerine Slyde, playing electric piano, so with two keyboards in the band, one of our early influences was Spooky Tooth – who we had seen as the VIPs at the Birdcage.

We started out playing mostly covers including that band's version of the Janis Ian song "Society's Child". In our earliest sets, other covers were mainly American including "Pat's Song" by Country Joe & the Fish, "Morning Glory" by Tim Buckley, "Love Me Two Times" by the Doors, "It Takes a Lot to Laugh" by Bob Dylan, "Apricot Brandy" by Rhinoceros, "Violets of Dawn" by Eric Andersen and a few old blues songs including "Spoonful", "Going Down Slow" and Bo Diddley's "Who Do You Love?"

These covers were less mainstream than the days of the local soul bands, who mostly performed similar songs, but despite our hint of difference, the question remained "so what?" What were our ambitions? Like many young bands, we wanted to move beyond the local scene; after all, three of us had already been full-time professionals and in my case, oddly, at that point I had more experience of that, than of being in a good regular local band. In addition, three of the guys had played quite regularly at Middle Earth and, having accompanied them, we had a taste for that scene alongside an excitement with the innovative and experimental spirit of the times. In particular, this offered opportunities to find an audience for music that would push us as much as them. If we remained a covers band, we could hardly compete with the top acts who were now writing virtually all their own material, all we might aspire to realistically were support spots in the clubs that were hiring those bands. In fact, over the 18 months of our existence, we played support to some of those new acts including Free (twice), the Edgar Broughton Band, the Deviants, Mott the Hoople, the Liverpool Scene, Atomic Rooster, Daddy Longlegs, Skin Alley and Junior's Eyes, as well as appearing down the bill at a couple of Festivals. But we wanted to stand alongside those bands, and while in Harlem Speakeasy, my years of watching the top British soul bands led me to doubt our credibility at that level, Rosemary was rather different. It was a band I quickly came to believe in, and a band still think might have 'made it' – and I was not the only one. In 2003, Portsmouth City Museum published an oral history of the local music scene, in which Steve Farrow – sadly no longer with us – said

> There have been a couple of bands I've been in that wrote their own material and one was in the late 1960s … called Rosemary … The song writing was good; the performances were good in their day and could probably match any band in England at the time (Stedman *et al*, 13)

It felt just like that. This was my first experience of being in a band that believed in itself and it made an incredible difference, even if I was not always confident yet about my vocals. Mick Legg, writing separately of the band, said, rather delightfully, in response to an online confession from DJ Pete Cross that he "could never work us out"

I could never work it out either. We were more of a social event than a solid beat band. We started out as a Spooky Tooth type band but soon evolved into something else entirely. My favourite band for material we did was Tangerine Slyde, but I really loved Rosemary because of the experimental nature of the music and I think we were the only local band that kept the same personnel from beginning to end. I had a hell of a lot of fun, met loads of great people and I'm grateful for that

Through my time in that band, I too learned so much that stood me in good stead over the years – not just musically. More broadly, after the successive fashions for American influenced genres like skiffle, rock & roll, rhythm & blues, and soul, all of which had excited me, we were trying to find an 'English' way of singing and playing. Richard Goldstein (2015) has suggested that

Pop music represented a certain idea of America to kids in other countries. In Britain, it meant funkiness and freedom from the propriety that confined them (51).

Maybe after a decade or more of drawing from all those thrilling Yanks, we were now sufficiently funky and free to 'do our thing'?

In Rosemary, we started writing, quickly and pretty prolifically. That had a consequence for us in terms of chasing gigs because there is no doubt that in part the flourishing of the nightclub/DJ/dancing/disco scene of the 1970s was a reaction against so many bands, national and local, playing more complicated songs that were often unfamiliar to audiences. Popular music does not attract a single, monolithic audience but among them are those whose preferences are for relatively unchallenging background 'muzak' during the day, and stuff to dance to at the weekends. Around Pompey a very clear example of a band that took the alternative route would be Gentle Giant, a cult 'prog' band of the 1970s with a number of albums released, who, in their previous incarnation, had been the very danceable, entertaining Simon Dupree & the Big Sound, reeling off the soul/Motown covers and enjoying a Top Ten hit record. Very soon, Rosemary's set consisted entirely of original songs too, which meant regular fans or those willing to listen hard might enjoy it, but the 'Friday night dancers' might not. It was, nonetheless, a strategy which briefly offered possibilities of real musical development as the 1960s drew to a close.

The audience that we pursued was a different one too from the days of Harlem Speakeasy, although to some extent it was one that was growing with us. It is often characterized simply as the college audience and if that is true to an extent, in terms of the newer venues, it ignores the majority who were not students who came to those gigs and followed bands like ours. Many of them had moved on from the mod scene and, particularly if they were working, had the money to go to gigs, buy albums and new clothes, score a bit of dope and maybe acid. That's how things were at the start of 1969 as in Portsmouth, we moved towards another summer of love. Indeed, however jaded things became in San Francisco and London, I've often thought that 1969 was perhaps *the* 'hippie' year in Portsmouth.

Beyond Portsmouth, it was more generally the year in which the transition in popular culture from mod was almost complete, with two utterly divergent options for those who were not simply moving towards, regular employment, and a life of quiet, domestic bliss. For those who still sought excitement and an involvement in a scene, it was pretty much a straight choice between a sharp very urban, rather macho post-mod/skinhead/casual look, dancing in particular to ska and soul. The alternative was a trip into the land of the hippies. In the 1960s, white British bands did not generally play ska, waiting for the next generation to find a creative outlet in that direction, but one of the clearest examples of a change from mod/soul to a British form of psychedelia is a 45rpm single by the Alan Bown! who sounded very different from the band that performed soul covers of Otis Redding, Willie Mitchell, Edwin Starr, the Impressions or the Temptations in their Birdcage days. The song is called "Toyland".

It opens with the sound effects of young kids at play, before we are told that Toyland is a place to go and blow your mind, in the company of a teddy bear, and a grey mouse, plus honey and buttercups. It is a mid-tempo song that starts with acoustic guitar and flute and the organ comes in and out, although there is little sign of Alan Bown's trumpet. As usual, vocalist Jess Roden gives a fine performance and the whole thing is catchy enough to have been a hit although it was not. It appeared as a track on the band's first studio album (1968) which also included the rather jolly, string-laden "We Can Help You", the orchestral/choral "You're Not in My Class", the mysterious, sometimes discordant "Storybook" and the shifting tempos and instrumentation of "Love is a Beautiful Thing" – it is perhaps no surprise that one of the band, John Helliwell, ended up in Supertramp. Lyrically some of this was (literally) kid's stuff, musically it was edging towards 'prog' before people were using the term.

It was also very English. For some reason, quite a lot of the new music on our side of the Atlantic was rather 'twee', drawing upon music hall (led by the Beatles), childhood, with lyrics about pixies, elves and Toyland, or funny stories about granny taking a trip to Hollywood. It could tend to be rather

Tolkienesque, a bit 'Alice in Wonderland', glimpses of Narnia perhaps, or at least the rural idyll of scarecrows, and little Emily playing games for May. It was not much like that in Haight Ashbury where the roots of American folk, blues, jazz and country were generally rather more visible – and broadly more to my tastes.

There was often a different sound too. While most of the new American bands emerged from a beatnik/acoustic folk scene, on the whole that was not the case in Britain; despite the tendency towards childlike lyrics, musically many of our bands had come thorough the jazz or rhythm & blues club scene and were accomplished players. In recent years, BBC4 has shown many compilations from its back catalogue, including in July 2016, an hour-long programme entitled "Psychedelic Rock at the BBC". It opened with the guitar-led Yardbirds and included the Who, Jimi Hendrix Experience, the Move and Cream, while there was also a number of bands and tracks featuring Hammond Organ, an instrument that owed much to the 1960s popularity of American jazz players such as Jimmy Smith, Jimmy McGriff, Big John Patton and of course the mods' darling, Booker T. The Hammond-led psychedelia in this programme, defined implicitly by the BBC, included Procul Harum, the Nice, Brian Auger Trinity (with Julie Driscoll), the Crazy World of Arthur Brown, Joe Cocker's Grease Band, the Small Faces, and the Moody Blues. Soft Machine, early favourites of the London counterculture were not in the show but might have been, adding another Hammond-based band and while some might wish to contest the idea that all of these bands and tracks can be defined as strictly psychedelic, they are indicative of the popular live acts around Britain in the late 1960s. Incidentally only one act on the entire show featured saxophones and they were the tongue-in-cheek 'Bonzos' – at the comedic end of anything remotely psychedelic. In America brass and reed sections would re-emerge through jazz-rock and jazz-funk, and they would have some influence on bands in Britain, including Portsmouth.

In addition to the rich sounds of the Hammond organs, most with Leslie speakers, there was the rather less substantial, if distinctive sound of the smaller keyboards like the Farfisa Duo which coloured the music of the early Pink Floyd and in America, Country Joe & the Fish and Sir Douglas Quintet ("She's About a Mover"). Given the guitar-dominated sound of the Bay Area, the Fish were pretty unusual in featuring that instrument on tracks from their first album, including "Not So Sweet Martha Lorraine", "Porpoise Mouth", "Section 43", "Love", "The Masked Marauder" and "Bass Strings". The Farfisa duo was also the organ that John Lytle played in my new band, Rosemary.

On some occasions, Rosemary were said to remind people somewhat of Pink Floyd or perhaps Love which is worth mentioning, not to make exaggerated claims, but to stress that however experimental we might have been in a local context, we were, in terms of instrumentation, style, gigs, audience and ambitions, operating within the context of the emerging rock scene. There was another more challenging, more 'radical' kind of musical experimentation back then with which we got slightly involved, not least because it had a significant thread in Portsmouth.

During 1968, in Portsmouth, the "Dance of Words" and the Arts Workshop were both College initiatives that had helped to offer new ideas and approaches around the city, and when the new academic year began in September 1968, there was another intriguing development at the College of Art – in its final independent year before Fine Art was taken into the new Polytechnic.

This was not merely a creative or cultural development but one that also embraced radical ideas in that 'political' year. Jeffrey Steele, a significant British systems painter and the new Head of Department, introduced an experimental music option to the fine art course with the support of Maurice Dennis who ran complementary studies but has also played banjo for decades in local traditional jazz bands. In the autumn of 1968, Ron Geesin, who would collaborate with Pink Floyd's Roger Waters on the soundtrack to the film, *The Body*, arrived as a lecturer – followed in 1969 by Gavin Bryars. Together, they explored the collaborative art/music practices of America's Black Mountain College (notably by John Cage), as well as the European avant-garde (Schoenberg, Webern, Stockhausen etc). There were a series of visiting lectures from Morton Feldman, John Tilbury, John White, Cornelius Cardew and others, with Cardew's Scratch Orchestra and Marxist-informed politics influential on the work.

During 1969, the students offered some Thursday lunchtime performances of newer music such as Terry Riley's 'minimalist' composition "In C", with some keyboards and amplifiers borrowed from local groups, including Rosemary. This enabled me to attend (although I believe attendance was unrestricted) and opened my ears to musical possibilities beyond those of the current rock scene. It was thrilling and enlightening and it was happening in the heart of Portsmouth. Subsequently, the better-known Portsmouth Sinfonia emerged from this project, involving many students and guests, including Brian Eno. In a spirit that was similar to that of Cardew's Scratch Orchestra, those players had to be either non-musicians, or to play an instrument that was unfamiliar to them.

An article in *Beat Instrumental* (September 1968) about Geesin, described how this new music was emerging through processes that produced "sometimes startling and always interesting sounds", and suggested that his recent album

A Raise of Eyebrows had "baffled many" but also led to some "disciples". They described the recording as

> Made up of humour, grunts, satire and poetry all held together by Geesin's musical virtuosity on guitar, 15-string contra guitar, six-string banjo, oil-drum, milk bottles, piano and many other implements not usually associated with music (14-15)

Geesin remained in an on-off relationship with the Polytechnic/University in Portsmouth for decades, and we worked together briefly in the same department in the early 21st century. In 1969, Gavin Bryars also arrived in Portsmouth and Steele and his colleagues began to develop their practice. Having begun in May 1968, Steele's retrospective account (1976) of this work focused on its political significance. He suggested the musical avant-garde of the late 1960s revolved around a major tension between the post-Schoenberg/Webern European tradition and the Zen influenced, often more playful work of John Cage in the USA – both of which had strong links with painting. The tension for Steele was essentially between "structure (and) academicism or mysticism". He then made a special claim for the art college work of 1969 and the early 1970s, based on the "dialectical resolution" of these issues, "in the context of provincial isolation and naiveté which gave Portsmouth music of that time its seductive quality" (297).

While the new work developed, some of the art lecturers were not particularly pleased that the music, performance and conceptual work had shifted from 'complementary' studies to occupy some students' whole time. Jeffery Steele who still lives in Southsea, stood down as Head of Painting to engage in the teaching and those debates, and suggested that these conflicts were typical of attempts across the fine art world to find a multi-disciplinary equivalent to cybernetics or the hope of "something comparable" to recent, "progressive" work in the USA's Black Mountain College.

Steele remained very interested in the established working practices of musicians of "very diverse opinions and temperaments (who) are accustomed to working together effectively", generally a key difference between (solitary) fine artists and (collaborative) performing artists (298). In the broader city context, here was an opportunity for Portsmouth to pursue aesthetically what other places had done in more overtly political/social ways, although it was of course a much smaller experiment. Encouragingly, it was not a project behind the closed doors of the academy. Most of the initiatives came from the students and a number of them mixed with some of us in Rosemary who came to see what was happening with our keyboards. In a separate initiative at the college, on one occasion Rosemary were provided with a whole day's rehearsal space in the graphics studio, in exchange for which the design students made photographs, films, posters and mock-up covers in a 'band' project.

Rosemary and the art/music students exchanged ideas, shared attitudes and equipment and entertained each other. Rosemary and other local bands played at the Art College dances which were very popular in the city, and members of Rosemary participated in the production of an experimental soundtrack for a graphics photo-film project. I have a vivid memory of my first viewing of films like Warhol's *Chelsea Girls* or the surrealist classic *Un Chien Andalou* at those lunchtime events, accompanied by live performances. In Rosemary, we believed ourselves to be exploring new directions in contemporary rock music but these occasions offered new ideas for the band to consider – particularly in the longer instrumental pieces which were becoming an increasing part of the repertoire.

There was however a crucial difference between Rosemary and the art student musicians. Our band consisted of young men who were becoming conventionally proficient on their instruments, moving from that first basic level towards new skills that were characteristic of many rock musicians in the late 1960s. In addition, the band was pursuing the economic independence of a professional career, moving towards writing and arranging all its own materials. By contrast, Steele notes that in the early work at the art college the students performed "rudimentary and banal material" on instruments "which they only later learned to play". In particular, "they inverted the explicitly stated premise…that long study and practice must precede any worthwhile achievement" (298). We were far more conventional.

Those of us playing in local bands might have been 'rock & rollers' but we valued and sought relatively conventional musical proficiency. We admired and noted each other's skills, debated the relative merits of, say, Clapton and Hendrix, and joined in with the dismissal of successful pop acts like the Monkees or the Love Affair, of whom it was said that they could not really play their instruments, or had not played on their hits. Regardless of how experimental, underground groups might be, they were almost always judged against fairly traditional criteria of musical and stage craftsmanship. By contrast, the art students explored the possibility that mistakes were better considered as "deviation", or a new direction in the same process. As a result, Steele recorded that "negative factors could now be transferred into the positive column", while John White described Portsmouth music as "soft, faltering and correct" (298). The emphasis remained on collaborative work which was clearly a central concept to so many of the social, political, cultural, aesthetic and economic projects in the counter culture.

Portsmouth music at the college became more explicitly political. In his retrospective account, Steele suggested that the avant-garde had little "revolutionary significance" because it was "inherently authoritarian", and failed to pay attention to the "real working circumstances of the majority of people". He described Cage's ideas as "preposterous", and reported that in 1971 John Tilbury had presented a paper to the Portsmouth students which was "the first specifically Marxist critique of the role of avant-garde music in a class society" (299). By 1971, the psychedelic underground and its music had largely disappeared and this political approach was confined to the academic context of the new Polytechnic's Fine Art department – except in the often-acknowledged issue of "the ideological effects of mass-produced music to which whole populations are daily subjected…" (299).

Perhaps the most public example of the art students' approach was the Portsmouth Sinfonia which assembled a set of orchestral instruments and performers, few of whom could 'play' in a conventional sense but who set about performing orchestral classics. They attracted significant media attention, and gave a performance at the Albert Hall in May 1974, which included Brian Eno, who in that same year produced their Transatlantic album … *Plays the Popular Classics*. In March 2017, *Uncut* magazine proclaimed the album 21st in their list of the 101 "Weirdest Albums of All Time". Although the Portsmouth Sinfonia emerged from the radical and experimental initiatives in the Polytechnic's Fine Art Department, they became eventually rather more of a joke. In January 1975, *Let It Rock* magazine carried a tongue-in cheek review of them playing at Cardiff's Concert Hall, written in the style of a football report, under the headline "Portsmouth Sinfonia: 6, Hundred Best Tunes: 1". It opened: "Since the Sinfonia's promotion to the first division after their thrilling victory at the Albert Hall last season, this match has become a regular fixture" and listed performances of "Also Sprach Zarathustra", "The Blue Danube", "Air on a G String", Beethoven's "Fifth Symphony", "the William Tell Overture", and "Hall of the Mountain King" (*Let It Rock,* January 1975). Having (apparently) disappeared, the Sinfonia enjoyed a Top 50 British hit single with "Classical Muddly" in 1981.

As we moved into our twenties, popular music was developing beyond an ephemeral sing-along/dance-along business into something more serious and sustained, while a new younger generation followed behind demanding their generation's pure pop. We had no idea at the time, but I suppose we were in the early stages of being the first *mass* generation for whom the music never ends. There had always been a few ardent fans, followers and musicians who made popular music their life's work or hobby, but now many of us began finding ways to sustain our involvement through life and often beyond musical performance and/or consumption. I have described for example, how Geoff and Martin designed posters and established themselves as Portsmouth's top light show and how this led to substantial careers in those fields, and there was also Nigel Grundy who became a very accomplished photographer and through a combination of ingenuity and bottle managed to photograph many of the major acts appearing in Portsmouth at that time including Pink Floyd, Ginger Baker, Julie Driscoll, Black Sabbath, and the 'Bonzos'. He started his working life with the city council's Parks Department but eventually lectured in photography at the University and now curates the excellent exhibition of popular music in the Guildhall, with his wife and Phil Freeman. Phil, one-time soul singer with two very successful local acts, the Soul Society and Image, was later another lighting man with, for example, 10cc and Take That, plus Live Aid in the 1980s. We were becoming more than mere consumers of what the entertainment industry had to offer, and also developing that D-I-Y ethos taken up significantly by the punks a few years later. To a greater or lesser extent, we were finding a way of staying involved in popular music and popular culture that has lasted a lifetime.

FREE CONCERT, SOUTHSEA COMMON, SEPTEMBER 1969

Rosemary performing.

THE COMMON PEOPLE

"There's Rosemary, that's for remembrance; pray, love, remember …"

William Shakespeare, *Hamlet*

As the 1960s embarked on their final twelve months, Portsmouth's permanent clubs, the Birdcage and Brave New World had gone, the Tricorn was still mainly a cabaret venue, and local promoters had to return to hiring available venues. The Guildhall continued to promote a range of concerts, but given the liveliness of the Southsea scene in the pubs and coffee bars, it made sense that many gigs took place in Kimbells, next to the Queen's Hotel, or in the larger ballroom on South Parade Pier. The latter would become a regular entertainment venue for the students of Portsmouth's brand-new Polytechnic, as well as independent promoters, and one of them, Philip Haines, presented a number of events there, including Roxy Music, in their early days and surprisingly supporting Rory Gallagher, plus Jeff Beck, Lindisfarne, Fairport Convention, America, Supertramp, and in March 1972, David Bowie – for a fee of £225.

After closing the Brave New World, Rikki Farr had gone back to Kimbells on a regular basis and his first Sunday night Blues Club of 1969, featured Ten Years After, plus a live BBC broadcast of Cream's farewell gig at the Albert Hall. Alvin Lee described the club as having the "best atmosphere in the country". Another popular British blues act, Savoy Brown, appeared there in the following week, and Rikki, by now running the Apache boutique on the corner of Marmion Road, also advertised a new Saturday "Progressive" Club at Kimbells offering "mad movies, light shows & full stereophonic sounds". He opened with Fairport Convention for 7/6d, and the following week came drummer Keef Hartley and his band, then Terry Reid, followed by Chicken Shack. Elsewhere, the Pretty Things, the Alan Bown! and local groups Concrete Parachute and Halcyon Order played one night at the Locarno.

Spinner reported "Pompey progressive favourites Heaven going to London on Tuesday to record an LP possibly for release on CBS…the songs are originals written mainly by bass player Brian Kemp". They did record it, at Southern Sounds in Denmark Street, and it still circulates around the city, but this is not the material that was eventually released by Heaven (mark two) on CBS in 1970 as *Brass Rock*. The term 'progressive' was now becoming more common than west coast, although the music still owed more to the experimental spirit of late 1960s than to what became known in the next decade as 'prog'. Local folk legend Jon Isherwood released a single, "Old Time Movies" and "Apple Pie" on Parlophone. It was a light pop item and sold very few copies, but in the early 1970s he received a royalty cheque for a small amount, which was worth more because George Harrison had signed it for the production company! Ironically, "Apple Pie" was a side-swipe at the Beatles' organization; for some time, Jon displayed the cheque on the wall of his Marmion Road shop – maybe he never cashed it.

Free, Blonde on Blonde, Glass Menagerie and DJ John Peel appeared at the South Parade Pier, and in this lively start to the year, Spinner observed that Terry Reid was "well received" despite a "low attendance" at Kimbells, but warned, "Portsmouth could well be witnessing the death throes of progressive beat". Parlour promoter Linn Harris suggested the scene was "played out", adding, "many progressive outfits are brilliant instrumentally but the youngsters cannot dance to them". Oddly the psychedelic scene in San Francisco's ballrooms at this time owed some part of its success to the fact that it allowed American audiences to dance, which had previously been a problem in their seated auditoriums – there was rarely any equivalent of a Birdcage club for *white* kids to dance to the best of contemporary black music.

The stylistic difference at Rikki Farr's Kimbells nights between 'progressive' Saturdays and 'blue' Sundays was not always obvious with Keef Hartley on a Saturday and the less bluesy organist Pete Bardens with his new band Village at the Blues Club. Sadly, the Saturday nights were soon abandoned, although Spinner reported that "the Blues club (was) still doing well", as Blodwyn Pig, led by former Jethro Tull guitarist Mick Abrahams, "went down a storm".

Locally, in early February 1969, St Margaret's Youth Club presented Heaven plus the debut of Rosemary (5/-) and Spinner reported the latter were "very well received". EXP were renamed In Grandma's Absence, planning to play "driving progressive music" while some members of the Inspiration were "reforming" under new name Wanted. They retained their saxophone-led sound but moved from soul towards the influence of Blood, Sweat & Tears and the Electric Flag. The *Evening News* ran an article on teenagers "floundering under the pressures of today's permissive society" but led with "Even the Oldies fall for *Hair*", about the new London musical, which would come to the King's Theatre.

Spinner predicted that the summer of 1969 in Portsmouth would "start with a bang with the arrival of the Mothers of Invention" adding "with the closure of the Middle Earth, London, it looks like the entire light show is shifting to

Pompey". It did not happen, but Portsmouth had its own good lightshows. In late February, South Parade Pier featured the return of the Gun, with the Deviants and Canadian blues band McKenna Mendelson. Rosemary played the Oasis, and there were also nine days of the Student Rag Week including 'Stweek' gigs every day in a disused Guildhall Square shop, featuring many of the Portsmouth groups.

In North End, the Oasis seemed to have as many different names as had once been the case at the Hampshire Terrace Club or Ricky's in Goldsmith Avenue. An advertisement announced 'officially' that the Parlour had "ceased to exist", replaced by a club called the Yeti, which local explorers struggled to discover, although it opened with the Grand Union Blues Band and Light Emporium.

By the early spring of 1969, Rosemary was settling into its style, introducing a few original songs, having played about a dozen gigs, including ventures into London and on the local student scene. On the whole people the people we might have hoped would like us seemed to do so, and we were also getting used to each other. None of us were working full-time by then. Steve, Brian and Dave had been 'dockies', and Mick had worked for the city council while John and I were the ex-grammar school kids, and therefore useless. Once Harlem Speakeasy split, I signed on, and even got the odd bit of 'dole' as an unemployed musician. Now, on my dad's urging I was signing on to cover my stamp; he was a wise man in such matters. After the members of Speakeasy left our flat in Fratton Road, I'd been dossing with pals in flats around Southsea until one landlord caught us and sent us packing. With no money, I went home for while – my folks were great; extraordinarily tolerant of something that completely bewildered them.

I was having too much fun to worry what other people thought. My hair was pretty long by now and the neat mod style no longer in evidence. I was mostly wearing T-shirts and Levis, and until they made me feet ache, a pair of knee-length, hi-heel, patchwork snakeskin boots, made-to-measure in the King's Road for £30. As crazy as that might have been, it was nothing to what I had worn on stage in Harlem Speakeasy through 1968. My Aunt Mary up in Derbyshire, had been so fascinated by this career development that very kindly she sent me a chunk of money to buy some stage gear and I spent a morning in King's Road, Chelsea in early 1968, by the end of which I had a couple of dyed, collarless grandad shirts, a long string of beads, crushed blue velvet trousers, a crocheted and fringed jacket and a silk floral hat. I am rarely a hat man, so that did not last long, as my very thick dark hair grew onto my shoulders and then well beyond, but the rest of it was sufficient. Clean it was, mod it definitely was not – it remains I think my greatest fashion crime, and my dad was sufficiently amused and bewildered to photograph me in front of a bush of his red roses. It is a picture that has been displayed quite frequently since those days, and perhaps needs putting away now!

In late March, Rosemary supported Free at Kimbells; on the next night, we played at London's Marquee Club, then on Tuesday 25th March 1969 came one of the great local nights – and a highly influential evening in my life. We had been listening to Country Joe & the Fish for a year or two via their albums, and John Peel, while in Rosemary their "Pat's Song" was one of the songs in our first set. As a consequence, we were thrilled to learn that they were coming to play at South Parade Pier courtesy of Rikki and his Apache Promotions – along with the somewhat folky Eclection, DJ Jeff Dexter from Middle Earth, and Explosive Spectrum Lights (8-12pm). The Fish line-up included Joe of course, and Barry Melton (who before the gig, taped interviews with members of the audience), although it was otherwise different from the line-up of the early albums, since Bruce, David and Chicken had been replaced. Within six months, this band would play at Woodstock where Country Joe's impromptu solo performance – notably his "F-U-C-K Cheer" and "Fixing to Die Rag" – gained considerable attention, not least since Joe is the only person to appear in two separate performances in the movie. When the band appeared in Portsmouth, their new album, *Here We Go Again* had just been released, and I recall Joe featuring the title song and another waltz, "Maria", as well as the riveting solo narrative of his setting of Robert W Service's First World War poem "Jean Desprez". It was not all classic psychedelia.

I am not sure why I recall those songs in particular, although I have always been a sucker for waltz-time, but perhaps I have a less clear memory of any of the more familiar songs from the first two beautiful albums, because by then I knew them pretty well? On the other hand, it is perhaps surprising that I recall anything much about the evening because on the way to the gig a group of us met up at Jim Lush's where someone had some acid, which was shared generously. I was off on my first trip.

Over the next couple of years, I took acid pretty regularly, in a variety of contexts, mostly in the local countryside or our seafront, and with my best pals including some of the other guys in Rosemary. This first trip might have been almost two years after Haight Ashbury's summer of love but it was quite magical and very gentle, and it sealed my relationship with Country Joe & the Fish for life. The timing I am sure, was another example of something more than coincidence. I had been smoking dope regularly now for about 18 months and to a large extent it was always my drug of choice – far more than alcohol – but for that brief period there was nothing to compare with acid, which I think justifies every positive claim made for it.

I cannot comment about the casualties for whom I have complete sympathy (and I knew one or two) but I have known more casualties from alcohol, motor cars and other drugs, to believe that there is the need for a strong case to be made against good quality LSD. Indeed, it has been interesting to read recently that scientific research and personal testimony is suggesting once again how beneficial it can be in certain cases of psychological distress – for example Ayelet Waldman's recently published diary account of how microdosing LSD has helped her with the mood swings of serious depression (2016). In December 2016, the *Guardian* published news from the USA that while in 1970, Richard Nixon's government had classified psychedelic drugs as having "no medical use … nearly half a century later, two trials in the USA may have proved that wrong". After clinical trials of a single high dose of psilocybin on 80 people who suffered illness-related depression and anxiety, they reported "in 80% of cases, the patient's distress lifted, and remained that way for six to eight months" (3.12.2016).

I did not need it to do that for me – I was a pretty happy guy when I started taking it, and a pretty happy guy when I stopped, at most a couple of years later – but more than that, I believe absolutely that it opened my mind to seeing the world in certain different ways and I often feel when engaged in conversations, or creative activities with other people, that many people who took acid have a subtly different take on life. The only problem can be back in 'reality' trying to make things work with people who obviously do not share that perspective; but I do not regret taking acid for one moment. Neither do I regret that I took it for the last time about 45 years ago – enough was sufficient.

Over the next 12 months the drugs came pretty regularly. I have never done heroin or cocaine but there were barbiturates and other, sometimes crazy, things – a bottle of Romilar balanced an initial intense nausea with a feeling not unlike acid, and a bottle of Dr. Collis Brown was similar. I have never enjoyed speed much, but it was available; not least because Rosemary had a mate called 'Slim' who was not, who shared his appetite-suppressing pills (Ponderax) which kept us up all night. The stupidest drugs of the lot were 'Mandies' (Mandrax) which just induced a kind of mental obliteration, although it helped to dull the pain when little Davey Evans, stuck a safety pin through my ear, in preparation for my first earring. Davey was another Birdcage boy who I had not known in those days, but he became a good mate for a couple of years – a mod who was transported by the then very fashionable Tolkien's hobbits, wore a green velvet jacket, and called me 'Strider' (Aragorn) and Mick Legg (inevitably) Legolas. We had a lot of fun, he hung out with Rosemary and somehow became a mate of Marc Bolan's bongo buddy, Steve Peregrine Took. After Rosemary ended, we drifted apart and one night a couple of years later, in a flat on his own, he took drugs once too often and accidentally choked to death on his own vomit. He was a lovely guy, from whom I learned a great deal that a 'straight' life could not have taught me.

Within a year or two I was over most of the drugs, although I continued smoking dope for some years. During this century, I have not used any drugs and these days I hardly ever drink alcohol either, but those experiences were all interesting in their own ways. They have left me too with a life-long conviction that the so-called 'war on drugs' is one of the stupidest, least productive, indeed most harmful strategies that the establishment has concocted. Drugs, like alcohol, can be harmful, while some (like LSD) can also have significant beneficial effects. Some are very dangerous, but that does not and never will stop people taking them, and all the 'don't take drugs' campaigns in the world will not change that.

Occasionally I find myself in conversations with people who have never taken recreational drugs but seem to know better than me why they should be banned. The advantages of legalizing recreational drugs are that, like alcohol, they can then be controlled more effectively in terms of potency and distribution, preventing for example so much damage from something like skunk. In addition, selling them legally would produce huge sums for the Exchequer (to be passed to the ailing NHS?) and would, to a considerable extent, disable the increasingly dangerous criminal activity around the black market which was always a concern but is now increasingly threatening, and often impossible to control. It would free the police to deal with other problems, and while there is a view that criminals would simply go elsewhere, it is not *that* simple for them. In the final analysis, we live in a world where people are going to take stimulants. We can pretend we are stopping that for the first time since Adam & Eve ate the apple, or we can acknowledge it, and deal with it sensibly, humanely – and profitably – for social benefits. Neil Woods was an undercover police officer, whose work was to catch drug dealers, but he has published *Good Cop, Bad War* (2016) and spoke about it and his belief in the legalization and control of drugs, in an article in *the Guardian,* in which he argued

> Fifty per cent of the people behind bars in this country are there for drug related reasons. Alongside that, 50% of acquisitive crime is committed by less than 0.2% of the population, and that's problematic heroin users. If we undercut the criminal gangs and prescribed heroin to addicts, most of that crime would disappear overnight (27.8.2016).

He added that evidence of the potential of such an approach can be found already in a partial strategy in Switzerland, while he also cited a recent global study that concluded unambiguously that the penalties – long prison sentences, even death – "have no impact on drug use". His message, the message of a 'narcotics cop', is that "drug policy should be about reducing not drug use, but drug harm".

That Country Joe & the Fish night in 1969, lives with me still, and eventually had amazing repercussions, but the fun was not over. On the following Sunday at Southsea's beautiful old King's Theatre, Rikki was at it again with Apache's "experimental concert" featuring Roland Kirk and Soft Machine. We took a box and crammed loads of us in, from where we could roll and smoke joints in privacy – all very enriching. Sometime around then too Rikki enjoyed a major coup with Led Zeppelin appearing at the Kimbells Sunday club, and later he repeated the 'posh' jazz night, matching Family with Indo Jazz Fusions. One week after the first King's Theatre night, Al Stewart, Alexis Korner, and Champion Jack Dupree offered an interesting mixture at South Parade Pier, then blues acts BB King, Fleetwood Mac, Duster Bennett and Sonny Terry & Brownie McGhee came to the Guildhall, followed there in mid-May by a Chrysalis tour with Jethro Tull, Ten Years After and Clouds. John Mayall returned to the Guildhall, while Rory Gallagher with Taste appeared at Kimbells blues club. The second British blues boom had arrived, alongside the taste for experimentation and novelty. It was still an extraordinarily exciting time on the Portsmouth scene, and there was no reason to imagine it might end.

Through the early summer, Rosemary were playing quite regularly around the city and central southern England. We were "well received" at the Oasis, but less so at the Whaley Club, a sailor's venue on Whale Island, where the young ratings did not think much of guys who looked like 'girls'. Still they paid us £18 which was around the going rate for a local band and we had no agent's fees to find. In our early months, Vic Brown from Gosport helped us out – he had been active at the Thorngate Hall and on the Gosport jazz scene for some years – but he did not really get Rosemary, and we drifted apart. We were a bit 'far out' I guess or perhaps a bit 'lively', and none of the local agencies seemed to fancy us much.

I think that was a shame, because we would have benefitted from working more regularly, musically and economically, although it meant we retained our independence. I tend to think that in various respects, through 1969/70, we shared many similarities of approach and audience with Heaven and Coconut Mushroom, but those two bands had strong local management and agency representation so, for example, in July 1969, Heaven spent three days recording and 15 nights of paid performing in the south and west, including Dorchester, Bristol, Salisbury, Maidstone and Southampton. Only one night was in Portsmouth, and they earned £330 that month. By contrast, Rosemary's busiest month in all of our 18 months, was December (always a busy month) 1969, with eight paid gigs worth just £135 (one was a 'fiver' expenses for a benefit). Our best month in terms of average income per gig was our final one, in July 1970, with five gigs worth £128, all local, with four in Portsmouth, and one in Gosport. That kept expenses down, but even without them, it worked out at around £20 each in a month. In addition, we rarely got the longer-distance gigs unless we went to London to play the major clubs – usually for at best, a fiver for the petrol!

Coconut Mushroom, like Heaven, had an agency, and worked more than us. For example, they had a date book of 11 gigs in central southern England in December 1967 – mostly paying between £15-£20 – turned professional in July 1968, and immediately departed for Switzerland where in a fortnight they earned £220. Returning to England, they added a further £81 with four gigs around the south coast, in September they spent five nights in Scotland (£105) and then earned around £230 with a two-week tour of Germany and Switzerland. After that work around the southern region continued to come in.

In Rosemary, after just three months together, Spinner previewed our "experimental" evening at the Oasis on 15 May, which would be "augmented by lights, verse and mime … (where) musical content will comprise entirely original content". From that point, Rosemary almost always performed only original material and Heaven too, still working on their album, featured a high proportion of their own songs, augmented of course by their version of Donovan's "Wear Your Love Like Heaven". Their own songs included a number with titles that seemed somewhat typical of English psychedelia including "Old Mad Walter", "The Day that Judy Came to Stay" and most obviously "The Gardener". They were a fine band and with organ, saxes, flutes and trumpets were more jazz-oriented than Rosemary. This commitment to song writing was at that time a development for local groups, while the experimental evening at the Oasis was something I was very keen to try in the wake of the impact of the Dance of Words and the stories of the Trips Festival and multi-media events in London.

Experimentation in presentation was not necessarily straightforward in Portsmouth, and not something we ever took to gigs outside the city, where we were just another 'rock' band, so what was its purpose? To offer a coherent explanation at this distance of almost half-a-century, is not unproblematic and I am very reluctant to speak on behalf of the other members of the band, but I suppose I hoped we could be at the cutting edge of whatever might be happening. We had experienced the local art students' project, and it seemed then that these multi-media events were shifting pop or perhaps rock tentatively towards an engagement with live art and happenings. With my interest in contemporary art I was perhaps the band member most keen on those initiatives, but the other guys in Rosemary, fine musicians, and all more experienced and competent players than me, were very tolerant and generally supportive of some of my suggestions, including trying out different kinds of venues and live events.

I have related going to a festival or two, and the Hyde Park concert and I had read about all the events in the parks and on the streets of Haight Ashbury, with their sense that the bands were *sharing* an experience with their peers, rather than simply hogging the limelight. By the summer of 1969 there was a community of like-minded people on the Southsea scene including some students, and it felt like a good idea to try to organize a free concert, so I telephoned Mr P Maunder the Manager of the city's Parks and Recreation Department about the possibility of one in the city centre's Victoria Park. He replied by letter on 26 June that the Parks Sub-Committee had "carefully considered" the idea but "could not agree to the request". Subsequently the *Evening News* reported that 'Roly' (AS Rowland) "in association with Mr D Allen" had applied to organize a similar event in Leigh Park Gardens, just outside the city featuring "modern groups … (with) guitarists, bongo players and a soloist folk singer". I have no recollection of that at all, but it was after the 26 June response, and I guess it was declined too – perhaps it led to a bout of bongo fury?

A number of articles about this issue then appeared in the *Evening News* and the idea was taken up by local drummer Paul Sevier and his pals, including Martin's younger brother Paul Richman, Richard Thomas, and a couple of others. Somehow, they worked the magic and obtained permission for an event on Southsea Common, almost opposite the Queen's Hotel in late September. This was great news, although we had no stage or power organized as we set about assembling a bill. Attempts to lure bands from London foundered, although Rikki Farr's brother Gary Farr agreed to play, and we sought sponsors. When none appeared, we raised the money ourselves which was pretty tough given that we were earning virtually nothing from gigs. Rosemary and a few other bands, organized events in Eastney church halls (St Margaret's, St James') working with two lightshows, filling the whole hall with swirling psychedelia and making enough to hire a generator and the scaffolding needed to build a crude stage. Then the local bands on the bill pooled their PA systems to make enough noise and we were away.

At this point we were pursuing the template in every detail. Just as the Stones had done in London, we invited a local chapter of the Hell's Angels to 'police' the event although we knew this part of the Portsmouth scene to be pretty gentle. We had however reckoned without an invasion of the local football supporters from Fratton Park, where ironically, I had spent the previous afternoon, as I still held a certain interest in sport.

The free concert took place on Sunday 28 September 1969, and featured Rosemary, Gary Farr (introduced by Rikki), Riverside, Internal Combustion, In Grandma's Absence, and Steve Kray. The London edition of *Rolling Stone* ran a report on the contribution from the "provinces" to the free, outdoor music scene, while the *Evening News*, the following day reported on its front page "Skinheads run riot at Southsea Pop Concert". In truth while this was a 'juicy' story for the newspaper it was a fairly brief, if noisy interruption, after which the concert continued. A later story reported that Paul Sevier, Richard Thomas and others hoped to repeat the experiment with a Council spokesman saying "it was an orderly crowd (and) we would be quite happy about the holding of another concert". *Rolling Stone* said 3,00 had attended – perhaps not including the skinheads, but mentioning visiting American sailors – and described Rosemary as "obviously, the crowd's favourites". Thank you, *Rolling Stone*.

I have no idea what motivated the skinheads to come, seeking to disrupt the event. Maybe they just hated hippies for being hippies? I wonder how many of them are still in Portsmouth and over the years have attended the Sunday afternoon free gigs on the Bandstand; perhaps the Heineken Festivals that ran for a few years on Castle Field, or these days, the huge weekend Victorious Festival on Southsea Common? If so, it is perhaps worth pointing out that the whole thing started with us. After the 'interruption', we were able to end the show on a somewhat chilly, grey afternoon with a smattering of rain in the air and the wind blowing off the sea. It was not quite the utopia of that first Hyde Park concert but maybe that is Pompey for you – I think you have to keep trying, although that particular free concert idea proved to be a 'one off' for the time being.

Locally, back in the summer of 1969, things had generally felt quite lively, although the news was not always positive. We often went to watch Polydor recording band Blossom Toes, who were regular visitors but they played at the Oasis "to under 100 people", while Spinner reported "poor audiences also for Steamhammer, and Beggar's Farm". I remember on one occasion with drummer Dave Pittard, seeing Blossom Toes, who for the first time in our experience were using a small backline, sending everything through the PA controlled by a guy out front with the mixer. It was a revelation – and they were an inventive and underrated band.

More positively on the audience front, Liverpool Scene & Gary Farr "packed the place" at Kimbells' Sunday Blues Club and the following Sunday the Pretty Things, now into their *SF Sorrow*, post-R&B phase, appeared with similar success. One of Spinner's main stories was about "Concert Experiments for Beat Fans", including reports of the Mothers of Invention's two shows at the Guildhall, which "astounded everyone" despite a near-empty first house. We went to that first one, bought tickets for the cheap seats and ended up near the front. They were terrific – and their quality was a challenge to those of us who thought we might be breaking new ground.

Kimbells Blues Club presented John Hiseman's Colosseum, while Pink Floyd appeared at the Guildhall. Spinner described their film soundtrack album, *More*, as "weird space-age", and reported that local band Dragonfly (age 14-16) were seeking to play in the band's (post-Syd Barrett) style. Spinner had championed Love previously and they influenced Rosemary, Heaven and Coconut Mushroom, so on the unsuccessful reissue of the single "Alone Again Or", he asked in his column "how could we ever let such an artistic group as Love vanish from the scene?" Unlike a few years earlier, this 'Spinner' (they changed from time-to-time) wrote mainly about live gigs and local bands, although with the 1970s looming, the Marina Discotheque with DJ Gary Buck was attracting customers for its record shows from Friday-Sunday, 9-1 pm. The Tricorn Club featured mainly cabaret acts including local folk group Weavers Green including another member of the Hugg family, while Kippington Lodge (with Nick Lowe & Brinsley Schwarz) also played there alongside DJ Pete Cross – another Birdcage boy. While this account is princi-pally about the music internationally, nationally and locally that was seeking to break new ground, it is important to note that some very good but more mainstream local acts like the Furys or the still soulful Image, continued to work regularly and were popular with their audiences.

Local newspaper adverts offered us "flared denim jeans" from 17/11d – 22/11d, and the news reported much excitement across most of the world in mid-July as astronaut Neil Armstrong took a first "leap for mankind" that was not eventually as large as many hoped at the time. Pompey's manager George Smith signed Dave Munks from Sheffield United, telling him to cut his hair, because "football may be part of the entertainment business but leave long hair for the television and pop stars". Long-haired Led Zeppelin appeared at the Guildhall with the Liverpool Scene and Blodwyn Pig, and on the following day, St Margaret's Youth Club hosted a "Galactic Implosion" with Rosemary, Rivendell & Parallax Theorem attempting "to create a complete environmental light show rather than just a way of glorifying a pop group". In July, Mushroom – increasingly omitting the Coconut – signed a song writing contract with Sparta Music, Heaven appeared at Manor Court Youth Club and returned to London for three days recording, plus a gig at Blaises Club. The Rolling Stones dedicated their Hyde Park free concert to the memory of Brian Jones who had died a few days earlier.

In mid-August 1969, the Woodstock Music & Arts Fair, took place in New York State over three days – you've probably heard of it. There were press reports of course but until the film appeared in 1970 the most comprehensive report was probably in *Rolling Stone,* which was now available locally. In the same edition, they reported on another significant festival that came two weeks later just across the Solent, and in anticipation of which the *Evening News* had carried a front-page photograph and interview with Bob Dylan. Because of this second Isle of Wight Festival, the usual pop page, was replaced by a "Festival Preview" on Friday. It began on 29 August at Wootton and featured Bob Dylan & the Band, the Who, Joe Cocker, Tom Paxton, Richie Havens, the Nice, Pretty Things, Family and others – including Heaven. Over the following days, the newspaper carried a range of stories including a photograph and tale of a chip van burning out, while on Monday, a by-line described "Dylan's Pilgrims in Slow Progress" as the "strange shuffling mass" returned home, plus photographs of John Lennon and Yoko Ono who were in the audience. In the following week, the newspaper's Jane Hunt Page ran pictures of Festival Women (including Rikki's wife Karole Farr) under the title of "Strange Trend in Young Society" which is "making us stop and think hard". She added that these "people of my own age group" have a "totally alien" lifestyle, conclud-ing, "I don't see what I'm missing". Spinner was more cheerful, declaring that Dylan was "still the tops".

I went over with Martin, both virtually penniless but we worked out a strategy with borrowed pass-outs that without surrendering them, got us in-and-out, produced some 'spares' and funded the weekend's travel, food and drugs. Martin is a pal of Ray Foulk now, but I guess we still owe him. On Sunday evening, tripping, I sat on my own for a very long time following the fine set by the Band, while the stage crew tried to sort out the sound properly. One of the delights of acid is that it challenges your assumptions about what *really* matters, and by the time Bob Dylan finally appeared, I watched a couple of songs and wandered away, although I could still hear him somewhere way off in the darkness. When it was over, I was surprised that so many people seemed in such a rush to leave, but maybe they had to return to work the next day; my next commitment was the next Rosemary gig on the following Friday at the Parlour (£27). Elsewhere (Allen, 2004) I have written that the film of *Woodstock* offers us a sense of the time when acoustic acts and amplified rock bands shared stages and headlines fairly equally – the 1969, Isle of Wight Festival was perhaps an even clearer example of that, especially with all the acoustic guitars on the Sunday afternoon, and to some extent it was repeated in 1970 with Joan Baez, John Sebastian and Joni Mitchell. With very few exceptions however (Sly & Family Stone, Miles Davis, Richie Havens) these mammoth festivals were predominantly white events, and unlike Windsor in 1967, not very bluesy. After the event, Michael Gray wrote extensively about the Isle of Wight Festival in *Rolling Stone* and described the voyage "from the appalling town of Portsmouth". Pompey is a city of course (with *two* cathedrals) so what does he know? We never invited him back.

The first Isle of Wight Festival had been a bit of a learning curve, while elsewhere in Britain the older festivals still retained a degree of respectability derived from the jazz and folk traditions, but by 1969 on the Isle of Wight a new pattern was set through which festivals and outdoor gigs became a part of the alternative lifestyle, even if just for a weekend for some participants. Graham Laker has stronger memories:

> Festivals weren't just about a bit of fun and some good sounds (as they are today) but were simmering hotbeds of revolution with an ongoing campaign for the legalising of marijuana, sale of alternative (and left wing) magazines – *Red Dwarf, I.T., Albion, Oz*, macrobiotic rice and the ridicule of the man in the suit with briefcase – 'Norman Normal'. Anything 'straight' was derided, such as the upper classes, politics (other than the radical left), vocal groups such as the Temptations with their synchronised dance movies and harmonies (a favourite target of John Peel), and holding down a sensible job (although many of us did).

I did not yet have a "sensible job", and after that festival I spent some time in Notting Hill where 'Slim' Brown was now living; I can recall visits to the Electric Cinema and the Roundhouse even through the haze of those days. He lived and I dossed in a big house also inhabited by other rock musicians and a couple of German 'sex workers' (not what they were called then). They seemed fun initially, until one of them borrowed a rather fine orange leather coat from me. When I asked for it back, she threatened me with a knife – and kept the coat. I hope she enjoyed it.

One London highlight at the time occurred in September, when the whole band came up to London and we took a trip across the city to the South Bank. 'Slim', who, as he might have said of himself, had 'more front than Woolworth's', then blagged us in backstage (I think he said we were the Pink Floyd!) from where we watched Fairport Convention, John & Beverly Martin and – honestly – Nick Drake, live! One of the recurring myths of that time is that it was later generations that discovered Nick Drake, but it is not true. There we were in the provinces in 1969, already loving Fairport Convention and when our roadie Davey Jones bought *Five Leaves Left,* probably on the basis of a review, and noting the presence of Richard Thompson on the session, we listened to it regularly, admiring the sound as another influence. Then, almost by chance, we saw that legendary concert for free. A couple of months later that lovely Thompson track "Time Has Told Me" appeared on the popular Island sampler, *Nice Enough to Eat.* We knew about Nick Drake, and I loved him then and still do now, even if his tracks have been hugely over-used on television soundtracks and adverts.

Back in Portsmouth, in late October 1969, Spinner predicted a "large crowd" for Portchester Youth Club's outdoor 'festival', featuring Heaven, Gold Dust, Paper (the "show stealers"), the Brew, Internal Combustion, Gorilla, and Switch. Sadly, the attendance was "disappointing", but maybe the last week of the month was a bit late to be keeping warm outside? Pentangle returned to the Guildhall that month, while Mushroom were back from a northern tour where they played at the Cavern Club. They were now doing lots of "recording session work" and had a delightful story of meeting John Lennon on the A3, after his Rolls Royce suffered a puncture. Colin Carter and Mick McGuigan helped him change the tyre and were invited back for coffee, with Colin confessing to being "completely starstruck". They made a rare Portsmouth appearance at the Oasis in November which Spinner called "as slick as ever". At the same venue on the last day of October, Rosemary "broke the house record" (and were paid £29), while Image and DJ Pete Cross were offering soul sounds at the Tricorn Club. The local Portsmouth scene was still alive, although there were fewer visiting acts in the clubs than a few months earlier.

In early November, the *Evening News* changed its design, and the pop page became smaller. There was a review of the Beatles' *Abbey Road* while the only local item news announced "Rosemary's scheduled appearance in the Oasis Club tomorrow cancelled because of London recording commitment". We had signed with the publishers (Warner) Chappells and in the West End's Orange Studios recorded two original songs ("If" and "One Hand Clapping") for a single scheduled for the Major Minor label. While in London we appeared at the Freakeasy Club with Atomic Rooster and DJ Jerry Floyd, and returning to Portsmouth, played for students at the College of Technology in Park Building. In mid-October, there were suddenly no local music stories in the *Evening News* but a range of articles about the swinging sixties. Mr R Bonner Bink, Conservative MP for Portsmouth South, complained that, "a permissive society is not a progressive one but an anarchist community". Spinner published a picture and criticism of a "sickening and incoherent publicity blurb" from Slade, at that time, the "first skinhead group". There was also a headline "Legalise all Drugs says Young Tory".

As the end of the 1960s approached, Spinner announced Heaven's LP was completed "but the company insist on releasing a commercial single first"; sadly, nothing ever emerged, DJ Pete Cross launched a "brighten up Portsmouth campaign" and students moved their regular gigs with local bands to the former TA Drill Hall, St Paul's Road. Popular culture through the 1960s had been remarkable in Portsmouth as elsewhere but as the decade approached its conclusion, there were signs of the energy fading. In a late November interview, Derek Shulman of Simon Dupree & the Big Sound suggested that Portsmouth was "a disgrace to the Pop World", adding that local beat fans had been "spoilt by an over-saturation of good sounds and are consequently now indifferent". He added that clubs had closed and groups were disenchanted with the city – for sure, he did not speak for Rosemary or the considerable number of people who supported us locally, and a week later in a "quick reaction", Gosport Promoter/Manager Vic Brown invited them to play at the Oasis "to try to better the groups which appear there". Shulman responded, qualifying his original statement.

The last month of the 1960s opened with the promise of "something special" at the Oasis with Pete Bugg's new drummer-less Mirkwood supporting Rosemary. Spinner reported that Mirkwood were "well received" as the two bands established another "new house record". Meanwhile, Rikki Farr and his wife Karole opened a second "Apache" boutique with "superbly styled clothes" in the Tricorn Centre, as the new Village shopping complex opened on 13 December 1969.

Meanwhile a week earlier across the Atlantic, the Rolling Stones promoted the chaotic free festival at the Altamont Speedway in California. Hell's Angels 'policing' the event, murdered a spectator in an act often seen as one of the major factors that contributed to the 'end' of the spirit of the 1960s. There is no doubt of course that it was pretty awful and one that we can see an account of in the Maysles' documentary film *Gimme Shelter*. All kinds of people have to take responsibility for what happened, but it is worth remembering that the so-called 'hippie dream' had been dealing with murder, serious drug problems, overcrowding and general disappointment in Haight Ashbury, for more than two years before that.

There were problems at Woodstock too, although to this day, that event retains a feel of something more positive. There again, two years earlier, for all the magic in the performances of Joplin, Redding and Hendrix, there had been tensions around money at the 1967 Monterey Festival. The whole summer of love/underground/ counterculture moment was of course ideal-istic – sometimes hopelessly so, but it was never a utopia. It might be that people were trying to "Turn On, Tune In, and Drop Out" but you cannot do that and simply overnight divest yourself of all the habits and attitudes of the previous twenty(ish) years. Those of us who explored the new ways beyond mere drugs and music, were mostly young and mainly naïve; we were learning a whole host of lessons very rapidly, and that included a recognition that declaring yourself for flower power and peace and love was not in itself sufficient to transform the world. As Barry Miles observed, we were engaged in "the great experiment of deciding how to live" and like most experiments there was trial and error as well as success, with blind alleys as well as new possibilities (*Guardian Review* 20.03.2010)

Another event said to bring the whole dream to a savage, almost unspeakable conclusion was the Manson murders. The truth of this is surely again – and setting aside that these people merely *resembled* hippies – that it is perhaps impossible to try to construct a more open, more trusting mini-society, *within* the larger context of a society that exploits and murders as America did, with for example, its own black population or in Vietnam. That is a long project, probably longer than one lifetime, and not something that can be achieved in a year or two with some imaginative rock bands and a supply of acid. Ultimately it demands the transformation of the greater society and that is not something that we baby boomers have achieved in the west – at least not for the better, and certainly not in 2017. But there have been some incremental advances which might offer a foundation.

In the late 1960s, things did not always go according to plan – assuming there was ever a plan. Joe Boyd and Richard Neville, two men at the heart of the London underground both wrote memoirs which identified the many difficulties or unpleasant situations that arose amid the idealism. Neville told of the "numerous scoundrels" that were attracted by the "underground scene" including thieves, bullies, junkies (and) paedophiles" (xii) and he admitted that when, years later, he "revisited the hipster fantasy movies *Easy Rider* and *Hair*" he cringed at "the pungent whiff of sexism and self-satisfaction" (360). Boyd meanwhile recorded that

> Beneath the surface, the progressive sixties hid all manner of unpleasantness: sexism, reaction, racism and factionalism. The idea that drugs, sex and music could transform the world was always a pretty naïve dream (164).

As the 1970s loomed, problems were developing within the London counterculture, which while apparently trivial in retrospect, indicated the sort of difficulties that can occur when young people are thrown together, trying to create a very new way of living with very few resources. I have made regular references throughout to *International Times* which played a central role in the underground and the emergence of the counterculture, but I knew nothing of the 'politics' around the production of that publication when in early November 1969, I bought a new newspaper very much in the graphic style of *International Times* (they even had tits on page 3) but called *International Free Press* (1/6d weekly) and promising on the cover, "The TRUTH about the October 13th Thing".

What did that mean? What had happened on that Monday evening, the day after my 20th birthday, as I finally passed beyond my teen age? The new publication described a 'revolution' among the staff of International Times, liberating some stock "in order to carry on the next issue in freedom". They claimed that the people controlling *International Times*

> Had become deeply involved with power, money and property. *IT* became institutionalized and exclusive … *IT* had set itself up as an underground newspaper – and in fact it was straight as hell

While this takeover was happening, Sue Miles, arrived with her husband and one of the founders, Barry Miles and others and – to the incredulity of the revolutionaries – "THEY CALLED THE FUZZ. They called the Fuzz. THEY CALLED THE FUZZ".

The revolutionaries added, "let us have some genuine HEAD POWER. We are committed to the ALTERNATIVE SOCIETY". I'm not sure what happened to their new publication except to say that it is not listed at all in the Wikipedia article about the British Underground Press, while *International Times* certainly continued, although in December it had to announce on the front cover, that the police had charged them over adverts which had been carried regularly in its early months because they were

> For the purpose of homosexual practices and thereby to debauch and corrupt public morals contrary to Common Law … (and) that they conspired to outrage public decency by inserting advertisements … containing lewd, disgusting and offensive matter.

International Times announced the need for some "heavy bread" and the setting up of a Bust Fund, with their financial position being "even more bizarre than usual as a result of the recent attempt to take over *IT*". London was closer to home than Altamont or Los Angeles, and in a day-to-day sense the pressures of combatting the authorities *and* fighting with each other must have put a strain on any hopes of effecting significant and permanent changes to society. By contrast, life in Portsmouth was fairly peaceful but I do not mean that the counterculture or even the new music flourished here.

Some aspects did well enough, and some did not, but in certain respects, there is a simpler explanation for changes in Portsmouth. For a start, there were not that many full-time hippies; it was a working-class city, in which most people accepted the likelihood that they needed a regular job and a regular wage. There were not hundreds of disappointed young people about to skip off over Portsdown Hill to set up communes in the Hampshire countryside – apart from anything else, there were not vast acres of unclaimed land just waiting for some hippies with seeds, guitars and a mime troupe, who were "going to make it". The tight island that is Britain is not like that, particularly in the south-east, although from the 1970s, squatting as a form of collective community living became increasingly common and increasingly political.

A number of people involved in the Portsmouth scene developed skills that took them on to creative careers, and many of the musicians from around then continued to play, even until today; rarely earning a real 'living' from gigs, but at least getting out to play and getting back enough to pay for new guitars, amplifiers, drum kits from time-to-time. That democratizing of music-making from the mid-1950s was in itself a remarkable revolution which is not dependent simply on professional success – indeed its great quality is perhaps the creation of a world where hordes of young people learned to play and then went on playing, carrying their ageing audience with them. Whether anything much more of the counterculture survived beyond that in and around Portsmouth is harder to establish, but I will address that question a little later.

On the Portsmouth music scene, life for Rosemary still seemed very hopeful, while the more experimental local bands continued playing in the city. Heaven, Rosemary and Shy Limbs appeared at the old Rock Gardens on 10 December, while Rosemary in turn thanked the Hell's Angels who had worked at Southsea Common's Free Concert by playing at a "Greasy Flower, Scorpio Benefit Concert" in Waterlooville, just north of Portsmouth, on 11 December. The gig also featured the Edgar Broughton Band, the Deviants and members of the Pink Fairies. The *Evening News* warned in a headline of an "Invasion by Hell's Angels" reassuring the locals that the police were "ready" but on the following day reported that Waterlooville's "biggest happening" with "several hundred people" had "passed off completely peacefully". Among those in attendance was 'Buttons', one of London's top Hell's Angels – I found them all quite delightful.

On 12 December, Granddad & Dragonfly appeared at the Southern Grammar School and Mushroom, now a four-piece, won a Southern Area "Search for a Group" contest with the Finals at London's Lyceum in January. Sadly,

Heaven's LP was "still not released" and would not be, and local guitarist and singer-songwriter Steve Kray was recording with Transatlantic although again nothing would emerge. Rosemary played at the Art College's Christmas party in Hyde Park Road and on Christmas Eve at Christ Church Hall Gosport with Heaven, offering what the advertisements called "Music-Lights-Colours" – all for just 6/- (30p).

The *Evening News* supported a government bill to curb gatherings like the Isle of Wight Festival, while as the year drew to a close, there were a number of review features including "Spinner looks at 1969 – the year when it all happened". He also considered the music of the whole decade and on the last day of December, there was a more general four-page supplement, "Farewell to the Sixties". He described a "remarkable decade of music" mentioning among others Cliff, Lonnie Donegan, Elvis, the Beatles, Rolling Stones and Bob Dylan, whose music he thought "became weird, lyrically nonsensical…and was, I strongly believe the forerunner of what we know today as the underground music movement." In this latter context, he wrote about *Sgt Pepper's Lonely Hearts Club Band*, Jimi Hendrix, the Mothers of Invention and Love, but considered the Beatles and Bob Dylan as the most significant. He suggested incorrectly that the next major impact would come from "an original big band", and published his latest poll in which the most popular visitors were in order, Pink Floyd, Family, Jethro Tull, Amen Corner, and the Bonzo Dog Doo Dah Band. Albums now dominated record sales while the newer rock bands appeared firmly in control of the live music scene, and even though the 1960s were ending, there was one more, huge Isle of Wight Festival looming.

Before their Christmas break, Portsmouth's students presented the 'Bonzos', Idle Race and Heaven at South Parade Pier, then both the year and that extraordinary decade concluded locally with various New Year's Eve events. Rosemary, Mushroom, Dragonfly and Internal Combustion played downstairs at Kimbell's, for what *the Evening News* still called "a Rave", while upstairs, the dancing was just as it might have been ten years before. It was much the same at Dorothy Whitbread's Dancing School in the city centre, while the Oasis offered a cabaret quartet and insisted, "collar and tie essential". Lace appeared at the Tricorn Club, Hayling Island's Sinah Warren offered a Ball and Buffet, while Ron Bennett, his band and blind pianist Bill Cole were playing the dinner dances at the Queen's Hotel in Southsea. On the music and entertainment scene, the new sounds had arrived and in terms of scale were perhaps dominant, but they had not *replaced* the old sounds, all of which survived as long as there was an audience to support them.

Did 1 January 1970, signify the end of all that excitement and the start of something different, more mainstream, perhaps less challenging? No, it did not, not least because history rarely divides that neatly into days, months, years and decades. Anyway, local bands like Heaven, Mushroom and Rosemary were still going and were hopeful of stepping up to the next stage with record releases which in those days were pretty essential in terms of a full-time professional career. In the event, Aubrey Small would be one of the big achievers in that respect.

Over a period of eighteen months, Rosemary made all kinds of approaches to all kinds of organisations – almost every one of them in London of course and including the rock magazine *Zigzag,* Joe Boyd's 'Witchseason', Andrew Lord/Lauder at Liberty Records and others. We were not alone of course, we had only a pretty poor quality two-track tape, recorded in John's basement and generally we got polite replies but little more. We went to All Saints in Ladbroke Grove and played for the guys who managed the early Hawkwind Zoo, but nothing came of that, then to an audition at the Fishmonger's Arms where a new agency/management company headed by a guy from the Riot Squad was interested.

Therein – and elsewhere – is an interesting tale about the entertainment industry, even in those days of undergrounds and alternatives, but I will come back to it after another account of interest from Middle Earth Records and a man called not Gandalf but Roger Chapman. He had been a student (Geography) in Portsmouth, but the company was in London. He was interested in us and came to see us play at the Temple in Soho (formerly the Flamingo). You will recall I had an unhappy time there in 1968, and my return, at the beginning of the 1970s, was a bit of a repeat. We appeared with Mott the Hoople and for the first time in my life I sang through a 300-watt PA which they allowed all four bands to use. I was so used to straining through my 100 watts with a band backline of Marshall stacks and the like, that I got a bit lost and did not sing very well. A few days later we learned that Middle Earth Records would only offer a deal if I was replaced.

This was distressing of course, however if we go back to the audition at the Fishmonger's Arms the opposite happened. The agency had a young bass player who had been working with Alexis Korner and they wanted to catch the fashion for jazz-rock by putting a band together around him. Without telling us, they were not *really* looking for bands, they were looking for individual musicians, they reckoned I looked and sounded right and I spent a few days in London, rehearsing with them. Why the difference? Who knows? Perhaps, simply, because I sang better in that audition than at the Temple gig, although more probably because they could hear that I could sing in the somewhat tougher 'bluesy' style they wanted, while in truth, some of the gentler stuff that we were playing in Rosemary was not quite right for my voice. My problems were rooted partly in a lack of experience; I had only been a solo front man for twelve months, and these days, I am a far better singer. In part, too, that has a good deal to do with learning how to sing through microphones and PA systems, over loud bands which is not a 'natural' skill – it must be learned. I did that, but sadly the record industry is not looking for promising 67-year-olds!

It seems from those two tales that I might have been either the weakest link or the best thing about the band, although of course I was neither. Rosemary is the only band in my life that started with six guys and ended with the same six guys, with not one change. On one occasion, Steve too was nearly lured away and we even auditioned replacements, but like me he came back. We were very tight, not just musically but inter-personally – all for one and one for all – and we were very tight with Pompey. In the end, it seemed all this was resolved when we made contact with an accomplished musician and arranger Phil Pickett at the song publishers (Warner) Chappell. He liked us and he liked our writing; he came to a couple of gigs and then stayed at my place, while we worked on some songs in our normal rehearsal space in a Stamshaw pub.

He took a different view of my singing. Early in the first rehearsal we tried out a new blues-based song, featuring Steve's fine playing on his Fender 'Strat'. It was not typical of Rosemary's sound but it suited my voice, which Phil commented on when we started working on some of our other, older songs. We did not change much as far as I can recall but he made a crucial observation that on some of the songs a key change might suit me better. It seems extraordinarily naïve now, but I did not know initially even what he meant, and I learned a very important lesson that day. Ever since, except where it would disrupt the whole feel and sound of the song, I do my best to ensure that the key is the one that best suits the vocal. But in my days in Rosemary I did not even know that was possible; I had not yet developed the understanding or craftsmanship required of a good singer.

We signed a contract with Chappell's initially for about 15 songs, almost all of which included my lyrics. Most were fairly opaque in terms of meaning although looking at them these days I can discern at least some significant influences. In a song called "Road" that ended with a long improvised instrumental on which I played (rare) harmonica I wrote a lyric about an exchange with a vagabond that owed something to Tim Buckley's "Morning Glory", and there were other narratives ideas that were influenced by my fondness for the lyrics on Bob Dylan's album *John Wesley Harding*. Other songs often included what I suppose might be cautiously called surreal juxtapositions of unlikely ideas or images, while the work was not often explicitly 'political' in content, because I have always been somewhat wary of mixing such things with the music.

Eventually Chappells signed a deal of some kind with Major Minor records and we recorded a single. The flip-side pinched its title, if not its meaning from Zen, "The Sound of One Hand Clapping", while the intended 'A' side, "If …" sounded a bit post-Cream. Again, I reckon my singing was quite strong, while the lyric addressed itself to materialism with a chorus that ran

> Don't concern yourself with walls
> Or with the buildings that will fall
> Because I think you're wasting time
> By claiming them as yours or mine

The title was a nodding reference to the recent film by Lindsay Anderson and a reflection of the opening line "If you're worried about my style, about the viciousness of smiles …" Cheery stuff huh? – and not at all British nursery rhyme psychedelic.

These days all I have of that recording is a crummy MP3 copy of an acetate that I copied onto a reel-to-reel when it was first recorded. We used to have an acetate around Pompey but it disappeared. Why do I not have the record? Because it was never released. Everything was in place, there was a release date planned for mid-April 1970 and then, for whatever reason it did not happen. I am not sure I ever knew exactly why, but it was something to do with a disagreement between the publishers and the record label, and apparently, nothing to do with us.

The band did a few more gigs around the city through May, June and July 1970, all paying reasonably well – including our one-and-only £40 gig, at the Oasis – but the heart went out of it. I was sick of being broke and got myself a not unpleasant job, labouring on the city's seafront parks. At the beginning and end of July we played two fairly big local one-day 'festivals' at the old Greyhound track at Tipner. The first also included an early run-out for Gentle Giant, plus the Keef Hartley Band, the Strawbs, East of Eden, Uriah Heep, Gypsy and Affinity (with Linda Hoyle). Our old mates Heaven were there too, but not all of them. Rikki Farr had taken them on, and just like the J Crow Combo, had split the original band, keeping just drummer 'Nobby' Glover, the very talented Ray King on various reeds and Dave Gautrey on trumpet, and adding three new guys from Southampton, giving them a heavier, more jazz-rock sound. They recorded *Brass-Rock,* but nothing much happened, although like the old Heaven they did get to play at the (third) Isle of Wight Festival.

Hardly anyone came to the 'dogs' – 10,000 were expected but fewer than 1,000 arrived and the PA was so awful, that we cut our losses and played long instrumental passages. *Melody Maker* reviewed it and said that with the "unbelievably bad" PA, hampering the sound, we were "very Pink Floydish" which we tended to be without many vocals. Following this, we played there again in something called 'Polk', a mixture of Pop and Folk, although in reality it was a folk event promoted by Jon Isherwood with the Settlers, Noel Murphy, the Tinkers, Diz Disley, Jasper Carrott plus Lee Sutton, a female impersonator, local DJ Pete Cross and us. I guess, along with Pete, we were the pop.

Again, almost nobody came, and that was it. On Saturday 26 July 1970 at Pompey Greyhounds, my music-making '1960s' came to an end. I did help put together another band called Gilbey Twiss, with Mick Legg again and some fine players including the now legendary Pompey drummer Bernie Fox. Mick and guitarist Denny Barnes wrote most of the stuff to which I added even gloomier lyrics, and we had a nice sax player called Mick Tuck, while briefly an old girlfriend of mine, Susan Hunt came in to sing. Mick Dillon and Alan Roblin got us some work, and we played a few gigs around the city but it was all a bit too rock-oriented for me and anyway fairly soon, Denny went off to join British blues band Sam Apple Pie, and that was that.

While some of my strongest dreams ended in the summer of 1970s, other things were happening that suggested changing times more broadly. By 1969 Britain's Labour Government was struggling with a number of issues and early in that year introduced a White Paper, "In Place of Strife", aiming to reform Trade Union activity. It never became law and to a large extent, what followed was by contrast, a decade of increased strife. The British economy was in trouble, while in August as the 'Troubles' increased, British troops occupied Belfast. By contrast the Divorce Reform Act and the abolition of the death penalty reflected significant attitudinal changes socially. In June 1970, Edward Heath led the Conservative Party to a highly unexpected victory in the General Election.

In the same month, Country Joe McDonald having lost his Fish, was singing solo in the rain at the Bath Festival in a fine line-up that also included Pink Floyd, the Byrds, Donovan, Jefferson Airplane, Canned Heat, the Mothers of Invention and Led Zeppelin. Quite a few of us went down from Portsmouth while, farmer Michael Eavis from Pilton near Glastonbury also attended the event and was inspired to organise a first festival on his farmland in September 1970, starring T Rex, Al Stewart and Quintessence. His tickets cost £1 and included free milk from the Eavis cows. It followed the rather larger third Isle of Wight Festival in late August, a somewhat tempestuous, event, again organised by the Foulk brothers and Rikki Farr. Acts included the Doors,

Miles Davis, Joni Mitchell, Donovan the Who and Jimi Hendrix. Ray Foulk has recently written two very interesting histories about the three Festivals.

Accounts of the 1970 Isle of Wight festival have tended to focus on the tensions between the promoters and the political activists (British White Panthers and European Marxists and anarchists) who demanded a free festival. It centred around two problems for the businessmen – the hill overlooking the site, which allowed a free view of the acts, and the somewhat flimsy fence which was vulnerable to attack. In a film of the event, *Message to Love,* Rikki Farr is shown devising a plan to allow the 'Free Festival Radicals' to paint the fence in exchange for free tickets, but later we see one of the Foulk brother promoters bewailing the purchase of 200 gallons of paint and 300 brushes from which had come chaos. The 'radicals' had covered each other in paint and shifted between Jackson Pollock-style action painting and slogans which in themselves are perhaps not untypical of the state of the British political underground by the summer of 1970. The slogans included Acid, Speed, Fuck the Guards, The Fence Must Die, Don't Buy, Entrance is Everywhere, LSD, Anarchy, Pigs Suck, Free, Commune, Out Demon? and Hendrix for God. Hendrix performed there, but sadly within a month was dead.

As is always the case, the vast majority of the people at the festival, including me, had a perfectly fine time and probably viewed the political activity and responses – including on-stage from compere Rikki Farr – as an additional element of the entertainment. Some of the White Panthers had organised a smaller festival 'Phun City' near Worthing in Sussex earlier in the same summer, which was intended to raise money for an *International Times* legal fund but ended in a drugged economic chaos, and raised nothing. The account in the 'paper by Mick Farren, suggests that a good time was generally had by all the participants even perhaps the bands, although they were not paid. What the underground could never explain was exactly how musicians and other full-time participants, might continue to function without reasonably regular remuneration.

One of the more varied and comprehensive contributions to the evaluation of the end of the 1960s came in Jonathan Green's oral history of the English underground *Days in the Life,* in which Green juxtaposed different memories and opinions. The respondents included people like Joe Boyd, Mark Boyle, Jim Haynes, John Hopkins, Barry Miles and Paul McCartney, and one of them, Geoffrey Robertson, a junior barrister in the *Oz* Trial of 1971, suggested "the 'alternative' society had…ended" by the time of the trial, which he felt was its "dying flourish" (397). As we have noted, they were mostly men and there was an unpleasant legal offshoot, described by Joe Boyd, involving Caroline Coon, the central figure in the still surviving Release organisation which provides legal advice and support to people who have been 'busted'. Green covered Release over pages 197-203 and published the views of five men about the organisation. One of them, Steve Abrams, an Oxford University postgraduate and the founder of the Society of Mental Awareness (SOMA), a drug research project, suggested

> Caroline (Coon) did a magnificent job for Release, but for reasons one can only speculate on, a lot of people in the underground, *the underground almost to a man,* resented her for it. There was tremendous hostility to her and the better she was at it, the more they didn't like her ... She had no interest in hyperbole or proclamations of philosophy, all she was interested in was answering the 'phone and getting people a lawyer (199).

The emphasis in the above is mine, but I imagine Abrams used those words carefully and they are an indictment of people (men) who were claiming to create a better, fairer society. It is greatly to Caroline Coon's credit that Release is almost the only tangible survivor from those days. More broadly, to some extent perhaps precisely *because* they were key participants in the swinging sixties, a number of Green's respondents also seemed to treat this moment in the early 1970s precisely like death, rather than transformation, or perhaps a moving on. This might be read in Green's subtitle for the final section: "In Conclusion: 'Some Kind of Golden Age" since the implication was that things were thereafter in decline. Sometimes this idea of a 'Golden Age' was merely fanciful – June Bolan for example remembered that "the summers always seemed to be good" (428) whereas in their review of the 20th century's summers, *Wisden Cricketers' Almanac* 2000, revealed that, in terms of sunshine, temperature and rainfall, the English summers of the 1960s were actually the worst decade of the whole twentieth century.

The opinions reported by Green were often contradictory. David May suggested that the 1960s had "an enormous effect" in, for example changing police attitudes, whereas musician Robert Wyatt took the view that the counterculture simply made the Establishment "more flexible" and therefore more able to retain control (425). Documentary film maker Jo Durden-Smith suggested there is little evidence that things changed significantly but noted – perhaps crucially – an absence of reflexivity in proceedings because everyone "was so busy, there was so much going on, who had time to sit down and analyse it?" (427). This may have also been because as Christopher Logue suggested the key figures in the underground were "intellectually flat and unadventurous" with no "self-knowledge" (439).

Had there been a greater reflexivity, it might have been more inclusive – for example in terms of gender, race and class. Despite artist Mark Boyle's view that the class system "faltered" and everyone "was mixing with everyone else" (426) it was predominantly a period for middle-class white boys who, in Richard Neville's terms, enjoyed the power that came with a certain kind of playing. In addition, if it was a 'Golden' Age for some people, this was less clear-cut in terms of feminism. For example, "hippie chick" (*sic*) and painter Nicola Lane suggested that in the 1960s, women were only needed for "fucks and domesticity" while film theorist/maker Laura Mulvey suggested that all the women did was "shorten their skirts". Activist/artist Jeff Nuttall on the other hand accused feminism of being "anti-revolutionary" in contributing to the "enfeeblement of a cultural movement that might have succeeded" (401-403). Addressing another popular account of the death of the 1960s, Mulvey challenged the orthodox (male?) view that the events of Paris in 1968 were a failure. For her they constituted a "generating point" because

> Whereas so many other political activities became dispersed and went into decline, after '68, feminism flourished (405)

While these broader social and political issues encouraged a variety of opinions even from those actively involved, there was perhaps a greater consensus around aesthetic practices, summed up clearly by poet Christopher Logue who said that it was a "very rich period" in "style, fashion, dancing, music etc. etc." (426). Mick Farren who was heavily involved in so many aspects of the underground believed that rock 'n' roll "was the key factor" (429), although it would be difficult to argue that there was much of any real significance that emerged through the British counterculture in the more traditional arts like painting, literature, poetry or theatre.

In positive mood, Andrea Adam, countercultural reporter for the USA's *Time* magazine, experienced the whole period in London and noted the "validity" of people's "urge to be less consumer-orientated" and to "lead a more communal", more caring life (427) although musician and medical doctor Sam Hutt recalled "an awful lot of posing". In terms of the legacy, Richard Neville suggested that after the "golden time", people's ideas "shrank to (their) own ambition" which led "basically (to) the reversion to materialism" (431). Similarly, textile designer and underground journalist Alan Marcuson seemed dismayed that his generation returned to the preoccupation with material success, whereas Andrew Bailey, his colleague on *Rolling Stone* and *Friends,* described that shift more positively, in terms of the entrepreneurial spirit of the underground – identifying particular successes like Richard Branson, Tony Elliot, Felix Dennis and Jann Wenner (430). Sue Miles was more critical, suggesting that it was "really about...ripping everybody off" (432) and Mick Farren wondered whether it was true that "all we got was MTV" (435).

Left-wing doctor David Widgery thought that eventually people "settled for the devil they know" (438) but Su Small, who worked for *International Times*, was happy to celebrate the spread of feminism, gay rights, wholefoods and a wider range of religions. It is not unreasonable to suggest evidence of some progress subsequently in most or all of those aspects – not least in terms of the growth of the 'self-help' movement, although that has required a degree of pretty thorough quality control. Interestingly, when the book was first published, Small was hoping that by the late 1990s

> The government will be mostly made up of people born the same time as us and I think some of them will have been exposed to things we were doing in the '60s (431).

Since then, the media has carried images of Tony Blair as a guitar hero, and tales of Bill Clinton trying, if not actually inhaling a joint. How might Small feel about her views now given a general swing to the centre right, and the maintenance of American and British aggression elsewhere in the world? A different and possibly more accurate view came from Duncan Fallowell, a student at the time and later a writer. He suggested

> Those who are moving into political power are the ones who lived through it without participating in it and actually hate the people who were liberated by it (441).

In 1986, Hewison also assembled a number of analyses of the late 1960s and the counterculture, and observed that while "certainly there was no political revolution", he could identify "marked social differences" over the decade from 1964. By contrast, he cited Sedgwick's 1975 view most of those who had engaged politically in the counterculture were "now leading very quiet lives", but also offered Martin's opinion from 1981, that "what was shocking in 1968, is often too commonplace today to require comment" (275). It is worth suggesting too, that had the late 1960s' counterculture been merely a temporary, ephemeral moment, it is doubtful whether so many cultural commentators, including many who did not experience those times, would be so keen to revisit them again-and-again; even if often from a critical viewpoint.

Recently, Baron Finkelstein, who sits on the Conservative side of the House of Lords, and is also a columnist in *The Times,* revisited two of the media's favourite reasons for the eventual failures of the counterculture, the festivals of Altamont and Woodstock. In a piece entitled "The 'silent majority' is on the march again" (4.1.2017) he referred to the then current V&A exhibition, listing as many negatives of those two events as he could find, although he did concede that the exhibition offered an "exciting tour of a gripping era". He then suggested that as "the liberals looked back on 2016", there was a parallel with the early 1970s' "hangover from the hippy experiment", before invoking Richard Nixon's "famous speech claiming the support of the 'silent majority'", who stood for "law and order … the flag and the military (and) a robust response to liberalism".

It is of course an interesting if somewhat dangerous strategy to invoke Richard Nixon and his supporters as standing for "law and order". Like Sandbrook, Finkelstein suggested that only the liberal elites and university students participated in the 'radical' sixties while "others felt left out", including "the young". Meanwhile Nixon (and Agnew) were apparently "*forced* to resign", not as a consequence of lying about illegal activities, but "*by* the media and elites" (my emphases). His article ended somewhat optimistically, with the hope that our world today might emulate the 1970s and beyond, in replicating "a balance between liberty and order", although it was fairly clear by implication, about the relative weightings in that balance.

People often suggest that the swinging sixties and counterculture simply ground to a halt around 1970, in which case I wonder why so many conservative commentators feel somehow compelled to refer frequently to those days as the root of all contemporary evil. Either it had an impact and a legacy, or it did not? Finkelstein takes a pretty gentle view of those times but his Conservative Party predecessors in the Governments of the 1980s were not said to be big fans of the 'progressive' decade. More recently, Thomas Frank an American political analyst, has described how the alarmingly right-wing adviser to President Trump, Stephen Bannon, wrote, directed and produced a documentary about the financial crash of 2008 entitled *Generation Zero*, in which he argued that the recent financial crisis was "not a failure of capitalism, but a failure of culture". And what exactly was that 'culture'? Apparently, Bannon pointed his finger directly at "the counterculture of the 1960s. Bell bottoms. Drum solos. Dope. That's the thing to blame for the financial crisis and the bailouts". I am probably with him on most drum solos, but Frank tells us that this point is made regularly in the film, with "footage … of hippies dancing and fooling around … thrown together with stock footage of dollar bills being counted … or mean-looking sharks, and then back to those happy hippies again". Frank describes the legacy that Bannon identifies, as "an epidemic of irresponsibility and self-indulgence". It seems then that there really was a significant legacy and one of the world's most powerful men has called it (*The Guardian* 11.2.2017).

Interestingly, Finkelstein chose to ignore Charles Manson. He and his followers attracted major headlines, encouraging people to write off the 'hippy dream', but they were not the only group to emerge from the counter culture who tried communal living, and these experiments occurred, partly in a utopian spirit and partly for a pragmatic pooling of resources and skills. They were probably more common in America, partly because there was more space and partly because their move to the country was initially a specific response to the severe overcrowding in San Francisco by the end of 1967. While there was less of this in the UK, as early as 1967, *International Times* was reporting on a group called 'The Tribe of the Sacred Mushroom', and to a lesser extent an inner-city version of sorts was the group who ran *Gandalf's Garden* in King's Road, Chelsea. Sid Rawle, known as the 'King of the Hippies' was involved in similar projects for many years, including the Tipi Valley community in Wales and the travellers who would often journey from one festival to another, via perhaps Stonehenge or Avebury. In 1985, they were attacked by the police in the Battle of the Beanfield – the largest mass civil arrest in English history.

For some reason, 2016 brought some attention back to these communities and 'cults', initially with a novel by Emma Cline, based to some extent on the Manson story, *The Girls*. It attracted quite a bit of attention, including an article in the *Guardian* asking what the "hippy horror means in 2016" (17.8 6-9). Crucially, Hadley Freeman observed

> The idea that the deeply racist, misogynistic and flat-out deranged Manson represented any kind of hippy dream is … deluded … But it is also a reflection of how, in fact, some of his beliefs weren't so different from those around him.

In particular, Freeman referred to the frequent assumption in such groups that a man "had the right" to have as many sexual relationships with as many women as he wished. He reported that in 2015, Karina Longworth produced a 12-episode podcast about Manson and said about this issue "it became gruesomely clear to me that the era of free love didn't leave every woman who was expected to participate in it, feeling more free".

Later in 2016, the *Observer* ran a story about the experiences of Lauren Hough who had been raised in a 'religious' cult set up by David Berg in California of the 1960s called the Family (27.11. 2016). Hough told how the Family had started simply as "hippies, travelling in caravans and living in camp grounds", which was generally a "happy" time, but then came the oppressive, control-ling and often cruel circumstances in which she, and other younger people lived, under the rule of their leader: "In another reality, another time, he'd have been locked up in an institution. In my reality and time, he founded a cult". When asked whether she blamed her parents for what happened, she said

> Well I know what an idiot I was when I was 19, the age they were when they joined. It's kinda hard to hold it against someone.

That is a generous observation but it raises the key point that however correct they might be in seeing the flaws in the dominant society, adolescents and young adults are not able to transform modern societies on their own.

I am not aware that there were any 'cults' in Portsmouth, although a number of people became involved in various religious and spiritual groups which offered an alternative to the dominant versions of Christianity. There were certainly people in Portsmouth who got involved in Scientology, Divine Light, Hare Krishna and Buddhist groups – I participated in one of the latter, called Soka Gakki International (SGI).

I have been seeking to describe the impact of these new ideas on a provincial English city. We were never cutting edge, never at the forefront of these new ideas, but we drew upon many of them in various ways. I would suggest that by 1969, we were noting increasingly what was happening in London, rather than America, through our trips to the capital, through the countercultural network and publications, through radio shows, through visiting bands, and on our own scene, with its particular reflections of our city. The idea that because of some rotten developments in America, everything was finished is frankly bizarre – or perhaps it is merely a convenient story. Perhaps the media had simply tired of the whole thing and wished to move on to something else?

The previous chapter brings the tale of Portsmouth's swinging sixties to the end of that decade, and marks a transitional point in my life. As I have said, that is very different from suggesting that everything simply ground to a halt, although what followed was perhaps less collective, and more individual or small-scale. The last two chapters of this book consider firstly, the often neglected spiritual and alternative healing/lifestyle aspects of the counterculture, and secondly, where life took me after 1970. That final chapter touches upon politics, and education but mostly music – including a return, 'full circle', to an extraordinary time that I enjoyed with some survivors from San Francisco and the original summer of love.

SPIRIT IN THE SKY

"These people live differently … This is essentially a religious movement;
a demand that we as humans live up to our spiritual responsibilities".

Kenneth Rexroth, *Berkeley Barb*

To date, this history has been one focused mainly on music, fashion and subcultures, beatniks and rockers the mods and the hippies. But as the counterculture grew, it embraced other things – sex and drugs of course but also 'alternative' approaches to daily living which might be spiritual, physical (especially dietary) or political – including the 'green' or ecological movement.

We were, on the whole, a privileged generation, and there was much that was ephemeral and hedonistic about sixties teenage life for many of us, often centred on an emerging sense of self and (sub) group identity. But approaching the end of those largely pleasurable days, and stimulated by new ideas emerging through the arts and counterculture, there was an opportunity to worry less about personal identity, and more about meaning in a broader sense. "What's it all about …?" as the sixties soundtrack enquired.

Su Small, who worked for *International Times*, noted the impact of the broader changes, telling Jonathan Green (1998, 431)

> Loads of things that were just laughed at in those days are taken
> for granted now. The fact that there is such a thing as feminism …
> gay rights, certain aspects of the arts, libertarianism, wholefoods
> … the acceptance of a wider range of religions.

In the respect of the latter two points, we are familiar today with alternative healing, yoga, Buddhism, vegan/vegetarian diets, and sometimes these things become fashionable, as with the recent focus on 'mindfulness'. Many of these changes were to be found around Haight Ashbury in 1967 and could be found in pockets of London if somewhat more disparate. Writing about the Californian world of young people in 1967, Jeff Berner, in an article called "Astronauts of Inner Space" wrote

There has never been a tribe of young people in history which took so much interest in life and its kaleidoscope of forms: Zuni culture, oriental music, Zen, British Digger Socialism, electronic composition, magics and religions from everywhere (Hill, 2016, 151)

Zuni culture is rather particularly north American, but otherwise these things began to spread – not least through the agreed free exchange of articles and information from underground publications on both sides of the Atlantic. But while some parts of the western world were beginning to explore 'alternative' lifestyles, healing and spirituality, there was not much in evidence in Portsmouth back then, although there is a good deal more today.

In terms of healing alternatives to orthodox medicine and the National Health Service, in Portsmouth's Kelly's Directory for 1967 we can find a Mr. Reeves in Chichester Road who offered acupuncture and massage, while in Southsea, Mrs. Cannings was the sole osteopath listed. The Radiant Health Centre was in Osborne Road with Delmonico's coffee bar next door and Minn's Music next to them. The only other health food shop listed was Rundle Johnson in Arundel Street, although I believe there might have been another in Fawcett Road. Today there are many health food stores, herbalists, vegan stores, acupuncturists, homeopaths and other healers around the city, offering a range of alternatives, while the biggest change of all, the digital revolution, gives most of us access to so much information about all these things – Buddhist chanting? Try YouTube. Throw the *I Ching*? It's online. Comprehensive astrological chart? That's there too. Alternative cures for enlarged prostate or varicose veins? You can find them – and the remedies can be bought in the city from herbalists or stores like Holland & Barrett, or online (I choose these as examples, because I have used them all).

What about these developments in the counterculture of the 1960s? The Whole Earth Catalogue, and formation of Greenpeace or Friends of the Earth, the discovery by young people of Buddhism, Transcendental Meditation, astrology, macrobiotics, alternative therapies, the *I Ching* and the mysteries of ancient Britain (among others) were sometimes contentious for the hard-line, more overtly politically active members of the counterculture, or for those who looked on from the outside. Perhaps as a consequence, these things receive comparatively little coverage in the histories of the period, compared to the coverage of revolutionary politics or sex, drugs and rock & roll. But they were there, and many have grown more significantly and become far more a part of mainstream society than other aspects of the period.

While we might suggest that there was a certain energy in the late 1960s which encouraged people to explore a range of alternatives to mainstream ideas, some of these alternatives ran parallel to the emerging counterculture, rather than being a direct product of it. In Britain for example the Wrekin Trust was formed in 1971 largely through the efforts of Sir George Trevelyan (1906-1996), an educator who committed to this initiative on his retirement. The website about him suggests he is "regarded by many as the grandfather of the movement for spiritual regeneration in Britain". The Wrekin Trust website, meanwhile, informs us that it is "an educational charity which supports learning so that people can reach their fullest development," and continues,

> We provide opportunities for the safe exploration of spiritual truths as we each understand them, encouraging people to draw on their own life experience and knowledge. We facilitate connection, dialogue and social action and have a multi-faith approach which embraces the arts and sciences. We include ecological and holistic approaches which foster sustainable ways of living.

In terms of its procedures, the Trust describes "taking ideas and findings back into mainstream society by making them relevant, grounded and accessible."

One examination of what is known as New Age ideas and practices was an oral history publication *Far Out: The Dawning of New Age Britain* which accompanied a Channel 4 television series. Akhtar and Humphries (1999) chose a title reflective of 1960s 'hip' language although the project's title indicated that many New Age topics, including astrology, yoga, natural healing, ley lines and witchcraft, could be found in Britain decades if not centuries earlier. Nonetheless, the introduction acknowledged the impact of the 1960s, suggesting that this is when the 'New Age' "seemed to emerge":

> Along with flower power, hippies and the counterculture. At its heart was a search for personal spiritual meaning, very different to anything on offer from the established church. It looked to the mystic East and the pagan past for spiritual inspiration… (6)

They acknowledged that some commentators felt the New Age was a passing fashion, but by the 1980s the "movement" was "firmly entrenched, with Glastonbury, the main place of pilgrimage." By Glastonbury, they meant the town, not the festival, although the latter has areas devoted to such matters – for example the Healing Fields, away from the main stages. Regardless of what happened to the fashions of the late 1960s, this New Age is still with us and has extended across the country, but it remains a strangely neglected aspect of so much of the history of the late 1960s underground and counter-culture, although Miles' recalled the Chelsea set and their engagement with Arthurian legends and the myths of Glastonbury.

One of the characteristics of the memoirs of British 1960s 'activists' is that they are London-centred because most of these writers spent their 1960s in the capital, even when they came from elsewhere. Barry Miles was from Gloucestershire, Sheila Rowbotham from Yorkshire, Brian Jones from Cheltenham and the Beatles from Liverpool, but it often seems (incorrectly) that everyone ended up in London. Yet the one major exception in terms of this part of the story is Glastonbury.

The Somerset town, a few miles south of Wells, might be seen as rather sleepy, architecturally dull, and somewhat cut-off, with no railway station and a rural bus service, yet Glastonbury is a most extraordinary place. While its name is best known now for the summer festival, which is actually a few miles to the east, for those with a deeper interest in spiritual and New Age ideas, Glastonbury offers much more on a permanent basis. The ruins and grounds of the Abbey, smashed by Henry VIII, are quite beautiful and replete with myth and historical fact; there is for example a tomb said to be the last resting-place of King Arthur and Queen Guinevere. Out of town towards the west is the gentle slope of Wearyall Hill with the 'original' Glastonbury thorn, where it is believed by some that Joseph of Arimethea visited when the Somerset Levels were sea – leading to the belief that Glastonbury is really Britain's ancient Isle of Avalon. Some believe too, that the boy Jesus came with him on one voyage, and it is that legend which is celebrated by William Blake in the opening lines of "Jerusalem". That tale tells of the exhaustion of the party (Weary-all) and how Joseph thrust his staff into the ground where it remained and grew into the thorn which still flowers every Christmas, when a cutting is sent to HM Queen Elizabeth. Back down the hill and moving eastwards out-of-town, in the direction of the Festival, is the Chalice Well, which has been restored into beautiful gardens with various springs and pools of pure water. Again, there is a tale of the Holy Chalice being lodged in the Well at the top end of the garden. Members, known as Companions, contribute to the upkeep of the Well, which attracts many visitors and also offers overnight accommodation.

Overlooking the Well and the town is Glastonbury Tor, the most familiar site in that landscape. Many locals and visitors enjoy the bracing climb to the disused chapel on the summit and it is the site of many festivities at various times of the year. As tales of Jesus, Joseph, the Abbey and the Chalice suggest, there has been a powerful Christian tradition in Glastonbury but now it inter-twines with other beliefs. Many pagan festivals are celebrated there, and visitors are often intrigued by the full range of 'New Age' practices. The High Street and attached areas are filled with herbalists, vegetarian restaurants and shops selling crystals, flower remedies, New Age music and books, Buddhist statues, water fountains and all the ephemera of this 'movement'. Some are obviously there for predominantly commercial reasons, but others seem more committed to an alternative lifestyle. There are a number of healing centres, public meetings and lectures, a library and many B&Bs, which cater for these interests.

Benham (1993) has written an account of *The Avalonians,* remarkable individuals who came to Glastonbury in the early years of the twentieth century and began its first 'revival'. Glastonbury did not suddenly 'happen' in the 1960s, but it was waiting to be re-discovered by a greater mass and as a consequence of the activities of Miles' friends from Chelsea, *Gandalf's Garden* and others, this occurred. But even for those who wish to pursue such interests this has not been unproblematic. Young people came to discover and explore, and they came again for generation after generation. Some showed little sustained interest in the more complex or esoteric aspects of the Glastonbury experience and for some years, casualties of the hippie lifestyle have congregated in the streets. They are mostly harmless, but some see them as the outward manifestation of a depleted spirit in Glastonbury, as if its deeper energies have been sucked dry and not replenished.

Benham offers a clear antidote to these concerns in his concluding paragraph, the first part of which supports the key thesis of this book, that what began around 50 years ago did not suddenly and rapidly disappear:

> The ideas which were once exclusive to the hippie and 'new age' community have gained wider currency among the general populace. Hopefully the post flower-power generation will see from this story of the earlier Avalonians that they did not invent the Glastonbury mystique for themselves and that the true pioneers…had the power to reach back…to retrieve the ancient spirit and make of it something to live by (273).

In *Hippie,*Miles acknowledged that the period led to a clearer focus on ecological issues, sexuality, 'natural' food, fashion, and eventually – in part reacting against a certain Hippie tendency towards misogyny – the women's movement of the early 1970s. In considering its legacy, Miles suggests

> One very durable aspect of the '60s counter culture that is still with us today and growing each year was the personal growth movement – new age therapy. The yoga classes and gestalt

therapy of the '60s developed into a mass-movement of self-examination and self-therapy among the middle classes (20).

One senses in the last part of that a certain scepticism about the obsession with "self" among the "middle classes" but Miles is correct in its legacy and he lists an extraordinary variety of alternative ways of approaching life which emerged or were developed in the period so that he can claim that "no other period can have produced such a quantity of such imaginative speculation and belief in such a short time" (22). In some respects, the relative 'invisibility' in the histories of many of the self-help, healing and spiritual aspects of the 1960s, is because so much of it was less declamatory, less attention-seeking and – while often practised collectively – ultimately private and personal. At its heart was a search for new ideas and ways of behaving which might replace those that seemed outdated and irrelevant, particularly to the younger generation.

In his comprehensive general histories of the decade, Sandbrook (2006) offers a chapter entitled "Heavens Above!" which considers changes in the Church of England and the church-going population, the representation of organised religion in popular cinema and television and the new 'search' for spiritual meaning – beginning with the Beatles' well-documented encounters with the Maharishi Mahesh Yogi. As an accomplished archival historian, he weaves the details of these events into an accurate and clearly written account. But elsewhere in his mission to persuade us that only a cultural elite were involved in all these changes, he revisits his generalisations about the well-to-do.

> For many…disaffected young Britons in the sixties, the solution to all this existential doubt lay in India or rather in their romanticised image of mysticism, drugs and spiritual enlightenment…However this appealed only to a small, affluent minority (441).

In my specific focus on Portsmouth I have asked, tongue-in-cheek, whether our story of the 1960s in the provinces was exceptional, and whether we were perhaps the only place outside Notting Hill or Chelsea that was a part of these new ways. Clearly, we were not for the most part affluent, but I do not believe that we were alone for one moment. In addition, I know still, a number of people from the city who in their younger days pursued that search for "enlightenment" and many are still engaged in that. In the late 1960s and early 1970s some went to join the Scientologists or locally, engaged with Divine Light or a local Buddhist group. Our number included dockyard apprentices, a former boy soldier, a machine illustrator, a couple of unemployed musicians and a handful of art students. By-and-large we had grown up in the ordinary streets of Portsmouth and attended the variety of grammar, secondary modern and technical schools. There may not have been an 'A' Level or more than a pound or two between us in those days, and I do not believe that our principal motivation was disaffection or existential doubt – even if that might have been developing. The primary motivation for our involvement in this scene whether it was music, fashion, drugs, sex or the search for nirvana, was a profound sense of openness and excitement – a positive, albeit sometimes naïve feeling that there was more to life than we'd been told to date. I've never doubted that, and now that I am 67, rather than in '67, I feel exactly the same; we learned to search, and found that searching brought its rewards as well as occasional disappointments, blind alleys or frustrations.

Having written in detail about the Beatles and the various cults, Sandbrook repeated the point that these spiritual quests and superstitions were "briefly fashionable among bohemians and bright young things". He continued to insist that the participants were "the well-educated and wealthy", adding that transcendental meditation "was never especially popular in the back streets of Bolton" (444). He offered no evidence for that claim, and I know little of Bolton, although it has a Guildhall that resembles Portsmouth's, but these things *were* taken up in the back streets of Portsmouth, which is often characterised as a working-class northern town that happens to be on the south coast. Far from being "briefly fashionable", transcendental meditation, and Buddhist groups survive in the city in the 21st century and I know others in Portsmouth who became involved in various alternative religions back then who are still engaged in personal project today, including for example, Buddhists, Christians, and Kabbalists – served too by shops such as Aristia (Albert Road) which sell the full range of New Age artefacts and books as well as running or advertising courses. Most aspects of this 'alternative' Portsmouth, are far more visible, accessible and mature now than was the case in the late 1960s.

While Sandbrook says something about some of these changes, Davie (1994) in *Understanding Post-War British Society,* offers a chapter entitled "Religion in post-war Britain: a sociological view" without mentioning any religions outside the major organised forms – mainly Anglican and Catholic Christianity. That makes it a somewhat limited "understanding" and shows how other forms of religious and/or spiritual beliefs have often been ignored or poorly documented – not just in terms of the 1960s, but also what has happened since.

I am emphasising the impact of this alternative in the late-1960s and beyond, while acknowledging that its roots can be traced in some respects to what we might call 'pagan' times; to the European Romanticism of 200 years ago, to Europe and Britain in the period on either side of the First World War; and more recently in the post-war inheritance from the beats and beatniks. In 1962 for example, Allen Ginsberg in the journals he kept during a visit to India (see also Miles 2001) recorded in notes for a lecture, four aspects of "organized experiment in consciousness" (93) as

> Thru jazz ecstacy and mantras
> Thru that electronic machinery
> Thru drugs
> Tantra & Zen meditation

The list is very similar to that which might have been produced in Haight-Ashbury five years later, with the substitution of psychedelic rock for jazz.

In the 1950s and 1960s, one of the most informed contributors to the new interest in spirituality was the Englishman Alan Watts, who settled in California and was neither a poet nor a musician. In 1936, he published the first of about twenty books, *The Spirit of Zen* and in the summer of 1958 he contributed "Beat Zen, Square Zen, Zen" to a special issue of the *Chicago Review* devoted to the new interest in Zen and eastern spirituality. The publication also featured pieces by beat writers Jack Kerouac and Gary Snyder, while Watts' article was subsequently published as a pamphlet by San Francisco's City Lights.

To a large extent, the counterculture was about dissatisfaction with contemporary western society and the politics of change. Graham Laker who had been a mod and was in Portsmouth at this time of change, recalls that in the late 1960s, "it wasn't just fashion or music this time, but a way of changing the old world-order – Peace, Love, turn on the politicians, make them see the error of their ways," although he admits "I was naive enough to believe that the political scene was on the verge of a great change. It was all a bit scary – to be replaced by God knows what?" He added,

> Of course, nothing of any significance did happen and this led to
> the angry protests/riots of Grosvenor Square, Paris and Chicago
> in '68, the rejection of authority by The Yippies and Black Panthers
> … and Haight Ashbury becoming a wasteland of junkies and
> panhandlers

Watts, and others exploring for us, unfamiliar religious ideas, offered an alternative to disenchantment, social chaos, political protest or anarchy. Towards the start of his piece, Watts observed that to the significant Taoist thinkers, like Chuang-tzu:

> Those who would have good government without its correlative misrule, and right without its correlative wrong, do not understand the principles of the universe.

Adding, that to westerners, this might seem "a weak-kneed lack of commitment to principle" whereas it is actually a vision of life in which good/evil; creative/destructive; wise/foolish are "inseparable polarities of existence" – yin and yang. Wisdom comes in learning to "ride" these polarities:

> It was always obvious to the Chinese, that a man who mistrusts himself cannot even trust his mistrust, and must therefore be hopelessly confused.

Watts sought to explain "the extraordinary growth of western interest in Zen" through the 1940s and 1950s, by referring to the search for "a reintegration of man and nature" and the recognition of the mystical in the natural. He spoke of the search for 'wholeness' in a culture where "the spiritual and the material, the conscious and the unconscious have been cataclysmically split". Further, for Watts, the particular attraction of Chinese Zen is embodied in the words of Lin-chi, "In Buddhism there is no place for using effort. Just be ordinary and nothing special". With such an approach, Watts identifies the awakened experience as possible for 'ordinary' people rather than "mysterious occultists" or 'skinny yogis'.

In order for westerners to understand Zen "deeply", Watts believed they must understand their own culture "thoroughly" and be "free of the itch to justify itself". Otherwise the western Zen

> Will be either 'beat' or 'square', either a revolt from the culture and social order, or a new form of stuffiness and respectability. For Zen is above all the liberation of the mind from conventional thought, and this is something utterly different from rebellion against convention ... or adopting foreign conventions.

Watts then discussed more specifically the writing of Kerouac, Ginsberg, Snyder – the beats – suggesting "it is always a shade too self-conscious, too subjective and too strident to have the flavor of Zen". The Taoist Zen of "nothing special" is then different from the fuss which mixes itself with "Bohemian affectations" in their work, although Watts ended rather delightfully by acknowledging that even his article was tending towards fuss, adding "if you want to spend your time hopping freight cars and digging Charlie Parker, it's a free country". Wisely, too, he reminds us that "there never was a spiritual movement without its excesses and distortions".

Watts was living and publishing in America, but he was an Englishman, born in 1915, and moved to New York in his early twenties to study Zen. In the 1950s, he went to California where he continued to study, publish and talk about spiritual matters. Is it significant that he was English? Perhaps not, but while it is common to see the counterculture's roots in California, specifically San Francisco, it is not simply the case that other places failed to bring anything specific or more local to what was happening. The spiritual element was possibly one of those, although we have a record of some of the things that were happening in Haight Ashbury in the late 1960s.

Charles Perry's fine history of the area (1984) revealed that in the "very early days" of Haight Ashbury "people shared the usual hodgepodge of bohemian traditions, dominated by the writings of the Beats" (257). The thought of these being considered "usual" (except in retrospect) is interesting to those of us from elsewhere; among the items he identified were yoga, Zen, the *I Ching*, Indian mysticism, Hinduism, occultism, Jung's archetypes, and astrology. Then there was psychology (notably Gestalt) and various writers were popular, including Gurdjieff, Marcuse, Huxley, Watts, AS Neil, Tolkien and of course Timothy Leary, although "Leary's style was not the Haight's"; for them, Kesey was "a more important psychedelic intellectual".

Perry reveals that Kesey had consulted the *I Ching* prior to the somewhat disappointing Acid Test Graduation, and its verdict was "Turning Point". He described the growing tensions in early 1967, between the Haight 'hippies' and the new Governor of California, Ronald Regan as a "race between the psychedelic revolution and the growing reaction". There was a "wave of fear", and a handout revealed that the *I Ching* was advising to "stay clean" but also leave San Francisco for a short while.

Perry makes a number of references to the *I Ching*, reminding us that the single volume edition had recently been published, after the original had been out of print in the west for some time – perhaps the oracle was waiting for its moment. The translation by Richard Wilhelm appeared in 1951 and then in various forms through the 1960s – my oldest copy of the single volume appeared in Britain in 1968, with its foreword by CG Jung who pointed out that the oracle "insists upon self-knowledge throughout … appropriate only for thoughtful and reflective people." Jung insisted that using the *I Ching* was in no way "occult"; adopting a "pragmatic" approach, linked to work in "psychotherapy and medical psychology".

Perry's eclectic "hodgepodge" was American and more specifically Haight-based, but it grew and spread across the western world in various ways. Back in Britain, and despite a real and growing interest in spiritual and religious practices, the Maharajah Mahesh Yogi was almost the only spiritual figure to warrant a mention in Marwick's major study of the decade (1998). Marwick mentioned Twiggy and the Twist, Woodstock and the working class and he also gave the consideration one might expect to topics like politics, drugs, crime, fashion, education, hippies, feminism, race, music and censorship. But religion occupied very little space, except where he identified how the established religions, in particular "fundamental-ist Protestantism" in southern USA, generally constituted a "ponderous obstruction on the paths to new thinking and freer lifestyles" (34). One might suggest that these new practices had the opposite effect, but it seems Marwick missed them. Meanwhile, he noted that Britain "was pervaded by…secular Anglicanism" which suited the country with Europe's lowest church attendance figures. Much later, Marwick addressed radical right-wing political views, informing us that

> Further out on the right were the fundamentalist religious cults and the anti-Darwinian Creationists in the United States, in their own way as rebellious and weird as the hippies." (501)

His only acknowledgement of any New Age ideas came yet again, in a section about the Beatles, where Marwick described how

> Oriental mysticism, transcendental meditation, Indian music and apparel were all coming into fashion among youth, counter-cultural and protest groups (459).

It is probably not insignificant, and in some cases, accurate, that Marwick sees these developments as subject to "fashion", and parallel to political radical-ism. On the same page, he mentions that "from August 1967 the Beatles had as their spiritual adviser the Maharajah Mahesh Yogi." Otherwise there is nothing more in over 800 pages, about these unexpected developments in spirituality and individual consciousness.

Miles (2002) offers rather more, describing the distinction between the hipper elements of London's West End and those in Chelsea with its "proper village atmosphere" and "beautiful people (with) money". He suggested they were "essentially an extension of Mary Quant's Swinging London, only with drugs" (232) and described them "experimenting with acid" and "spending entire evenings discussing flying saucers, ley lines and the court of King Arthur".

> There was first a trickle, then an exodus of people from Chelsea moving to the West Country to study the Glastonbury Zodiac, the ley lines and to hunt for traces of King Arthur (233).

Like their counterparts in San Francisco they read authors such as Hesse and Gibran but also British topics and authors including Tolkien, John Michell on flying saucers, 'magician' Aleister Crowley, Alfred Watkins' work which stimulated the interest in ley lines, plus their "special interest in books about Camelot" by authors like Geoffrey Ashe. Miles suggests that it was both an "important side" of the British counterculture and one which "had no counterpart in the USA". He suggested that Chelsea's King's Road led "straight to Glastonbury" in the late 1960s, with its tales of Arthur's tomb, the Zodiac in the land, the visits of Joseph of Arimathea and the boy Christ, the Chalice in the garden well and the Tor, on a direct ley line from Cornwall – another part of the land replete with Arthurian legends. The journey from London to Glastonbury conveniently passes close to the mysterious stones at Avebury and Stonehenge, before the Tor looms in the distance.

In itself of course, not all of this history is necessarily spiritual, and even where it is, much of it is rooted in Christianity rather than anything from the East. That made it harder to untangle from the institutions and traditions of the Christian Church in England that constituted one ruling element of conventional society that was being challenged by the counterculture. The attraction of the Arthurian legends however was enhanced by its link to 19th century Romanticism and the retelling of those tales in the artworks of the Pre-Raphaelites or Aubrey Beardsley the poems of William Morris and Tennyson and the reprinting after two centuries of Malory's account. There is much in the Chelsea underground described by Miles that is essentially romantic, and it has been one key thread running through British culture.

Although Miles did not identify similar ancient indigenous practices in the USA he might have considered the impact of native American culture on hippie communes and rural life. From the USA, two photographic records, by Lisa Law (2000) and Peter Simon (2001) include images which confirm involvement and interest in spiritual practices. Law shows Ginsberg, Snyder and others chanting on stage at San Francisco's "Human Be-In" in January 1967, Ravi Shankar on stage at the Monterey Festival six months later, and the Buddhist Suzuki-roshi teaching meditation. There are also pages of photographs of a group studying Kundalini Yoga with Yogi Bhajan; "a very charismatic Sikh" (92-107), astrologer Alan Oken and a Hare Krishna student in Santa Fe. Simon, who includes an autobiographical text, offers a chapter entitled "Searching for the Spirit" which includes images of Leary, Ginsberg, Hare Krishna practitioners and Ram Dass, who had collaborated with Leary in the LSD experiments of the 1960s. Simon recorded how he had begun to develop a significant interest in spiritual practices at the Tree Frog Commune, not least through a girlfriend who practised meditation, and after his "hippie and druggie daze" had left him "bottomless", he began to study with Ram Dass. It is not an untypical tale.

Lisa Law, so far at least, is unusual in this chapter's account of spiritual and New Age ideas in that she is a woman. It may be more than coincidence that the tendency for countercultural histories to ignore or critique spiritual or New Age ideas is at least partly that many of the 'historians' are male, despite the fact that many women have influenced and sometimes led these ideas. For well over a century, these women have included Theosophists Helena Blavatsky (1831-1891) and Alice Bailey (1880-1949), and others such as Katherine Maltwood (1878-1961), Dion Fortune (1890-1946), Margaret Hone (1892-1969) who was a founder member of the Faculty of Astrological Studies, Mary Caine who in 1969, reignited interest in Maltwood's idea of a Glastonbury Zodiac, and current astrologers Melanie Reinhardt and Liz Greene. The Faculty of Astrological Studies runs a number of 'live' and online courses and currently all its lecturers are women. In addition, it is frequently the case that over the past half-century, the huge number of New Age workshops on a wide range of topics held across Britain, have attracted more women than men – despite which a search of Wikipedia on the topic "new political directions in the 21st century" for the New Age, lists four authors who write on the subject. All four are men.

One sympathetic man, Tobias Jones (2007, 1), has noted how "hundreds of books" have been written "about the counter-culture or about hippie communes and dysfunctional ashrams" and he suggests that they employ a "stand-offish voyeurism", in which too often, the writer's intention is "to pry into alternative types and conclude they're doolally, if not actually dangerous". He adds

> It's much easier to sell a book which shores up our complacency by denying the alternatives, than one which challenges it by quietly listening …

Perhaps photographs and films are sometimes a more appropriate way of representing this element of the 1960s than written texts, although even from *within* the counterculture, Green's correspondents in his oral history of the "English Underground" (1998) offer some generally dismissive memories. For example, members of the Hare Krishna movement had been provided with offices to live and work in, but Tony Elliott remembered "this unbeliev-able smell" and Graham Keen called them "sluts (and) really awful slobs". Barry Miles expressed gratitude that George Harrison was more "receptive" to them (232-3) but there is an indication here that the counterculture did not always welcome organised religious groups, however 'alternative'.

This is confirmed by Green in a section subtitled "Religion: A mental disease if ever there was one" where, over two pages (296-297), leading underground figures criticised the new spirituality. Designer Nigel Waymouth described "endless Scientologists and Sufis" and his "contempt" for *Gandalf's Garden*, while publisher Nicholas Saunders suggested that the latter organisation attracted "people who didn't quite fit in…who felt a little lost" (which one might suggest is a frequent prerequisite of any underground involvement). Writer/singer Mick Farren believed that religion attracted anyone "looking for another daddy", while writer and artist Jeff Nuttall suggested that "religiosity was the stumbling block of the whole damn thing" adding that faith and a "belief in human freedom just don't mix". The Beatles' press officer Derek Taylor recalled how Apple employed a "special *I Ching* thrower", who was, presumably, not terribly effective.

Su Small (*IT*) admitted to being "much more worried by people who get into cults than drugs" although she offered no evidence about the long-term effects of those two options and it does not follow that an interest in spirituality leads to membership of a dangerous cult. More circumspectly, engineer and designer Jonathan Park acknowledged that in that "tremendously godless" time, relief from stress was available in "two forms", heroin or God, adding "a lot of people got into one or another" (296-297).

More positively, Dr Sam Hutt did recall the spiritual foundations of the early LSD experiences, derived from the ideas and publications of Timothy Leary:

> The first acid trips were extremely serious. A day fasting before reading *The Tibetan Book of the Dead, the Psychedelic Experience*; having Krishnamurti playing on record while you are tripping (177).

In *All Dressed Up*, Green (1999) considered spirituality in his section about "Hippie Trails: on the Road" (224-233), describing travels which were not necessarily for esoteric purposes. In Green's oral history of the period, *Days in the Life*, Paul McCartney offered some interesting observations about the Beatles' encounter with their 'Guru', the Maharishi Mahesh Yogi. He stressed that what they were exploring was "not a religion" but simply "a system of meditation" and recalled at the time, being introduced to the *Bhagavad Gita* "and stuff like that", including "bits of Khalil Gibran (and) … *Siddartha* … (which) all seemed the same kind of thing". He spoke also of the difference between Indian and western music and added

> Then you started to get the idea: one note, one concentrating, one lessening of stress, one reaching of a sort of new level did seem to

get you in touch with a better part of yourself. It was a very hectic
world … and this inner peace seemed a better thing (232).

Jonathan Green suggested that this searching was not "new", but that
while there had always been "small bands of dedicated seekers" or perhaps
"cranks", the 1960s "gave such crankery a new lease of life" (229). Elsewhere,
he mentioned trepanning, the process of drilling a hole in the skull in order
to say 'high' forever, while a D-I-Y guide to trepanning appeared in *Gandalf's
Garden*.

A more predictable critique of these developments came from journalist
and broadcaster Bernard Levin (1970). He suggested "there was no amount
of manifest absurdity that could deter those who wanted to believe from
believing" (39) and reserved his strongest attack for astrology, although
he invited reciprocal criticism by focusing on the general 'pop' astrology
as published in daily newspapers. Levin added "in the circumstances, it is
hardly surprising that the sixties also turned out to be the great age of the
flying saucer" (40).

Despite the relatively slight coverage of these spiritual aspects in many
countercultural histories, some attention was paid to them at the time. For
example, page seven of *The Guardian*, 25 May 1968, carried a number stories
which encapsulated the traditions, contradictions and upheavals which
occurred as the 1960s drew to a close. In the right-hand corner, Anthony
Pearson wrote about the pleasures of spending five days at London's
National Angling Show, while diagonally opposite Edward Greenfield's
column discussed the merits of recorded performances of Brahms, Dvorak,
Schubert and other classical composers. In such articles the traditions of
high culture and recreation must have seemed secure, but there were two
other larger, illustrated articles.

The largest by Terry Coleman ("Egotrips for Editors") focused on "periodi-
cals about the arts, the various forms of anarchy and the high life and its
attendant mysteries". These were broadly speaking the magazines of the
British counterculture or, as the manager of *Better Books* in Charing Cross
Road suggested, a dozen "hippy" magazines. Coleman described other
titles as more moderate, including *Private Eye* and somewhat surprisingly,
Oz. Among the more 'hard-core' titles were *Encounter, International Times,
The Black Dwarf, Whisper & Shout, Fire, The Running Man*, and *Gandalf's
Garden*.

Gandalf's Garden, named after Tolkien's wizard of course, ran to six editions
before the venture was abandoned along with their headquarters in King's
Road Chelsea. It is generally considered the first of the alternative spiritual

magazines, although Hutchinson is not untypical in his view that the magazine was "so committed to the acid generation that during its short existence it made parody of the underground press redundant" (1992, 100).

One example of unwitting self-parody was an article in Issue 5 on distinguishing between a "Brother of the Spirit" and a "plastic hippie". *Gandalf's Garden*, drawing upon a poem by Adrian Mitchell which they had published in Issue 3, suggested a "symbol of communication" might be to hand someone a leaf. The article advised that both "Underground" and "Overground" people would understand but "Upground dwellers" would not. It seemed pretty bonkers, but many of the articles were more focused and 'acid' was hardly a concern of the magazine. Rather, it drew attention to topics such as the Glastonbury Zodiac, Trepanning, the Atlantis myth, ecology, the Aetherius Society, clairvoyance, radical Christianity, Buddhism, Meher Baba, British-based communes and the "Revolutionary World Mind". In Issue 5, an article by Hapt (*sic*) suggested that

> Before the Golden Age can happen in our visible world (and it is already happening on the *inner planes* – the seeds are sown and germinating – and many of us are living here and there at-One-ment) it must be consciously lived in the hearts and minds of those who understand. They have to act as channels by projecting the future lifestyle so strongly into the 'etheric recording field' that it will be picked up unconsciously by more and more people as the *Age of Consciousness* develops. This is the only form of revolution that will be of any lasting use (5).

Gandalf's Garden was very considerably focused on spiritual topics, but during the summer of love, *International Times* would intersperse pieces about drugs, politics, new cinema, performance and rock & roll, with these other interests. In July 1967 for example, it carried a large advertisement for Running Man books, including a series by George Ohsawa about Zen Macrobiotics, Zen Cookery and a companion volume to the first of those, explaining "the principles of Yin and Yang". There were also a number of titles about sex and sexuality and another by Masters and Houston, *The Varieties of Psychedelic Experience.*

In the same edition, anticipating in a modest way the later success of *Time Out*, a "What's Happening" listing included a lecture on "the Elements of Yoga" in Hampstead and a "Discourse in Vedanta" at the Ramakrishna Vedanta Centre in Holland Park. That edition also carried an advert for an album *Ecstatic Music of Morocco* with recordings of dervishes in Tangier. By the time of the previously mentioned *International Times* 'Pop Supplement' in March 1968, a year renowned as far more 'political' across Europe and the USA, the spiritual dimension had faded somewhat, but was taken up by *Gandalf's Garden*. Did this suggest emerging 'factions' within the counterculture?

One of the key characteristics of what happened in the late 1960s is that while almost every new 'thing' had its antecedents – cool music, drugs, fashion, sex, trips to exotic countries – only in the late 1960s was this so widespread, so essentially 'democratic'. Suddenly these things were not the preserve of a social, cultural or economic elite – we could all join in. Joe Boyd outlined a history of previous 'bohemian' moments through Europe and America where the (mainly) middle-classes might indulge an appetite for a 'bit of rough', including the 18th century *Beggar's Opera* the next century's *La Vie Boheme* and in the 1920s, white audiences braving Harlem for a night of jazz and black dancers. Post-war, in America again, the beats and the abstract expressionist painters brought a new wildness to culture but always these manifestations were to be consumed securely, mostly by a small social elite, prior to a return to 'normal' life. By contrast, Boyd points out

> What London witnessed in the spring of 1967 was more than an
> endorsement of a new musical style, it was a mass-immersion in
> the sub-culture that gave rise to it (158)

In terms of the spiritual/religious motivation, Green (1999) suggests that the voyagers were "turning against the Judaeo-Christian ethic, so laden with guilt and work ethics" (226), but while he acknowledged that these eastern 'alternatives' could be pursued without travelling, it was exciting to travel in pursuit of the truth. Nonetheless many people (including me) did find opportunities on our doorsteps. For me, largely by chance, it was the SGI, a Japanese form of Buddhism based on the 13th century teachings of Nichiren. I cannot recall the precise circumstances, but a friend or friends met up with a small group based in Albert Road, Southsea and I went along to encounter an evening based mainly on the repeated chanting of "Nam-Myoho-Renge-Kyo" and the twice daily recitation of a set 'service' in Japanese and based on the Lotus Sutra.

For more than fifty years since then, I have used it, like the *I Ching,* on-and-off to help me focus or deal with an issue on my life. One aspect of this specific approach to Buddhism that surprised me, at least in the UK, was the extent to which discussions revolved around chanting for material benefits (job, car, house etc.) as if this was the way to engage young westerners, whereas in the late 1960s many of us were interested precisely in finding 'another way'. Despite that, and a total lack of interest in any occasional sectarian disputes that separate various Buddhist groups, I am entirely persuaded of the benefits of the chant, albeit with no clear way of explaining it – and no desire to offer one. For some time since discovering this particular practice, I pursued it intermittently and with less self-discipline than I might have, but in the past couple of years I have chanted each morning and evening for around 20 minutes, these days accompanying recordings that are available on YouTube.

There is no specific 'guru' in my chosen form of Buddhism, and Green, cites Sue Miles sceptical identification of "Indian travelling salesmen" including Meher Baba (Pete Townshend's guru), Bhagwan Shree Rajneesh, Swami Bhaktivedenta (Hare Krishna) and most famously Maharishi Mahesh Yogi for a short period, guru to the Beatles, Jagger and entourage. In addition, there was Bernice Martin's "do-it-yourself kit of spiritual self-development" which might offer

> A generalized dabbling in the literature and history of the occult, mandalas (Jungian or other), tarot cards, astrological prediction, yoga, techniques of mystical ecstasy (with or without drugs) in meditation and expanded consciousness (230.)

I suppose I have been something of a 'dabbler' myself. I take the view that exploring as many alternatives as possible, helps to clarify what might 'work' for me. In addition to my interests and practices, for over thirty years I've been married to an astrologer who is also a long-term practitioner and student of the Kabbalah. Some years before I met Lou (although we once lived about 10 doors apart as kids) she, like me, set out to the Bath Festival of 1970. She was hitching on her own after work in a local factory, on a Friday evening and on the way, got a lift to Oxford and as the rain began, headed west, when a car with three 30-somethings from London stopped. One of them she remembers as something of a "bohemian poet" with a "phenomenal knowledge of astrology".

They were intending to look for a west country property and as the rain got heavier they invited Lou to stay with them for what she still recalls as a completely "fabulous weekend" – with no sexual complications. They took her to Glastonbury on Saturday, Lou's first visit there, for her first trip up the Tor, where her bohemian friend pointed out how to identify the Glastonbury Zodiac in the surrounding landscape. They went also to the Chalice Well which stimulated her interest in the Arthurian legends, and she has a memory that the hippies in Glastonbury at that time, matched Miles' descriptions of the smarter Chelsea set. On the Sunday, although missing her future pal Country Joe, they went horse-riding and viewed properties before dropping Lou off at the Festival in time to hear one of the last bands performing. There she met up with her pals, but felt no regrets for what she had missed, because her weekend was the "magical spark" for what she considers a life-long journey, including her engagement with astrology. In our relationship, Lou is the very much the teacher in these matters, and since we both believe completely in karma, we do not consider our meeting as a coincidence, or matter of chance. As I write this nearly fifty years later, she is preparing to return to Glastonbury Abbey next weekend for a three-day astrology course presented by the Faculty of Astrological Studies, culminating on Sunday afternoon with a celebration of a moon eclipse in the Chalice Well Gardens.

Together Lou and I have taken New Age holidays in Europe, and spent many days in Glastonbury, particularly in residence at the Chalice Well, where we hold a Companions' membership. On two occasions, we came very close to purchasing properties in Glastonbury with the intention of moving there, but I guess Pompey would not let us go. I have been on New Age workshops over the years which have made variously lots of sense, a bit of sense or no sense at all, and these days I feel able fairly quickly to evaluate the potential value of such experiences. I'm not interested in making judgements about other people, but to take the Chalice Well in Glastonbury as one example, I am intrigued by the Avalonians, mainly intellectuals or creative individuals, who in the early decades of the twentieth century rebuilt the spirit of Glastonbury around the Well, its gardens, the Tor, the Abbey and other centres of that fascinating town. But these days, the Well has a celebratory culture which I find too ritualistic and performative for my needs. It's perfectly fine for those who enjoy it, but I love the moments of quiet in the garden and I find no need for the bigger events.

After all these years, my D-I-Y kit is much smaller than it once was. Chanting "Nam-Myoho-Renge-Kyo", sharing my wife's knowledge and wisdom, and the *I Ching* are about all I need – alongside continuing to find creative outlets in music or the visual arts. Our house is full of beautiful crystals but I have no real idea whether they make any difference and again, no great desire to find out. At 67, I guess my next great adventure will be death, so perhaps it will be time to look out my old copy of the *Tibetan Book of the Dead*?

Back in the 1960s, there were suddenly a number of ways of finding out about the various alternatives. As with most things it will have been easier in London but not impossible elsewhere, although one thing that helped was a voyage to King's Road, Chelsea with Martin, probably in 1968, when a walk to the far end – indeed World's End – revealed the *Gandalf's Garden* shop where we were welcomed in with a cup of jasmine tea and walked out with a copy of their "Mystical Scene" magazine.

Issue one was published in May 1968, while some of the young people of western Europe were engaged in a serious attempt at political revolution, whereas from the 'Garden' came a "soulflow from the pens of … mystics, writers, artists, diggers, delvers and poets". Inside were features on a Scottish Tibetan Monastic Centre, Yoga (for Western Bodies), Vinoba Bhave "known as the saint of India", Emanuel Swedenborg, the eighteenth century "inner space traveller", the sprouting of Digger philosophy, poems including one by Christopher Logue, thoughts from DJ John Peel who was being told by Marc (yes that one) to write of "badgers and water-voles and … river banks". Peel had read a book about the artist Paul Klee but not understanding it "felt sorry for the author". He was a fan of Captain Beefheart advertised as coming soon to the Middle Earth (followed by the Fugs). Less cheerfully came an article on the USA's defoliation of Vietnam.

Gandalf's Garden continued in the vein for six issues. Its magazine format resembled *Oz* (magazine) rather than *International Times* (newspaper), but the illustrations were rather more rural or perhaps Tolkien-inspired than the more lurid sexual psychedelia of *Oz*. Articles in future magazines included "Mescaline, Mysticism & Meditation"; the Anti University of London; the Living Communes Forum; "the Key to Self-Realisation", Steiner Schools, Sufis, the Selene Community, Aleister Crowley, Atlantis, Astrology, Buddhism, Meher Baba (who got another feature in *Rolling Stone*), the Mysteries of Glastonbury (including the Zodiac), the Aetherius Society, Hand-Reading, Gandhi, Hare Krishna, Trepanning, the Cosmic Continent and a "Hip Glossary".

It was a pretty comprehensive coverage of this gentler aspect of the counterculture – and they acknowledged the role of the new music scene with another column by John Peel, plus features on Tyrannosaurus Rex, Junior's Eyes, the Third Ear Band, UFO's darlings Soft Machine, and Britain's eastern-rockers Quintessence, the band that included Raja Ram, Shiva Shankar and Maha Dev in a band "whose lifestyle radiates love and good vibrations". Raja Ram explained "we feel playing music is a very spiritual thing, it's like doing holy work …". On 9 November 1969, Quintessence appeared at a 'Benefit' for *Gandalf's Garden* at St Pancras Town Hall, along with a classical sitar ensemble, Indian dancers and Barney Bubbles Light Show. Tickets from the magazine's 'Shoppe' were 10/-, but sadly, it was not enough.

That was issue six of *Gandalf's Garden* and the last one, as the 'Shoppe' in Chelsea closed too. There were no farewells, and it was probably published optimistically, but while *International Times*, *Oz* (briefly), *Rolling Stone* (including for a while a London edition) and other countercultural publications continued, the most 'spiritual' of them did not. In that last edition, an article about the 'underground' press (underground? A "sloppy word"), suggested a circulation world-wide of all the publications approaching one million. Nonetheless, the article warned

> Only a few of the largest papers are making a profit worth mention-
> ing, while most papers are losing money hand through fist. Yet they
> continue to be published

This last edition carried a quarter page advert for a new monthly magazine (3/-) called *Vishtaroone* which would "soon try and expound and expand upon the evolutionary moves towards a better universe spiritually, physi- cally and artistically". *Vishtaroone*, based in Dorset, proved short-lived and it is difficult to discover much about it. A website "Letters of Note" reveals correspondence between the editor and Marc Bolan and suggests incor- rectly that there may have been just one issue, yet there was certainly a second in May 1970, which carried an over-optimistic advert for another *Gandalf's Garden* and perhaps it was last edition of *Vishtaroone* too? If so, it had much to commend it as an introduction to their "spiritually based venture". Among a range of pastoral/eastern images and poetry, *Vishtaroone* offered articles on "Tao (the mystic universal principle)" and its symbol for Yin & Yang, Zen macrobiotics ("the application … of Yin & Yang"), sex and sexuality ("Come together" with an emphasis on 'together'), "Pastoral Commune: Is It Possible?" and "The Book of Change (*I Ching*)". These articles would be sufficient to give the newcomer a reasonable start, even with the less optimistic 1970s looming.

In terms of those who travelled in search of enlightenment, Jonathan Green cites a piece from back then by Duncan Campbell in one of the other underground 'papers *Ink*, in which Campbell identified six varieties of overseas 'trippers', as those on the "Religious Trip: the guru-collecters, Hare Krishna folks, Divine Light cavalry, Buddhist converts and searchers after nirvana, truth, light or a cheap temple to stay in" (225). He also mentioned the somewhat elusive 'cultural' trippers who went to India "to study sitar or tabla or learn Sanskrit". Campbell suggested that the latter generally "look down a bit on (the) drug-crazed religious freaks".

By 1969, *Gandalf's Garden* had a very different view of revolution from that held elsewhere in countercultural publications. *International Times* survived its internal take-over but was prosecuted for seeking to "outrage public decency", and in its last edition of the 1960s, suggested that "the establishment…don't seem to want to try and communicate with alterna- tive social groups". The rest of that edition (number 69) focused on music or social/political questions around education, housing and the inner cities except that, like *Gandalf's Garden,* they featured a piece on Meher Baba. *International Times* actually had a regular correspondent, John Michell, who was an authority on the British esoteric and spiritual traditions, who in 1969 published *The New View Over Atlantis* concerning ley lines, landscape mysteries and natural energies, focusing on Glastonbury and the idea of the "astrological New Age" – a moment which had been less seriously celebrated in the song from the musical *Hair,* about the dawning of the Age of Aquarius.

In his preface to the third edition Michell (1983 9-10) observed that the "old" thinking which had led to "modern technological civilisation" had now reached "exaggerated and dangerous extremes" but he warned "it is neither possible nor necessary to regress historically". What he preferred was to find older "principles" that

> May well provide the basis for a new form of science, better adapted than the present variety to the interests of the living earth".

In some cases, a "new form of science" began to develop in deliberately earth-bound ways. It manifested itself in ecological movements, communes, vegetarian and macrobiotic diets and could be found in articles in most of the underground magazines. In the United States, *the East West Journal* resembled the appearance of *International Times* or *Rolling Stone* but proclaimed itself devoted to "serving a world macrobiotic society". Issue seven included a feature on London, where we learned that this aspect of the new age had its own ideological splits. An interview with the proprietor of a Hampstead vegetarian restaurant revealed that a leading macrobiotic writer had accused him of sentimentality. He in turn defended his more catholic approach on the basis of attracting "the average man", adding that the *East West Journal* was "too exclusive – all those Oriental logos".

One of their articles, which was not overly "exclusive", featured a health food shop in the "sleepy town of Maidenhead". The spread of health food shops and herbalists is another characteristic of that period and since, but is often overlooked in the 1960s chronicles. Now we take them for granted with most towns and cities having quite a few, and when political bureaucrats tighten controls on healing products, thousands of customers protest through petitions and campaigning letters. Brown rice, vitamin supplements, soya milk and herbal teas have become features of the staple diets of many ordinary people, which was not generally true in the 1960s.

Evidence of the spread of interest in such matters can be found in the willingness of the media to examine and represent them. To take one example, the *Observer,* 26 October, 2003, carried a half-page news article on film-maker David Lynch's practice of Transcendental Meditation. That week, he had appeared in a press conference to launch

> A $1 billion fundraising campaign to build 100 'peace palaces'
> across America, part of a plan for 3,000 buildings across the globe,
> one in each major city (News, 23).

Lynch told reporter Paul Harris that "Peace could be on the earth this year". He was clearly a little optimistic but at least he was trying. In the same newspaper (29) the highly respected weekly column of David Aaronovitch carried the subtitle, "We'll believe anything these days". He examined with some scepticism the idea that Princess Diana psychically foretold her own death, and the results of a television programme examining whether prayers by others could aid patient recovery. He suggested that the majority of people today would rather risk "fat-headed gullibility" than "bonehead smugness", concluding that we are all "barking".

In the magazine section of the same edition, Polly Vernon examined our consumption of self-help books ("Feel the Fear & Read it Anyway…"). She reported that "even the most standard issue self-help disciple has an average of 12 help books". These books include titles like *Feel the Fear and Do It Anyway*, *Men are from Mars Women are from Venus*, *A Course in Miracles* and *Chicken Soup for the Soul*. Although twice as many women buy such books as men, the divide is not absolute and there is a wide age range. Sales are huge, rising in the early twenty-first century from £30m – £38m per year. It is a part of the growing 'Mind, Body & Spirit' movement, which includes major public events, glossy magazines like *Kindred Spirit* and a general obsession with well-being which the traditional organs of the state do not always satisfy. The article in the *Observer* identified Eileen Campbell as the self-help pioneer behind this cultural explosion, and recounted how she began this work, "after she returned, thoroughly enlightened, from a tour of the then relatively uncharted hippy trail in the mid-1970s".

This is just one example from just one Sunday and just one 'serious' British broadsheet. At the same time, the worldwide Anglican Church seemed poised to tear itself apart over the appointment of a Gay Bishop in the United States, and *the Sunday Times* carried a piece by India Knight from her forthcoming book suggesting that since we were spending more than £237 billion in shops in 2003, "you could argue quite convincingly that it has become our national religion" (News Review 6.4). By contrast there has been an extraordinary transformation in the lives of many thousands of people through the growing impact of the ecological, alternative and New Age movements since the 1960s. It begs the question why this is so often treated as nonsense or perhaps a minority issue, since so much of it has a positive potential.

Even at its most sceptical, the *Observer* found such topics newsworthy.

Meanwhile, every weekend, the *Sunday Times* publishes advice about alternative therapies and relatively lengthy horoscopes. It is hard to imagine similar coverage fifty years earlier. This example from 2003, while not chosen arbitrarily, was not isolated either. On 8 January 2017, the *Observer Magazine* carried a range of pieces all of which might be seen as having their roots in the late-1960s. The first showed a very stylish long-haired male model in a floral display of the latest fashions from 'House of Hackney', while two of the main articles that week were by food critic Jay Rayner attending a challenging silent retreat, and reporting on others following similar "wellness' activities, and American writer Ayelet Waldman reporting on her "micro-dosing LSD" to address "a near-suicidal depression". Towards the back of the magazine there were regular columns, including one offering advice about a sexual relationship, another ("A Brush with Greatness") in which Rick Wakeman described working on a recording session by David Bowie in 1969, Lucy Siegle's "Ethical Living" about the "Eco Guide to Taking Action in 2017", and Nigel Slater's "Food & Drink" recipe for "Midweek Dinner" – nothing less than Spiced *Lentil* Soup. The hippies are still everywhere.

In August 2016, the *Observer Magazine* in another of the weekly series "A Brush with Greatness", published an article by Paul Webster describing a 1973 meeting in Hydra with Marianne Ihlen – the woman for whom Leonard Cohen had written "So Long Marianne". He related how she prepared lunch for them, hoped they might forge a friendship with her son and then afterwards

> We sat among the cushions scattered over the stone floor while she gamely tried to explain the *I Ching*, a text compiling centuries of Chinese wisdom, fashionable in the 1960s.

Portsmouth's oldest surviving 'New Age' shop, is Aristia in Albert Road, exactly opposite the first school I attended, 60 years earlier. It opened in 1989 and stocks everything you might expect, including the *I Ching*, other books such as *Tibetan Book of the Dead* and *Bhagavad Gita,* and

> Ascended master pictures, Books, Copper discs, Music, Essences and sprays, Quartz and Metal singing bowls, Incense and smudge sticks, Tarot and Oracle decks and the home of the Crystal Oversoul range of images and products.

Topics there might include astrology, ley lines, crystal healing, while their visitors might chant, meditate, refuse meat, discuss rising signs, karma and reincarnation, support green issues and turn away from many of the more ostentatious and materialistic practices of their peers. While Aristia, and similar shops in many other towns and cities, survive and attract new customers, we might wonder more broadly whether every consideration of the legacy of the late 1960s' counterculture should acknowledge that the spiritual or New Age element is increasingly ubiquitous – without necessarily being seen merely as a product of those extraordinary days of the late 1960s. Miles, 2003, for example, noted

> Casting the *I Ching*, reading tarot cards and calculating astrological signs are now practiced by millions of people, very few of whom first read about them in the *San Francisco Oracle (372)*.

That aspect of the western world changed significantly in the late 1960s and it has not ceased since.

AFTERMATH

COUNTRY JOE McDONALD with REET, PETITE & GONE.

Southsea Bandstand, 2001

AFTERMATH

This book has brought together on the one hand, some fairly well documented aspects of the swinging sixties and the counterculture from across the western world, with a more detailed and less familiar history of Portsmouth, including aspects of my life during those years. While I have challenged the idea that the extraordinary changes of the late 1960s, simply ended as a consequence of a few, mostly American, events, I accept that the 'collective' experience of the 1970s and beyond, was by comparison, somewhat fragmented and dispersed as people often followed preferences in smaller groups or sometimes individually.

Any attempt to write a comprehensive account of the legacy of those times would require at the very least, another complete book, so while this final chapter is very much about what followed, it is also the most personal part of *Autumn of Love*. It is largely about how I believe those times impacted on the person I became – and true to those times, I am still 'becoming'.

At the start of this book I noted Dominic Sandbrook's claim that

> For most people in Britain, the Sixties didn't swing at all. As well as reflecting all the gaudy excitement of the period, I also wanted to reflect the lives of millions of people who felt left out or alienated by the cultural changes of the day.

What I have tried to establish throughout this book is that there was a good deal more swinging going on in provincial Portsmouth than Sandbrook seems willing to acknowledge, and that since Portsmouth was never leading the changes in those days, it is surely reasonable to suggest that the same situation might have obtained elsewhere.

None of this is to dispute that there were millions of people who were only slightly affected by the changes of that decade, although whether that left them feeling "left out or alienated" is another matter altogether. My father was in his mid-40s at the start of the 1960s and lived through them as quietly and kindly as he did most of the rest of his life. He did not enjoy much of contemporary or popular culture, particularly from the USA, but it would be wrong to suggest that he was not touched by what went on, given the life enjoyed by his son, and since his slightly younger daughter would embark on a four-year foundation/fine art 'degree' (Dip AD) as the 1960s drew to a close. The people my father loved and cared for, filled his house with the new music and fashion, with contemporary art and, in my case, with noisy disputes about political issues, which sometimes distressed my rather sensitive mum. She on the other hand, was interested in what my sister and I were up to, even came to see a couple of my gigs, and rather liked Ray Davies singing "Waterloo Sunset".

Some aspects of our lives might have left our parents feeling alienated, but I doubt whether my dad in particular ever felt "left out", other than in the sense that he chose and preferred to be. My folks led quiet lives, enjoying a modest lifestyle, through the decade. Ted Brooks tells an interesting tale that when he and his brothers and sister got involved in the local mod scene, their dad both observed and approved of the considerable care they took over their smart appearances – although he was less impressed as the clothes became more flamboyant and the hair longer, towards the late 1960s

But Sandbrook's other point is that those of us who were not "left out" or "alienated" were, by contrast, living lives of "gaudy excitement". There is no doubt that some aspects of those days were gaudy, in the sense of being too bright, highly decorated, and even tasteless or vulgar, but while our decade was the one that shifted from black & white 'realism' into technicolour dreams, through fashions, or graphics on our television and cinema screens and the Sunday magazine supplements, colourful is not the same thing as "gaudy", and I have tried to show that as we moved through adolescence towards early adulthood, it was possible to take a more rounded, mature and ultimately enriched approach to what was new.

For example, at 13 I bought my first pair of jeans, joined the Beatles' fan club and giggled at their witty seasonal flexidisc, which we received at Christmas. Within three years I was listening to "Tomorrow Never Knows", enjoying the Duke Ellington Orchestra at the Guildhall, and studying contemporary painting and sculpture. By 19, as the sixties drew to a close, I was reading Marcuse, using the I Ching, debating the merits of communal living and writing and performing music created by my band. Why would it have been otherwise? In what senses were those latter experiences merely "gaudy"? They were a part of growing up, and they have stayed with me in certain ways, as I have continued to grow. They were a part of 'becoming'.

Graham Laker has identified growing up in 1960s Portsmouth very succinctly for our generation of boys at least. He describes our route to the Summer of Love as:

'62: Young rockers – quiffed hair, Bobby Vee lookalikes
'63: Beatle clones
'64: The Rolling Stones became 'our ideals'.
'65: Turned into smart, pill popping mods.
'66: Well turned-out stylists.
'67: Summer of Love, hippies.

We did not know each other until the end of that story in the late 1960s, but it is very similar to the tale I have related, with a slightly older generation perhaps adding beatniks at the start.

One of the followers of the Pompey Pop Blog is Dave Glass, who grew up in Portsmouth but many years ago, moved across the seas to Norway. He once suggested, delightfully, on the Blog that were he to "write a book about that all-too-short period in my life when pop music was central to it, the title could be *From Charlie Drake to Nick Drake*", as in, "he's a bit moody, more Nick than Charlie". Dave also imagined travelling musically about the city, where North End's Soul Parlour brought to mind Paul Kossoff's guitar, the opening to the Action's "In My Lonely Room" suggested the Birdcage, at Kimbells it would be J Crow Combo playing "Pink Champagne" and passing the Rendezvous, Graham Bond's version of "Wade in the Water". He lived in the middle of Portsea Island but Billy Manning's seaside funfair brought back Freddy Cannon's "Palisades Park" or the Everly Brothers' "Ferris Wheel", while the Drifters' "Under the Boardwalk" transports him to the seafront promenade – an evocative environment denied to those stuck in London

I have suggested that, in Britain in particular, it makes no sense to suggest that the hopes and dreams of those days disappeared in the few months that covered American events like the Manson murders, Woodstock, and Altamont. While I have lived through considerable changes over the past 40+ years, this story has no clear ending and perhaps never will. Writing this book is simply one more consequence of the days that began back then.

Nonetheless, as the 1960s turned into 1970, I was no longer a teenager, the dream of a professional career in music was disappearing rapidly, and my life seemed to be following a more conventional path. By mid-summer I was playing less music, in full-time employment at last, studying part-time in preparation for what would become a much longer career, and in the early stages of a relationship with a young woman who would become, briefly, my first wife.

Presented that bluntly, the synopsis is perhaps almost a personal equivalent of the grander tales that the historians tell of Woodstock, Manson and Altamont, bringing the 'hippie dream' to a conclusion – but as with that account, I do not believe it. Things changed of course, but just as the world could never go back to the way it was in the early 1960s, so my life in 1970 and beyond, was one that would have been unimaginable just three or four years earlier. As I moved from teenage to adult life, I carried with me certain values and attitudes that I had developed in those few years. Much of my recent life had been a novelty, and like all such things, elements of it were superficial and ephemeral, but the more robust aspects of those experiences did not merely look forwards to a new world, but also built on much of what had gone before. Just as the psychedelic music of the San Francisco bands grew from the roots of the "old weird America", or the Beatles incorporated elements of British music hall in their *Sgt Pepper* album, so the best of the social and cultural elements of the counterculture drew on older political, social and spiritual ideas, derived from issues such as ecology, democracy, and equality. Miles (2003) noted that while much of what we call New Age existed well before the 1960s, our time was one of "*rediscovery*, as well as a time of invention" (my emphasis, 372). Another who came to acknowledge the value of the deeper roots was Robert Hunter, the lyricist for the Grateful Dead, who said that his purpose in writing was

> The exaltation of my spirit through other spirits. Traditional tools and forms are often apt for the purpose such as the 'Come All Ye' forms so popular in sailor songs and union ballads (Hill 2016, 8).

In March 1970, while still hoping that Rosemary would release the single and become fully professional, I started working as a labourer for the city's Parks Department on Southsea seafront, where I stayed for 18 months. After Rosemary split in the summer, Mick Legg and I were founding members of the rock band, Gilbey Twiss, but that did not last long, the band calling a halt early in 1971. I sold my (Selmer) PA system to a local band, Fernhill (formerly Dragonfly), and went to their next gig, to make sure everything worked properly – it happened to be at Brighton University, supporting Rod Stewart & the Faces, which was fun. Fernhill included Mark Lundquist, who went on to play with a version of Cliff Bennett & the Rebel Rousers, and often with the SAS Band, fronted by Spike Edney from Landport who, over the years has worked with so many big names, including keyboards with Queen. Guitarist Mark still plays, but also runs an agency and has worked with Procul Harum, the Commitments, the Drifters and others.

Having decided my hopes of a *professional* music career were over, I started attending evening classes at the Art College again, before, in September 1971, I began a four-year, full-time degree course, studying to teach Art in secondary schools. I graduated in the summer of 1975, and began a 10-year career as a comprehensive school art teacher.

The musical retirement did not last of course. At college, I met a fine blues/folk/roots acoustic guitarist called Bob Cooper-Grundy and we started working as a duo – much as I had done in the 1960s with Pete Gurd. In 1975, we increased that to a seven-piece jug/skiffle/blues band called Skys is Cryin', including fiddle, mandolin and washboard and entered a national student talent contest – mainly because the sponsors were offering free beer! One of the newcomers, Denis Reeve-Baker, played guitar and mandolin, and more than 40 years and at least half-a-dozen bands later, we are great buddies and still playing together in two bands. Skys is Cryin' won four rounds of that student competition, including the Final at Hammersmith Odeon (now the Apollo), where we appeared supporting Steeleye Span. The MC was Bob Harris and the judges included Alan Bown, who was clearly destined to play a part in my life – but while we took home £750 in prize money, it did not lead to much beyond a few years of some interesting gigs. Most of these were on the folk scene, although around 1978, in an effort to attract more interest, we entered one of those old *Melody Maker* competitions and went through from our regional heat at Southampton University, which led us to a semi-final at the Marquee Club. We looked for the most part like old hippies and there we were with dobro, washboard, mandolin, and harmonicas, playing old American songs – a bit like a Harry Smith tribute band. This would have been fine except that virtually all the other bands that day (plus their noisy supporters) were younger punks/new wavers. It could have been dodgy, but I think they figured we were rather quaint and no threat and in the end, they rather enjoyed us. It was my second gig at the legendary Marquee Club but I never got a penny from either – and this time we did not make the Final.

Continuing to play, as I have done ever since, provides a clear link with the 1960s, and after 50 years I can claim to have been reasonably successful as a semi-professional local musician. I am writing this around Christmas 2016, a period of three gigs in 10 days and I wonder whether they will ever stop? Music has been a constant blessing in my life, but my involvement in it reaches back before the days of the counterculture, so the bigger legacy from those days, was probably through politics, experimental mixed/multi-media art; to a greater degree the spiritual and 'New Age' ideas, and perhaps most-of-all, on my life in education

There is no longer anything like the four-year degree course I did in the early 1970s. We came to be characterised as the dangerously 'progressive' generation, the liberals who believed in child-centred education and caused years of disorder and dismay in the country. It is such nonsense that it would take too long to address it usefully here. In truth, the vast majority of my fellow students, and even more my subsequent fellow schoolteachers, were pretty ordinary, liberal-minded, yet socially fairly conservative people. Most cared about the 'kids' and did their best to address some serious difficulties that some youngsters brought with them, but they were not interested in anything 'revolutionary'. In addition, through the 1970s, they were dealing with the first big upheavals in a generation in the schools, including the raising of the school leaving age, declining job opportunities and apprentice-ships for teenagers, and most of all, the shift from the bi/tri-partite secondary schools to an under-resourced comprehensive system that was never actually 'comprehensive'. There was also the famous Ruskin College speech by James Callaghan in 1976 which ushered in a period of increasing interference in the daily working of schools by central government. That is a tendency that persists to this day and if all these changes over the past 40 years have been so fine, why have there been so many, and why do we still hear about so many 'failing' schools?

In my student days, I had one year as Social Secretary, promoting a number of local and national acts in a variety of venues, including a fairly odd night with Status Quo at the Guildhall and an even odder one with the Radha Krishna Temple at the college. In addition, I involved myself in student politics, which had grown from the spirit of 1968, and by the early 1970s was fairly lively. My political views have always been broadly left of centre, but around the world of students in those days, the array of groups on the far left often bewildered me; sometimes recalling that parody in Monty Python's *Life of Brian*. They included the International Marxist Group and a couple of Trotskyite organisations (I think), the Workers' Revolutionary Party and the International Socialists (soon to become the SWP). On one occasion, a few of us joined a caucus meeting to learn precisely how many weeks it would be until the Revolution – and I am not being entirely tongue-in-cheek here. During the call to 'arms', a couple of guys wandered in by accident, looking for a different meeting and apologized, but the man running the meeting (were they always men?) went berserk, and shouted and swore at them for having the temerity to make this genuine and very slight mistake. I've never forgotten it, and while I have not experienced anything like that in my years as a pretty inactive member of the Labour Party, you hear stories. Maybe the hard left just attracts all the bad-tempered people?

In case you might have forgotten, the Revolution did not arrive in the 1970s, despite the 'victory' by the miners and the defeat of Heath's Government – although you might argue that a very different revolution arrived a decade later, and is not merely continuing but growing more alarming almost by the week. Apart from the sheer absence of humanity in that exchange above, I was struck too by the absence of humour and imagination on the left. Both elements had been more apparent in parts of the counterculture, but it seemed there was no longer any '*play* power' and it would be difficult today to accuse the left of either humour or imagination in any noticeable quantities. Back then, I witnessed one example however, during a speech in the main hall to the whole conference. During a gay rights debate, a male delegate dressed like a Young Conservative presented a ranting speech against the evils of homosexuality and how the NUS should reject any motion of support. As the audience got restless, another young man – quite possibly his boyfriend – walked to the podium, they embraced and kissed and walked off hand-in-hand. It was a kind of delightful political theatre, but not something the conventional left would normally try.

In a broad sense, the 1970s were often more *effectively* 'radical' than the late 1960s, and among students there were more protest marches and demonstrations – certainly about grants and educational cuts, but also wider political issues, such as protesting the visit to Britain of the Portuguese Prime Minister Caetano who led a repressive regime at home, and in Portugal's African countries (Mozambique and others) – I guess it might be considered preparation for the proposed visit of President Trump. I made up for missing '1968', by participating in marches, and we ran a local 'Third World First' group that raised money and distributed educational material abroad. There was another Friends of the Earth-type group at college run by a really nice guy called Steve Jones – one of their projects was a Dutch 'white bicycle' scheme for Portsmouth students, although I am not sure it worked perfectly.

What my 1,000 fellow students shared in common was education and schooling. The early days of the underground in London had been associated with something called the London Free School, although in those days 'Free Schools' were very different from what that means today – they were essentially 'free' from government and local authority control, setting their own curriculum. The people involved in the London Free School were those who developed the UFO club, *International Times* and other initiatives, and Boyd has noted that the two things that survived from then are Release, the drugs and legal support charity, and the Notting Hill Carnival; it seems however there was not really much in the sense of a 'school'. The early-1970s Free Schools were generally fairly short-lived and perhaps mostly resembled extended versions of 'home schooling', with volunteers teaching small groups of children, largely free from the state system. There were such free schools at least in Liverpool, Manchester and Islington, London and while I was a student, I visited the last two, as well as a remarkable purpose-built progressive comprehensive school on the outskirts of Leicester called Countesthorpe College. These visits informed my degree dissertation on the 'Radical Tradition' in English education. I am not sure you could do that now.

These initiatives challenged many of my assumptions about teaching. Until the 1970s, 'progressive' schooling was generally only available if you could pay considerable sums to attend schools like AS Neil's Summerhill, Bedales near Petersfield or Abbotsholme, but suddenly an alternative might be available to 'ordinary' young people. Alongside these developments, there were a number of other initiatives – Rank & File was the radical wing of the National Union of Teachers, and there were publications about pupils' rights such as the magazine *Libertarian Education* which I sold at college, the one-off *Great Brain Robbery* and a couple that for somewhat different reasons became infamous, *Schoolkids Oz* and the *Little Red Schoolbook*. I still work a little in teaching, although no longer with schools, which must be a relief to some people. It all seems such a long time ago, and of course some of the ideas were half-formed and even crazy, while other aspects have remained with me – centrally the importance of being respectful of anyone whose education you are charged with supporting, although I cannot pretend that over 35 years I always met that aspiration.

After graduating, I worked in local comprehensive schools, mostly as an art teacher, introducing photography and video cameras into my art room, which led me towards an increasing involvement in media & film studies. In terms of discussions around issues like representation, agency and industry, that work was clearly 'political' – and I make no apologies for that since I believe adolescents need and deserve (non-partisan) political education. Over the past forty years, I would expect generations of Media Studies students to have had a pretty good grasp of what is currently described as 'fake news'. In 1985, after ten years in the classroom, I spent three years working on a very large, national project about all the arts in schools across the age range 5-18, during which we collaborated with the Arts Council, Crafts Council and British Film Institute. That government-funded project was one of a number based on a commitment to the idea that the most effective curriculum development should be teacher-led. It was easy to support that idea and I think we produced a good deal of evidence in its favour, but during the three years of the project, Prime Minister Margaret Thatcher and her henchman Kenneth Baker introduced the Education Reform Act, which included the National Curriculum. That was the end of the brief period of teachers being thought of as the ones who knew best. I moved on to the Education Department at Portsmouth Polytechnic, and while it was becoming the University of Portsmouth in 1992, I was gradually moving away from schools and into teaching arts and humanities subjects to undergraduates, which is eventually where I settled. A secondary school today, would seem like a foreign land to me.

I am relating these tales because it seems to me that my approach, my beliefs, my values in this professional work – and my overall commitment to teaching which, post-retirement, I still do on a voluntary basis – owes *something* to the influence of the counterculture. This is partly to do with a suspicion of authority, especially when it exercises itself simply to assert its right to do so. What the counterculture offered was a sense that I was not alone and that there were strategies for dealing with the difficulties in alternative ways – or at least alleviating the irritation. One of the constant positive strategies in my life is to get back to creative work, which has mattered throughout my life. It can take various forms, including of course visual art, but ultimately music has been the constant great factor; a world away from the world, with the stage, in Dick Heckstall-Smith's phrase, "the safest place in the world".

Since the late 1960s and Rosemary, which I do think of as a genuinely psyche-delic band, I have never again played anything to which I would apply that label, although some of my music-making is related to it. I have mentioned that my next venture was a rock band and, despite an abiding admiration for the music of Hendrix and Cream, I discovered early in the 1970s that on the whole, rock music was not for me. There were exceptions of a kind, mostly American, such as Little Feat, the Band, Steely Dan and later, the 'new wave' of Television or Talking Heads for example, but on the whole I did not like it very much. I remember anticipating eagerly the first Led Zeppelin album but I found it disappointing, and when I saw them a couple of times I was not at all fond of them. The evening that sealed it around the same time however, was a Portsmouth Polytechnic gig featuring the latest band to cause some excitement, Black Sabbath who seemed to me not merely loud in a very dull way, but literally depressing – there was not a thing about them that I found uplifting. A few years ago, BBC4 put out a celebratory programme about heavy metal that tried to argue it was the product of the environment of the 'Black Country'. Apparently if you grew up and then worked around Birmingham and the west midlands, it was inevitable your music would reflect that experience. It was a pretty unconvincing example of cultural determinism, since it conveniently ignored acts such as the Moody Blues, the Spencer Davis Group, Traffic, the Rockin' Berries, the Fortunes, Duran Duran, plus the Move, the Idle Race and all the Roy Wood/ Jeff Lynne projects and the ska/reggae influence on acts like the Beat, UB40 and Steel Pulse among others.

During the 1970s, I reverted to my earlier days, playing acoustic blues and string & jug band stuff – very much of the kind that the guys in the Grateful

Dead, Country Joe & the Fish, Jefferson Airplane, the Byrds and the Charlatans had played in the early 1960s, and influenced at that time by some fine American musicians such as Ry Cooder, Taj Mahal, Dave Bromberg and others. Bob & I wrote a Blues column in the student magazine and in 1976 I enjoyed a three-month spell as a radio blues DJ on Portsmouth's Radio Victory, deputising during the summer for the regular jazz guy Tim Colwell. I loved that hour every week, and about 20 years later I had another much longer spell doing much the same thing on our local BBC Radio Solent, which I eventually extended to a broader, roots, thematic thing – a bit like a modern-day Harry Smith.

In the early 1980s, I had a brief, delightful spell, playing in London with a large (11/12 piece) rhythm & blues, rock & roll band called the Operation. It included some of my buddies from Skys is Cryin' and we were mainly a busking band in the early days of the 'new' Covent Garden. When their singer went off around the world they called me up, and I'd travel to London every weekend, after school on Friday. Eventually the singer returned, but we simply expanded and soon got picked up with the other buskers to entertain the great and the good at the opening of the London Film Festival that year, where the punters included Prince Charles and (the then) Lady Diana! The other singer, Andy Rankin, left to join a newly formed Irish 'punk' band, switching to the drums – they were called the Pogues, and did pretty well, especially at Christmas.

After that, I returned to Portsmouth and through the 1980s played with a core of the same local guys in three successive rhythm & blues bands, Steel Mill (very much 1964-style), the Reds (more contemporary, Fabulous Thunderbirds, Ronnie Earl etc.) and the Notorious Strawboys who included a pedal steel and were a bit more 'rocky', a bit western swing, even a bit country. In the Reds, I reunited with my pal Denis from Skys is Cryin' plus Rosemary's Dave Pittard on drums and Brian Kemp from Heaven on organ – poor Brian was killed in a road accident, after which there was a big tribute night to him on South Parade Pier. He was a fine talent and his work remains with us in the album recordings he did with Heaven and later, as the keyboard player with my pal Mark Andrews and his Gents, who also included at one time a fine local drummer, Mr Lenny Tench.

Those 1980s bands were playing just local gigs – in Steel Mill we had a Friday night residency in the pub next door to the old Birdcage, 'Charley Hurdles', which was rather special, and often full to bursting. I came to love playing locally on a scene where you entertained your mates and made new ones. In the Reds, some of our more special gigs were for Birdcage boys Chris Abbott and Jim Lawrence, who began what became another legendary Pompey club, Basins. It started as a rhythm & blues club for our generation but soon became popular with the younger generation who came to see contemporary post-punk, reggae and somewhat quirky acts, but we have two claims to fame – we were the first band *ever* to play at Basins when it opened at SPECS in Palmerston Road, and we were the only band to appear at all three Basins venues; that one, plus Kimbells and finally the Tricorn. In particular, we played a number of support gigs to Wilko Johnson, while one of the finest of local bands, Emptifish were riotous regulars, supported by the Shakin' Sharks and Pompey's 657 crew. They (Emptifish & the Sharks) got back together in 2016, including a terrific performance at the Victorious Festival on Southsea Common.

I would not suggest that what I am describing here is countercultural – at least not beyond the link with a local community – but I think it was interesting in the way it reflected a couple of key aspects of what developed during and beyond the 1960s. Firstly, we were local musicians in our 30s, 40s, mostly in relationships or married, with homes and jobs, but still choosing to continue playing on a regular basis as semi-professionals – and there were plenty of us out there doing that. Secondly, within the context of the normal compromises that occur within bands, we were playing the music we wanted to. We were, in that sense, very different from acts who sought more frequent and better paid work by playing current or past hits, or perhaps following the growing fashion for tribute bands and taking gigs at parties, weddings and the like, for audiences that were not bothered about much except having a dance and maybe singing along. I'm not really describing the Blues Brothers' "Rawhide" sequence here, but art it ain't – and if the retort is that neither were we, that's fair enough, but at least we were playing what we wanted to play, and getting gigs for as long as our audiences liked it.

Nonetheless around 1991, the Notorious Strawboys reached its natural end, and in my 40s with a new job at the University, it felt to me again like a natural point to retire from the world of rock & roll in the pub or club on a Friday night. And while it was not at all the end of my musical career, since then it has generally consisted of gentler acoustic sounds, rooted in the past.

That phase began with a band called Reet Petite & Gone, which started in an 'open mic' night in a local pub, just around the corner from where I now live at the harbour-mouth end of town, where I first met acoustic and dobro guitar player Stewart Carr. At some point, we started playing together in each other's homes and my old pal Denis joined in. I added washboard (played with wire brushes) to vocals and harmonica and we played country/folk blues, jug band stuff and a few 'odds & ends' in that style. Fairly soon, we recruited Nick Evans, the multi-instrumentalist pedal steel player in the Notorious Strawboys, but playing mandolin with us, and we set off on a middle-aged adventure. When we retired from regular work in the late 1990s, we had played all over England, notably on the folk and blues scene and including the festivals at Glastonbury (twice), Cambridge (Folk) and others from Cornwall to Kent and Portsmouth to Redcar. We made four albums, mostly self-funded, with one on a 'real' label, we appeared on bits of television, and did a rather special live show for the Paul Jones Blues Show on BBC Radio 2. There was also a regular residency at the RMA Tavern in Eastney where again we played to our mates and our local community. It was all rather fine and rather fun. We were all working regularly during the day however, and in the end, it was too demanding, so again we pretended to retire, although we got back together every now and then, for the occasional gig. Then something quite extraordinary happened, for me, almost more remarkable than the record contract in 1968, and ultimately more rewarding.

I hardly drink these days, not because I have had any problem with alcohol, but because I feel better for it. But this extraordinary moment in my life emanated from a couple of somewhat drunken evenings. On the first, at home, I watched yet again the *Woodstock* film and got a bit misty eyed about Country Joe & the Fish. Unlike 1967, or even 1987, I now had access to the internet so I went searching for them, and found Country Joe's site with the shop, and news stories, and photos, and an address in Berkeley.

So, entirely speculatively, I sent Joe two of the albums made by Reet, Petite & Gone with a note explaining how much I'd always loved their albums – especially the first two – and how I'd seen him in Portsmouth 30 years before. I thought nothing more about it, but after some months he replied, saying that our recordings reminded him of the early pre-Vanguard, acoustic sound of his band in Berkeley.

I was thrilled by this but did not pursue it. Then I went to an evening at South Parade Pier, where I had first seen Country Joe & the Fish all those years before, and this too was a nostalgic evening – a Birdcage reunion with Pompey mods and Jimmy James & the Vagabonds. It was all rather delightful, and I spent quite a time chatting to my pal and local promoter John Roberts, who like me was a big fan of Country Joe & the Fish. He was also a local musician and had always liked Reet, Petite & Gone, so he kept pressing me to say what it would take to get the band back together. In the end, after yet another whiskey, I told him that if he could set up a tour with Joe, we'd do it. I was not really serious, nor was I thinking we might play *with him*, at best, simply tour as the support act. John took me at my word, contacted Joe and set the whole thing up, with us touring as his back-up band.

It was almost that simple. In the summer of 2001, John collected Joe from Heathrow and brought him to my home, where we lived above Old

Portsmouth's Sallyport Tearooms, which my wife Lou ran from 1996-2008. Joe stayed with us and we spent lots of time together chatting about the old days among other things. The guys had learned some of Joe's songs before he arrived and we rehearsed acoustically in our lounge before setting off on tour. For the most part we played Joe's songs from the early albums but in our amplified acoustic, 'skiffle' style. A privately recorded CD exists of the performance at London's Borderline Club and is typical of the performances on that tour with a set that includes, "Superbird", "Janis", "Flyin' High", "Not So Sweet Martha Lorrainne", "Death Sound Blues", "Who am I", "Thought Dream", Here I Go Again" and of course, the F-U-C-K cheer and "I-Feel-Like-I'm Fixin'-to-Die". Other songs included the political/social content of "Tricky Dicky" (Nixon), "Save the Whales" and "Summer of Love". Joe often played an additional solo set, including his Florence Nightingale song "Lady with the Lamp", selections from the album *War, War, War,* and there were often amusing recitations about the great banana hoax or the cheer.

The great night was probably that Borderline gig of which Max Bell in the *Evening Standard* (26.7.2001) said of Joe – "a counterculture superstar for a while":

> Looking at the small stocky figure … it's hard to equate the two eras, but as soon as he opened his mouth or blew upon his harmonica the memories flooded back … (He) began with a song yearning for the "Summer of Love" (and) thereafter he got down to his lampooning business with mini historical songs about discredited Presidents Nixon and LBJ, the hippy nemesis. Ole Joe wasn't alone in his ramblings since he was backed by the British jug band Reet, Petite & Gone who added appropriate dollops of Dobro, mandolin, slide guitar and snare drum to a well-worn mix … the troubadour won everyone over with his tall stories … good to see he hasn't lost his sense of humour.

That last point has always seemed important to me. I love Joe's gentler songs and sharp lyrics, I love the band's psychedelic sound, but in addition, they were always also one of the funniest of the bands from that period, when quite a lot of what emerged on stage could be a little 'po-faced'.

The tour began at the same South Parade Pier venue, almost exactly 32 years after that magical night in 1969, and having crossed the country, it ended on a Sunday afternoon with a free concert in Pompey blacksmith Pete Clutterbuck's beautiful Bandstand, on a blazing hot Southsea seafront – again almost exactly 32 years after the first free one on the Common. Despite Altamont, Manson, austerity and everything else, these things are never really over unless you allow them to be. Why would I wish to do that?

It did not finish there either. Joe came back in 2005 and brought three of the four guys from the classic line-up of Country Joe & the Fish. Missing was Barry Melton, who is now a lawyer, and apparently is unwilling to play with the others as Country Joe & the Fish, insisting on his right to be 'the Fish', so they called themselves the Country Joe Band – but there they were, Joe, Bruce, David and Chicken. They arrived in Portsmouth with John Roberts one summer evening when I was playing at the RMA in a new band with Denis, which had moved away from the blues. We had just started playing our take on "Woodstock" when entirely by chance, the guys walked in and played a short unplanned set, including Chicken, with no kit, drumming the room. I toured with them for part of that summer, taking my car to ease the load and they took it in turns to drive with me, which meant all kinds of different tales. David was a Buddhist and I took him to meet and chant with the SGI group in Portsmouth, Bruce related his years with the famous San Francisco Mime Troup and he and I talked politics more than the others. They had button badges saying "Fuck Bush" and Bruce had written a new song "Cakewalk to Baghdad". With Chicken, I talked mostly jazz and painting, while Joe and I knew each other by then well enough to range around topics. It was simply a delight, not least a lovely day at Fairport's Cropredy Festival, where they shared the bill with Jah Wobble, and were very well received.

Here's a strange thought about Country Joe & the Fish and their belated relationship with Portsmouth. As far as I am aware, the version of that band that made the first three albums Joe, Barry, Bruce, David and Chicken is the only major band from the days of Haight Ashbury from which all the members are still alive. The Portsmouth point is that the same thing can be said of 'our' two local hit-making bands of the 1960s, Manfred Mann and Simon Dupree & the Big Sound. But how many other successful bands from that time can you name that, at the start of 2017, were still all with us. Not the Beatles or Rolling Stones of course, not the Who or Small Faces, not the Kinks or Beach Boys, not the Doors or Cream and so on. Maybe it's something in the Southsea air?

Joe came back solo in 2007. He was 65 and seemed pretty tired of life as a solo artist on the road, but generally gave good performances, although he was not always cheerful. The highlight of that tour was a lunchtime spot at the Isle of Wight Festival, followed by Keane, Paolo Nutini, one of the Spice Girls and a top-of-the-bill bunch called the Rolling Stones. We had luxurious facilities backstage – our own mobile home, shower, bed, drinks, food, bowls of fruit, while the Stones, nowhere to be seen, had taken over the whole of a hotel behind the site. No-one was allowed on stage when they did their early morning sound check and their guitars – maybe 30 or more? – hung at the back with police 'do not cross' tape keeping them safe. There was an outdoor TV studio and Joe did an interview and then played very well – although afterwards some guy hassled him about doing the "F-U-C-K Cheer" with kids present. John (spoons) and I (washboard) were called up to play and sing on "I-Feel-Like-I'm-Fixing-to-Die", and there's a video recording of it somewhere on YouTube. It was rather fun and John and I wore specially made T-shirts with a huge F on the front. We had backstage access for the day, but late in the afternoon, Joe felt tired, so we went back to Portsmouth without seeing the Stones. It often felt to me in that week, as if those few years with Joe were at an end, and indeed he has pretty much retired now, certainly from overseas tours. 2007 was not always such fun, but I'll be grateful to John and Joe for ever for those wonderful experiences.

Subsequently, John has organized and often 'sponsored' tours with a number of guys from way back. Chicken disappeared but Bruce and David returned with Greg Douglass from the Steve Miller Band and Roy Blumenfeld from the Blues Project (Monterey Pop again) as the Former Members, and on a couple of occasions I got to sit in with them on harmonica. Then 'Grandpa Banana' from the Youngbloods came over and Reet Petite & Gone, back together yet again, supported him at the much-lamented Eastney Cellars; David La Flamme toured with a version of It's Beautiful Day, including Steve Browning of the Reds 'depping' on bass guitar, and Barry Melton came solo in 2010 when we supported again, and ended up with a big band, jamming "San Francisco Bay Blues" at the Pier. When they came to Portsmouth, John would usually bring them to our place for lunch or supper which was always such a pleasure – they were lovely guys, all of them. In the summer of 2016, Ross Hannan promoted a fine event at Dimbola Lodge on the Isle of Wight where Bruce Barthol did a solo spot, and Barry 'the Fish' Melton and Grandpa Banana played a really excellent acoustic duo set of mostly the old tunes from way back. As I finish this book, I'm planning with John, a Portsmouth Guildhall gig to launch its publication, featuring Bruce Barthol, just a couple of days after the fiftieth anniversary of Monterey Pop.

And so, it goes on. Denis, Nick and I have a six-piece acoustic band now called Scarlet Town that draws upon a broad range of material including English folk songs, Bob Dylan, Country Joe and the Grateful Dead, Gillian Welch, Pentangle, Alison Krauss and even (sometimes) "Morning Glory" by Tim Buckley, which we used to do in Rosemary back in 1969. We play here-and-there around town, including a fine club called Barebones run by our double bass player Dave Jordan. It is *completely* acoustic, entry is free with a collection, and you bring your own food and drink. It is a delight, harking back to the folk clubs and coffee houses of the 1960s.

In October 2014, Denis and I ran a skiffle workshop at the Guildhall (Portsmouth Civic Trust) as part of Portsmouth's annual 60+ Festival. The participants ranged from a few experienced players, to people who had never performed before and mostly came to sing or rattle a washboard. They enjoyed themselves, so we kept it going and did it again a year later from which we have assembled the Southsea Skiffle Orchestra. Virtually everyone is over 60, most are quite a bit older, there are around 35 of us and we play every month at the Guildhall, as well as other gigs around town at some of the bigger venues like the Kings Theatre, Theatre Royal and Victorious Festival, and to local groups, mainly pensioners. We rarely charge, being pleased to play for charity, and the collective spirit and sheer fun of the whole thing is not that remote from the 'Play' aspect of Richard Neville's *Playpower*.

Nigel Grundy has made a number of written and photographic contributions to this book, for which I am very grateful. He wrote to me about the Guildhall's historical project (PME) that he leads these days, working in particular, with his wife Audrie and Phil Freeman

> These days, I curate the Portsmouth Music Experience exhibition at the Guildhall, I am surrounded by the imagery and music of the 1960s and it is very pleasurable when a visitor sees or hears something that sparks a memory and they say, 'I had forgotten about that' – then we are off talking about those old days, and the minutes fly by, or in one case, two and a half hours! Without exception, everyone I talk to has very fond memories of growing up in the 1960s, especially if it was in Portsmouth. The most frequently used word in our visitors' comments book is 'memories'.

For those of us who were there in the 1960s, one day, relatively soon, all this will be over. Will the legacy be a positive one? In these disconcerting times, it's often difficult to be optimistic, but those last examples are about self-help, creativity, and being positive in our sharing with other people. Maybe those of us who have no significant power, can nonetheless 'play' in ways that help ourselves and others. The Beatles were over optimistic back in 1967; the world is more complex than they suggested, and I guess they knew that. But it's not a bad idea to begin (and here, to end) with LOVE. In 2002, Barry Miles, one of the key figures in Britain's counterculture, confessed that the participants might have been "naïve, distorted, arse-backwards and hopelessly idealistic" but what we were "stumbling towards" was, he suggested, "something better" (304). We might still be stumbling, but the journey is still worthwhile – and perhaps as urgent as it ever was.

GOODNIGHT & THANK YOU

SOUTH PARADE PIER.

Sandy Denny & Fotheringay in the old Ballroom, which burned
down during the filming of Tommy in 1974.

Photo: Nigel Grundy

GOODNIGHT & THANK YOU

Bibliography & Text References

Akhtar M & Humphries S 1999, *Far Out: The Dawning of New Age Britain,* Sansom & Co

Allen D 2004, "A Public Transition: Acoustic and Electric performances at the Woodstock Festival" in Bennett A editor 2004, *Remembering Woodstock,* Ashgate (111-126)

Allen D 2016 *Forever Changes: Living with English County Cricket,* Moyhill

Anderson P 2013, *Mods: The New Religion – the Style & Music of the 1960s Mods,* Omnibus

Anthony G 1980, *The Summer of Love: Haight Ashbury at its Highest,* Last Gasp Publishing

Arts Council of Great Britain, 1991, *Ready, Steady Go* (exhibition catalogue)

Barnes R 2000, 'Introduction' in Rawlings T 2000, *Mod: A Very British Phenomenon,* Omnibus

Benham P 1993, *The Avalonians,* Gothic Image

Bennett A & Kahn-Harris K 2004, *After Subculture: Critical Studies in Contemporary Youth Culture,* Palgrave

Boorman J 2003, *Adventures of a Suburban Boy,* Faber & Faber

Boyd J 2005, *White Bicycles: Making Music in the 1960s,* Serpent's Tail

Campbell J 1999, *This is the Beat Generation,* Secker & Warburg

Carr R, Case B, Dellar F, 1986, *The Hip: Hipsters, Jazz & the Beat Generation,* Faber & Faber

Chapman R 2010, *A Very Irregular Head: The Life of Syd Barrett,* Faber & Faber

Cline E 2016, *The Girls,* Chatto & Windus

Cohen S 1972, *Folk Devils & Moral Panics,* MacGibbon & Kee

Cohn N 1989, "Today there are no Gentlemen" in *Ball the Wall: Nik Cohn in the Age of Rock,* Picador (255-315)

Cohn N 2004, *Awopbopaloobop Alopbamboom,* Pimlico

Davie G 1994, "Religion in post-war Britain: a sociological view" in Obelkevich J & Catterall P 1994, *Understanding Post-War British Society,* Routledge

De Groot 2008, *60s Unplugged: A kaleidoscopic history of a disorderly decade,* Harvard University

De Rogatis J 1996, *Kaleidoscope Eyes: Psychedelic Music from the 1960s to the 1990s,* Fourth Estate

Didion J 1967, "The Hippie Generation" in *The Saturday Evening Post,* 23.9.1967 (25-31 etc.)

Diski J 2010, *The Sixties,* Profile Books

Foulk R with Foulk C 2015, *Stealing Dylan from Woodstock: When the World Came to the Isle of Wight,* Medina

Foulk R with Foulk C 2016, *The Last Great Event with Jimi Hendrix and Jim Morrison,* Medina

Fryer P 1967, "Map of the Underground; The Flower Power Structure and London Scene" in *Encounter* (magazine, London) October 1967 (6-20)

Ginsberg A 1956, *Howl,* City Lights Books

Ginsberg A 1970, *Indian Journals 1962-1963,* City Lights Books

Goldstein R 2015, *Another Little Piece of my Heart: My Life of Rock and Revolution in the Sixties,* Bloomsbury

Gray A 1981, *Lanark,* Canongate

Green J 1998, *Days in the Life,* Pimlico

Green J 1999, *All Dressed Up: The Sixties and the Counterculture,* Pimlico

Gross H, 1968, *The Flower People,* Ballantine Books

Hair R & Smith TR editors 2017, *Harry Smith's Anthology of American Folk Music: America Changed Through Music,* Routledge

Hebditch I 1999, "Weekend" in Hewitt P editor 1999, *The Sharper Word,* Helter Skelter

Hebditch I & Shepherd J 2012, *The Action: In the Lap of the Mods* (privately published)

Hebdige D 1979, *Subculture: The Meaning of Style,* Routledge

Henke J & Puterbaugh P editors 1997, *I Want to Take You Higher: The Psychedelic Era,* Chronicle Books

Hesse H 2001, *The Journey to the East,* Peter Owen

Hewison R 1986, *Too Much: Art & Society in the Sixties, 1960-1975,* Oxford University Press

Hewitt P 1999, editor, *The Sharper Word,* Helter Skelter

Hewitt P, 2000, *The Soul Stylists: Forty Years of Modernism,* Mainstream

Hill S 2016, *San Francisco & the Long 60s,* Bloomsbury

Hutchinson R 1992, *High Sixties: The Summers of Riot & Love,* Mainstream

Innes B 2002, *Snapshots of the 60s,* Brown Reference Group

Jones L 1963, *Blues People: The Negro experience in White America and the music that developed from it,* William Morrow & Co

Jones T 2007, *Utopian Dreams: In Search of a Good Life,* Faber & Faber

Keill C 1963, *Urban Blues,* University of Chicago

Law L 2000, *Flashing on the Sixties,* Squarebooks

Le Grice M 1977, *Abstract Film and Beyond,* Studio Vista

Leary T, Metzner R & Albert R, 2008, *The Psychedelic Experience: A Manual Based on the Tibetan Book of the Dead* Penguin Classics

MacInnes C, 2001, *Absolute Beginners* Allison & Busby

Maitland S editor 1988, *Very Heaven: Looking Back at the 1960s,* Virago

Marcus G 1997, "The Old, Weird America" in *Anthology of American Folk Music* (booklet) Smithsonian Folkways

Marwick A 1998, *The Sixties,* Oxford University Press

McKay G 2003, "Just a closer walk with thee: New-Orleans style jazz and the Campaign for Nuclear Disarmament in 1950s Britain" in the journal *Popular Music* (261-281)

McKay G 2000, *Glastonbury: A Very English Fair,* Victor Gollancz

Michell J 1983, 3rd edition, *The New View Over Atlantis,* Thames & Hudson

Miles B 2002, *In the Sixties,* Jonathan Cape

Miles B 2003, *Hippie,* Cassell

Mojo Music Guide 1: Psychedelia: 100 Masterpieces nd

Muggleton D 2000, *Inside Subculture: The Postmodern Meaning of Style,* Berg

Neville R 1971, *Playpower,* Paladin

Neville R 2009, *Hippie, Hippie, Shake,* Duckworth Overlook

Oliver P 1968, *Screening the Blues,* Da Capo

Palacios J 1998, *Lost in the Woods: Syd Barrett and the Pink Floyd,* Boxtree

Perry C 1976 "What a Long Strange Trip It's Been" in *Rolling Stone* no 207, 26.2.1976 (3)

Perry C 1977, "The Gathering of the Tribes" in Obst LR 1977, *The Sixties,* Random House/Rolling Stone (188-192)

Perry C 1984, *Haight Ashbury,* Rolling Stone Publications

Putowski G & Ensor J 1968, Programme: "Dance of Words", Portsmouth College of Technology

Rees D, Lazell B & Osborne R 1992, *Complete NME Singles Chart,* Boxtree

Roberts D Editor 2004, 17th edition *British Hit Singles & Albums,* Guinness World Records

Ross DA, 1995, "Director's Foreword" in Phillips L, 1995, *Beat Culture and the New America 1950-1965,* Whitney Museum of American Art, New York

Roszak T 1970, *The Making of a Counter Culture: Reflections on the Technocratic Society & Its Youthful Opposition,* Faber & Faber

Rowbotham S 2000, *Promise of a Dream: Remembering the Sixties,* Penguin

Sandbrook D 2005, *Never Had It So Good: a History of Britain from Suez to the Beatles,* Little Brown

Sandbrook D 2006, *White Heat: A History of Britain in the Swinging Sixties,* Little, Brown

Savage J 2016, *1966: The Year the Decade Exploded,* Faber & Faber

Sclanders A, 2017, *Minutes to Go,* Beat Books Catalogue number 74

Selvin J 1992, *Monterey Pop,* Chronicle Books

Selvin J 1995, *Summer of Love,* Plume

Simon P 2001, *I and Eye: Pictures of My Generation,* Bullfinch/Little, Brown & Co

Shipley M, 2015, *Psychedelic Mysticism: Transforming Consciousness, Religious Experience & Voluntary Peasants in Postwar America,* Lexington Books

Stedman J 1995, *Portsmouth Reborn: Destruction & Reconstruction 1939-1974,* City of Portsmouth

Steele J 1976, "Collaborative Work at Portsmouth" in *Studio International* November/ December 1976 (297-300)

Thompson H 1967, "The Hashbury is the Capital of the Hippies" in the "New York Times" 14 May 1967 reprinted in Kureishi H & Savage J 1995, *The Faber Book of Pop,* Faber & Faber

Tickner L 2008, *Hornsey 1968: The Art School Revolution,* Frances Lincoln

Waldeman A 2016, *A Really Good Day: How Microdosing made a Mega difference in my Mood, my Marriage and my Life,* Corsair

Watkins A 1925, *The Old Straight Track,* The Lost Library

Watkinson M & Anderson P 1991, *Crazy Diamond: Syd Barrett & the Dawn of Pink Floyd,* Omnibus

Watts A 1997, *Zen and the Beat Way,* Eden Grove Editions

Willhelm R (translator) 1967, *I Ching or Book of Changes,* Penguin Books

Wolfe T 1971, *The Electric Kool-Aid Acid Test,* Bantam

Website References

Aristia (New Age Shop), Portsmouth 2016: *http://aristia.co.uk/* retrieved September 2016

BBC 2004 *Why I Hate the Sixties*, Youtube *https://www.youtube.com/watch?v=VJM-xA8PcQ8* retrieved December 2016

BBC 2007 Boris Johnson & Portsmouth: *http://news.bbc.co.uk/1/hi/england/ hampshire/6521603.stm* retrieved January 2017

Better Books (Andrew Sclanders): *www.betterbooks.com* retrieved February 2017

Bolan (Marc) 1968 poem in *Gandalf's Garden http://www.lettersofnote.com/2011/01/ im-sending-you-poem.html retrieved October 2016*

Cooper, Mick: The Portsmouth Music Scene: *http://michaelcooper.org.uk/C/pmsindex.htm*

Gaskin, Stephen, obituary *http://www.telegraph.co.uk/news/obituaries/10946714/Stephen-Gaskin-obituary.html* retrieved December 2016

Pompey Pop Blog 2010-date, *https://pompeypop.wordpress.com/*

Roszak T 2001 *http://www.sfgate.com/books/article/When-the-counterculture-counted-2835958.php* retrieved December 2016

Sandbrook D nd *http://www.dominicsandbrook.com/books/white-heat-1964-1970-v-2-a-history-of-britain-in-the-swinging-sixties/* retrieved October 2016

Trevelyan, Sir George *http://www.sirgeorgetrevelyan.org.uk/* retrieved January 2017

Watts A 1958 *http://highexistence.com/beat-zen-square-zen-and-zen-a-1958-essay-by-alan-watts/* retrieved December 2016

Windsor Festival 1967: *http://www.ukrockfestivals.com/1967-windsor-festival.html* retrieved November 2016

Wrekin Trust Home Page *http://www.wrekintrust.org/* retrieved January 2017.

Pompey Pop

Allen D 1998, *Almost: 40 Years of Southsea Rock & Pompey Blues* Minerva

Allen D 2009, *Here Come the Sixties,* University of Portsmouth

Allen D & Cooper M, 2011, *Pompey Pop Pix,* Moyhill

Allen D 20   *The One in the Middle: Paul Pond, PGS, Portsmouth & Pop,* Portsmouth Grammar School Monograph number 25, 2013

Francis K 2001, *Seaside Rock: the 60s Southern Scene and the Beat Group that transcended a generation,* Lorcas

Grundy N 2012, *My Back Pages: Portsmouth 1962-1972 – Aspects of my Life and the Portsmouth Music Scene,* Southsea Press

Grundy N & Foulk R, 2016, *The 1968, 1969, 1970 Isle of Wight Experience,* Portsmouth Music Experience.

Jackson J 1999, *A Cure for Gravity,* Transworld

Stedman J, Lee S, Ball K, 2003, *Singing Out: Voices of Portsmouth Rock and Pop Musicians,* Portsmouth City Museum & Records Office

N.B.
Portsmouth City Library holds a 'Pompey Pop' Archive on the third floor, Local History, section.

Magazines & Newspapers

Except where indicated, UK publications. Most precise date references are in the text. The main sources included: Gandalf's Garden, The Guardian, International Times, Observer, Oz, Portsmouth Evening News, Rolling Stone (USA), Sunday Times, The Times, Time (USA).

ACKNOWLEDGEMENTS

Not for the first time I record my considerable gratitude to David Cronin of Moyhill Publishing for all his help and guidance in enabling this book to see the light of day, and once again, I thank my wife Lou for all her kindness and patience in supporting my endeavours.

In terms of refreshing my memories and feeding my understanding of those days, I would like to thank Andrew Sclanders of 'Beat Books' *(https://www. beatbooks.com/)* who keeps enticing me with real treasures, many of which appear in my bibliography.

I am very grateful to everyone around Portsmouth who supports the project that I call 'Pompey Pop'; not least to everyone who follows the Blog, and especially all those whose comments and ideas have contributed to this book. Most particularly I am grateful to Mick Cooper who has walked with me along this chosen path for some years now, and to Nigel Grundy who has contributed thoughts, memories and photographs to this publication. More than that, Nigel, his wife Audrie and 'soul man' Phil Freeman have been the driving forces in the marvellous exhibition of our city and our lives, known as Portsmouth Music Experience (PME).

That exhibition is housed at Portsmouth's Guildhall and I wish to thank Andy Grays and all his staff for their support of that historical project – and for providing us with a venue to continue playing through our 'swinging sixties' and beyond. I offer thanks to to my friends Martin and Geoff, for bringing light to my life, to the other guys in Rosemary, which was very special, and to John Roberts and Joe McDonald who, with my great pals in Reet, Petite & Gone, created a dream, and made it come true.

Finally, if you were a part of the scene that I have described in these pages, whether fan, promoter, style icon, DJ, mystical traveller or (especially) fellow musician, thank you.

Together we enjoyed something kind of wonderful, didn't we?

**"Don't adventures ever have an end? I suppose not.
Someone else always has to carry on the story."**

Bilbo Baggins – *The Fellowship of the Ring*

Index